Grace and Wisdom

Patrick G. Kerwin
1889 - 1963

Chief Justice of Canada

A biography
Stephen G. McKenna

Library and Archives Canada Cataloguing in Publication

McKenna, Stephen G., author
        Grace and Wisdom : Patrick G. Kerwin, Chief Justice of Canada /
Stephen G. McKenna. -- 1st edition.

1. Kerwin, Patrick, 1889-1963. 2. Canada. Supreme Court--Biography.
3. Judges--Canada--Biography. I. Title.

KE8248.K47M35 2017   347.71'03534   C2017-901614-8
KF345.Z9K47M35 2017

Petra Books
petrabooks.ca
Design and editing:
c. 84,000 words | 344 p
Bookman 10/12, 9/9, Optima 10, Arial 10
6" x 9"

Front cover sketch of Patrick Kerwin by George Lonn (1909 - 1999).
Back: Author photograph by Paul R. McKenna, 2017

Unless otherwise noted, interior illustrations are from the Family Archives.

While the best efforts have been made to identify copyright holders and sources,
the author is responsible for all content. Should the reader have any questions or
corrections, please email the author at contact@chiefjusticekerwin.ca

Dedication

To my grandmother, Georgina (Mace) Kerwin,
who accompanied my grandfather throughout his life journey.

To my mother, Isobel (Kerwin) McKenna,
for her patience, bravery and, of course, her stories.

To my wife,
for her kindness, love and unwavering support.

Patrick Kerwin, 1935.

Contents

Preface

This biography began through an ongoing curiosity about my maternal grandfather, Patrick Grandcourt Kerwin. From my perspective as a child, he was a kind and attentive grandparent with a warm smile and gentle demeanour. I saw him often, as my grandparents regularly came to our home for Sunday dinner. As well, it was a treat to visit my grandparents' spacious apartment, which often meant sitting with "Papa" in his study and sharing a delightful glass of ginger ale as he smoked his pipe while we chatted. This went on as our grandmother hovered, ensuring that I, as well as my brothers and sisters, did not get too rambunctious or tire him out because, after all, his work as the Chief Justice of the Supreme Court of Canada was no regular nine-to-five job; he was a very busy man.

My grandfather died at the age of 73, when I was only eight years old, but my memories, affection and interest in him continued. My mother, his eldest child, told and re-told numerous anecdotes about her father, family life and her father's career. There were stories of his life in Sarnia, her grandparents' and family stories in general that she had heard as a child that were repeated for our benefit. As a young person, I did not always fully absorb these family tales. In later years, as I began wondering about his life and the path that led him to become the Chief Justice of the Supreme Court of Canada, my mother was willing to once again share some of the family lore. This time I decided to take notes.

I have brought together research, history, stories and pictures as well as information provided by family and others who found this to be an interesting subject. Visiting Patrick's hometown of Sarnia and investigating his father's career in Great Lakes shipping proved to be fascinating as well as informative. As time and research went on, my thirst for knowledge about his life and career increased. Not every life lived leaves a deep trail of evidence; fortunately, the life of a lawyer, judge and Chief Justice of the Supreme Court of Canada left a trail that was somewhat easier to follow.

During my research, I made a special trip to Sarnia and Guelph in order to see the place where he was born and the city where his law career took shape. Having visited these places previously, it was interesting to return to these Ontario cities to see them from the viewpoint of my grandfather's life.

Touring the city he was born in and trying to find the homes in which he grew up and lived were of special significance. The home where he was born, 116 Essex Street in Sarnia, is still there and looks like a fine home by today's standards and, perhaps, was an even nicer home in the 1880s. The Gavin family home at 112 Elgin Street no longer exists and has been replaced by a parking lot for the business next door.

The location of the liquor store on Front Street was a bit harder to find. During that trip, I found the building I had thought it was in and, later, with the much-appreciated and on-going assistance provided by Randy Evans (of the Lambton County Law Society), the location was confirmed: 210 Front Street North. The building still exists today but not the third floor where the Kerwin family lived while Patrick's father operated the liquor store at street level.

While in Sarnia in the summer of 2011, I sat in what is now a park at the mouth of the St. Clair River, where the waters of the Upper Great Lakes flow past at a tremendous rate. I saw older teenagers acting like fearless young adventure seekers as they hurled themselves into the fast-paced current, floating from the mouth of Lake Huron down the river and under the bridge to the U.S.A. Speaking about this to a local man who was walking his dog, his response was, "Yes, it's a crazy thing to do, but we've all done it when we were younger." This made me wonder if Patrick and his brother, Vern, shared this exhilarating experience as well.

During my visit to Guelph I saw the home on Park Avenue where Patrick and his young family lived for a decade and a half. The home looked spectacular and must have gone through some changes over the years to bring it back to its original form. In the early 1970s, my mother (Isobel Kerwin McKenna) and I were driving through this part of Ontario and we toured through Guelph so she could show me around the sites of her hometown: where she went to school, where her father's office was and, finally, the home where she grew up. Much of it was very interesting but, unfortunately, the state of the family home at that particular time was far removed from what she remembered. The porch was gone and the house looked like it had been divided into apartments. My mother sighed and urged me to drive on and did not look back as we drove away. The exuberance she felt as we entered the city had been replaced with keen disappointment. I sincerely wish I could have let her know that the home is again as beautiful as it ever was, with its spacious porch reinstated as well as mature trees in the neighbourhood. Unfortunately, she died in July of 2009, two summers prior to this trip taking place.

From my viewpoint, Patrick's story is one of triumph: only eight years old when his father died, he entered the workforce at a young age and acquired an excellent education; he pursued a successful and varied career in law that saw him rise to the pinnacle of the profession. He was an adaptable man with a strong sense of self-discipline and duty.

Above all, he was a man whose service to the public was known to encompass, in the words of Governor General Georges Vanier, "grace and wisdom".

This is the story of a great Canadian.

Acknowledgements

In researching this project I was fortunate to share this interest and passion for the story of our grandfather, grandmother and family with many others. What finally set me going on this project was discovering that my cousin, Patrick James Kerwin (son of Patrick Kilroy and grandson of Patrick Grandcourt), had already done quite a bit of research on the Kerwin family. While reviewing his collection, I felt the determination required to act on what I had always thought was an interesting idea — to capture my grandfather's life and career from a personal point of view.

Also of invaluable assistance was being given access to the 'Kerwin Archives' as amassed by my Uncle George Kerwin; his daughter, Shawn Kerwin, was kind enough to let me search through and copy, scan or read the multitude of items in her home that had been collected. Her brother, Michael, provided valuable information as well as anecdotes that were new to the conversation. Other family members shared bits of history or anecdotes as well.

While in Toronto a year later, I visited Osgoode Hall and the Law Society of Upper Canada and would like to note the tremendous assistance provided by the archivist, Paul Leatherdale, in learning about my grandfather's life and aspects of the school as well. It was fascinating to tour the building where Patrick was educated, the hall where he sat for exams and later as an exam invigilator, and the courtrooms where he sat as a student and later as a Judge.

Back in Ottawa, while researching the books Patrick had charged out of the Library of Parliament, I was fortunate to have Barbara Pilek (Chief, Branch Libraries and Information Service, Library of Parliament, Main Library, Centre Block) as my most-knowledgeable and agreeable guide. Getting to stand in the beautiful Library and touring the collections held downstairs was a unique and compelling experience. My thanks to her for taking the time and for her on-going enthusiasm for the Library of Parliament's well-being.

I contacted the Registrar of the Supreme Court of Canada, Roger Bilodeau, to tell him of the biography and asked to meet. In doing so, my wife and I were very generously given a behind-the-scenes tour of the Court by the Registrar himself, my first since the fall of 1962. Some things had changed, such as the Court Library and the level of security, but much of it seemed the same.

The Judges' Chambers are beautiful, spacious and full of books — some are very old while others look ancient. All in all, I have to agree with the assessment of *Maclean's Magazine* from years before, it is one of the most beautiful buildings in the capital.

I would also like to tip my hat in thanks to David Lee, a member of the Québec Bar, who went through the manuscript with a fine-tooth comb ensuring that not only was the legal jargon exact, but also providing invaluable input and comments.

I would like to thank His Excellency Governor General David Johnson and the Right Honourable Chief Justice Beverly McLachlan for their encouraging comments after reviewing the draft manuscript.

Lastly, I would like to acknowledge those who were kind enough to provide input, guidance, and encouragement. To one and all, may I offer my heartfelt thanks for your contributions and willingness to assist in this endeavour.

—Stephen G. McKenna

"Justice delayed is justice denied" [1]
is as true today as it ever was.

—Chief Justice Patrick Kerwin speaking at the opening
of the Superior Court of Québec
Montreal, Québec, 1957

---

1 Legal maxim attributed to British PM Gladstone, 1809 –1898.

Chapter 1

Young Patrick and his Family
Sarnia

Patrick Grandcourt Kerwin was born on October 25, 1889, at the family home located at 116 Essex Street in Sarnia, Ontario. Shortly thereafter, on November 17, 1889, he was baptized at the Our Lady of Mercy Catholic Church. Essex Street consisted of one- and two-storey homes in a middle-class neighbourhood only four blocks from Front Street, where the docks and stores were located. According to my grandmother Georgina, Patrick's wife, Patrick's mother chose her son's imposing middle name after she had "read it in a book somewhere — she was like that".

At the time of Patrick's birth, Queen Victoria was Canada's monarch and she continued to reign just into the next century. The Prime Minister of the day was Sir John A. Macdonald who was the leader of the "Liberal-Conservative" Party during Canada's 6th Parliament.

His parents, Patrick Kerwin Sr. and Ellen (Gavin), had been married four years by the time Patrick came along. He was not their first child; a daughter, Frances Mary, had been born to them in February 1888, but lived only a month. Patrick, however, was not destined to be an only child; his parents later provided him with a brother, Leo Joseph (known as Vern to all), born in 1892. According to family lore, Ellen's father had received a letter postmarked Vernon, Florida, and she liked that name so much that, soon after the birth and officially naming him Leo Joseph, she decided he was to be known as Vernon. Despite the fact that his first and second names had already been registered, the name stuck. A sister, Frances Ellen Letitia, was born in 1894.

~

The family name, Kerwin, is an Anglicized version of a Gaelic (Scottish/Irish) name, O'Ciardubhain, and it has been spelled as Kirwan, O'Kirwan, Culwen, Curwen, Kerwen, Kervyn and Kerven, among other variations. The name is believed to have originated in

1

Patrick Kerwin Sr., Patrick's father, circa 1890.

Scotland. For the Irish Kerwins, even though this name is commonly associated with the Galway district on the western shores of Ireland, the name can be traced back to County Wexford, in south-eastern Ireland.

That is where Patrick Kerwin Sr. was born in 1853, the eldest son of Martin Kerwin and Mary Hogan. The names Mary Cloak, or Clark, appear in some records and it is not known why this is. Martin Kerwin, according to family accounts, followed the occupations of miller and gardener to provide for his family.

Patrick Sr. was the first of many children born to Martin and Mary, but the only one born in Ireland. Soon after his birth, the family immigrated to Canada, making their way first to the Hamilton area, where five more boys and one girl were born. They then moved to Petrolia, and finally to Sarnia, Ontario. In Canada, the Kerwin sons tied their fortunes to the water becoming sailors on the Great Lakes.

In late 19th-century Ontario, where intercity roads were poor or non-existent, shipping on the Great Lakes was a vital and thriving enterprise. Ships, and later the railroad, were important in bringing settlers further inland to western Canada and the U.S.A. as well as providing goods of all manner to the city of Chicago, the fastest growing city in North America at that time. In Sarnia, Our Lady of Mercy Catholic Church — where Patrick Sr. would later be married and his children baptized — was located on a rise just off the river which made the steeples visible for quite a distance. These became an important reference point for all Great Lake mariners as they approached Sarnia from the St. Clair River or Lake Huron.

As was the norm for the time, Patrick Sr. would have started sailing at a young age, perhaps 12 to 14 years old, and worked his way up the ranks as he learned his trade. Prior to marrying Ellen Gavin, he had become a Captain of ships and, as well, diversified his career as an operator of tugs and an Inspector of Hulls and Equipment.

Schooner *Sligo* under sail on Lake Huron, circa 1880. *A Great Vessel Type: Archaeological and Historical Examination of the Welland Sailing Canal Ship, Sligo,* Toronto, Ontario, by Kimberly E. Monk, Department of History, East Carolina University, August 2003.

Before his eldest son was born and for some years after, Patrick Sr. worked as a ship's Captain on the Great Lakes and had ownership in two vessels as well as a number of tugs and scows plying the fast-moving waters of the Sarnia basin. The *Sligo* was the first ship Patrick Sr. had part ownership in. It was a Canadian-built vessel and, according to the *Marine Record*, "Captain P. Kerwin and others have purchased the schooner *Sligo* from Graham & Horn, Port Arthur, for $6,000. Captain Kerwin will sail her".[2] His second was the *Sovereign*, purchased by Patrick Sr. in 1890. This propeller-driven steamship was a bulk carrier of cargo that included wheat, wood, iron, coal, and vegetables, among other goods and commodities.

The *Sovereign* sank on October 25, 1891, twelve miles southwest of Lamb Island Lighthouse on Lake Superior while on a heading to reach Buffalo, NY, *enroute* from Port Arthur (now Thunder Bay), Ontario. Details of the loss indicated the ship was overwhelmed in a storm as it released its load of grain. All hands, including Captain Patrick Kerwin Sr., were saved as they had transferred to the *Sligo* that was in tow. The value of the vessel and cargo was estimated at $28,000.[3]

---

2 *Marine Record*, Apr. 7, 1887.
3 Karl E. Hedin, *The Great Lakes Guide to Sunken Ships* (Branden, 1993), 219.

3

Patrick Kerwin Sr.'s ship, the propeller-driven steamship *Sovereign* in Port Arthur ON, circa 1890. greatlakesships.org.

Sailing these ships and working to make a profit was the life and career of Patrick Kerwin Sr.; it was a career that, after almost two decades of toil, would allow him to marry and support a family as he was now a man of some means. Any woman who accepted his proposal would have to understand that he would be away for many months of the year. Patrick Sr. married Ellen on January 7, 1885. The church registry indicates the surname as Kirwan[4] and that Patrick Sr. was 31 years old and Ellen was 16 years old. Being a minor, Ellen required her parents' permission to marry.

Ellen (Gavin) Kerwin, Patrick's mother, was born in London, England on January 10, 1868, to John Gavin, a shoemaker, and Catherine (Kate) Welton. John and Kate immigrated to Brantford, Ontario in Canada in 1870. Ellen had many siblings, but as was sadly common in those times, some died as infants or young children. Even though documentation and family stories indicate Ellen Gavin as a native of England, one early census showed her nationality as Irish. According to my grandmother, Georgina Kerwin, Patrick's mother was not impressed at this designation as Ellen was quite proud of her English ancestry.

The Gavin family originally settled in Brantford, Ontario, but moved to Port Huron, Michigan, just across from Sarnia, Ontario, and then, later, to Sarnia. The impetus for the move from Brantford seems to have been the extreme embarrassment that Ellen Gavin's mother, Kate, felt at having given birth to Canada's first set of quadruplets. At the time, even having twins was regarded as something of an oddity. Although none of the babes survived, having quadruplets was perceived as catastrophic to the family's good name at the time.

---

4 This spelling variation later normalized to Kerwin in all documentation.

Patrick Kerwin and his mother, Ellen (Gavin) Kerwin, circa 1891.

With mother, Ellen (Gavin) Kerwin, circa 1893.

Many years later, Ellen repeated to her son Vern that her mother's horrified description of the event was that the babies "came like rats". Nevertheless, Queen Victoria sent a plaque to commemorate the unusual birth, which was discovered by Vern after his grandmother's death and a cash 'bounty' rumoured to be fifty pounds, a small fortune at the time. Recent correspondence with the Royal Archives at Windsor Castle [5] indicates the amount paid was probably closer to two or three pounds. Never spoken of in Kate Gavin's lifetime, the unfortunate quadruplets have lived on in family lore.

As a young wife in Sarnia, Ellen became adept at raising her young family for the most part by herself, as her husband was away for much or all of each sailing season, usually April to November, with his only extended time at home occurring during the winter months when the lakes were "iced up".

For the first six years of his life, young Patrick lived in what was, for all intents and purposes, a one-parent family for the better part of each year. Fortunately, both sides of the extended

---

5 Mrs. Jill Kelsey, Deputy Registrar, Jan. 31, 2012.

family in Sarnia were very supportive and equally understanding as many of Patrick Sr.'s brothers were sailors of the Great Lakes as well. This was a common way of life in communities near the Great Lakes.

One can imagine Patrick, as a young boy, running down to the docks to watch ships coming and going, being loaded and unloaded and all the activities of the adults around them.

The smell, textures and orchestra of sounds, including the creaking of old cranes, shouting of instructions, and birds hovering above waiting for a morsel, must have been exciting for any youngster.

It is not known what influence Patrick felt from the years he was exposed to his father's and uncles' careers with the ships and boats. However, we do know that Patrick Sr.'s son learned the value of honesty, hard work and devotion to his faith. These traits from his father would serve young Patrick well in the years to come.

Courts are established to settle disputes.

—Justice Patrick Kerwin in an address to graduating students,
Osgoode Hall, Toronto, June 29, 1950

Chapter 2

Growing Up
Sarnia

While Patrick was still a child, his father sold his ship the *Sligo*; and with the sinking of the *Sovereign*, Patrick Kerwin Sr. made arrangements by 1894 to become a land-locked merchant through the purchase of a liquor store in Sarnia.

The store had a favourable location — just across the street from the docks on Front Street and very near Ferry Dock Road, where passengers travelled to and from Port Huron in Michigan, and almost opposite John Gavin's, Patrick Sr.'s father-in-law, shoe-making store. This most likely meant that Patrick Sr. was putting everything they had into the business; there was no fallback plan, so it had to work. It is interesting to note that the store also had a telephone, a device that was not yet installed in most homes of the 1890s.

To announce his career change, he placed the following advertisement in the January 4, 1895 edition of the *Sarnia Daily Observer*.

Business Change

P. KERWIN

Desires to announce to his friends and the public that he has purchased
the liquor business formerly carried on by Mr. Wm. Coutlee,
and will continue the same at the old stand, East side FRONT STREET,
nearly opposite the Post Office.
I shall keep on hand the best and most Popular brands of

Wines, Ales

- AND -

LIQUORS

and shall make a specialty of Superior Liquors,
imported in packages for Family use.
Prices Reasonable.   Prompt delivery.
Telephone 121.
Trial Order solicited.

P. KERWIN

DIED.

In London, on Saturday, January 15th, 1898,

Patrick K. Kerwin.

THE FUNERAL

will leave the residence of his father-in-law, Mr. John Gavin, North Elgin Street, on Wednesday, Jan. 19, at 8:30 a. m., for the Catholic Church, thence to the cemetery.

Friends and acquaintances will please accept this intimation to attend.

Sarnia, January 17, 1898.

Patrick Kerwin Sr.'s Funeral Card, 1898.

Photos from the period when Patrick and his family resided above the liquor and wine store show it as a three-storey building with the liquor store on the ground floor, and the second floor occupied by the offices of a savings and loan company (possibly the London Loan Co.). Patrick Kerwin Sr. and Ellen with their three children, Patrick, Vernon and Frances lived on the third floor.

Patrick Kerwin Sr. decided, it is thought, to give up sailing the Great Lakes and become a merchant on Sarnia's main street as he was becoming increasingly unwell. By late 1896, only a few years after becoming a store owner, Patrick's father was so ill that the doctors transferred him to the Asylum for the Insane in London, Ontario, to treat his diagnosed condition, paresis, which can cause dementia. Paresis is defined as "a condition of muscular weakness caused by nerve damage or disease," [resulting in] "partial paralysis". General paresis is an "inflammation of the brain causing progressive dementia and paralysis".[6]

Patrick Kerwin Sr. died at the Asylum in London on January 15, 1898, with the Ontario death record showing him as a merchant, Roman Catholic, age 45. His body was returned to Sarnia for the funeral and interment.

This left Ellen Kerwin, a 28-year-old widow, with three young children (ages 8, 6 and 3½) to raise by herself year-round, not just during the sailing season, and now, with no income. She sold the stock in the family liquor store and moved in with her parents, John and Kate Gavin, at the family home located at 112 Elgin Street. This arrangement seems to have worked out fairly well, all things considered, as Patrick managed to earn good marks at school and was able to take piano lessons as a youngster. By all accounts, he became quite a good player both with sheet music and by ear. Young Patrick also learned how to

---

6 www.en.oxforddictionaries.com/definition/paresis Accessed Mar. 2017.

play the trombone in high school which led to him playing with a local band.

Frances, Patrick and Vernon Kerwin, Sarnia, circa 1897.

For his primary education, Patrick attended the Sarnia Separate School, starting in 1895. The teaching staff at the time consisted of two Sisters in charge of the girls' school and two lay teachers in charge of the boys' school. By 1901, the school was entirely in the charge of the Sisters. The lessons taught at this four-room school proved to be effective and beneficial as Patrick became a studious youngster who showed no signs of wanting to

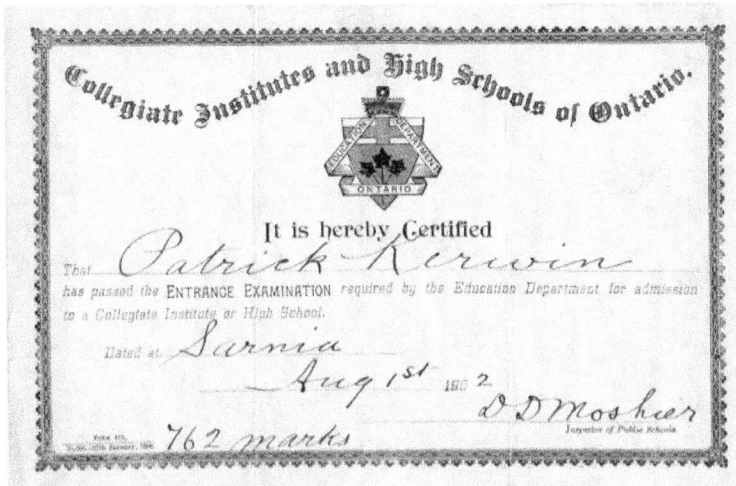

Patrick's Certification of having passed the Entrance Exam to attend High School, 1902.

follow in his father's careers as a Great Lakes Captain or liquor merchant.

Patrick passed the entrance exams for secondary school, scoring 762 marks, well above the 550 required to pass, and began attending the Sarnia Collegiate Institute on London School Road in September of 1902. This new Collegiate had just been opened and dedicated in 1891 to replace the old Collegiate. The building cost the Sarnia School System $21,000 to erect and the boys and girls had separate entrances, as was the custom. The design reflected the Victorian architecture of the late 1800s and was considered very grand by those who attended the opening. Sarnians were very proud of this new structure, and it was said that the slate roof was so good it lasted until the building was demolished in 1976.

In a family anecdote shared by Patrick's son, George, he tells of being with his Uncle Vern (Patrick's brother) in Sarnia when a municipal storage shed was being torn down just across the street from the Gavin family home at 112 Elgin Street. As they watched the work unfold, Uncle Vern picked up an undated stray ledger that lay near his feet, and happened to open it to a page where there was an entry about one of the Kerwin boys being fined, "5 shillings for throwing rocks". George said of this, "it's the sort of story I wouldn't believe — except I was there!" Vern declined to confirm or deny that it was his Kerwin family or that of their cousins.

Sarnia Collegiate Institute where Patrick attended High School, circa 1898.

According to an oft-repeated story in our family, Patrick, at the age of fourteen, decided to quit high school and get a job to help out with the family's finances. As the eldest son, he took his position very seriously and felt that it was up to him to provide for his mother and siblings. The ambitious young man quickly found a delivery job with a local butcher shop. This was a job where getting all the deliveries done in a timely manner was important as his cargo was freshly-cut meat. Patrick's tasks included loading the orders onto a one-horse wagon and making deliveries to private homes in the morning with this routine being repeated for the afternoon run as well. Patrick, having been a good student, enjoyed reading very much and would bring a book along on his route. After a short time on the job, the book interested him so much that he pulled off the road to read for a while. When customers complained, Patrick was summarily dismissed from his job. Patrick was later quoted as saying that, "getting fired as delivery boy was the best career move I ever made".

After this episode, he and his mother approached a particularly helpful Sister at the high school to see if something could be done to finance the young man's further schooling and help the family finances. On Patrick's behalf, this Sister approached the local Member of Provincial Parliament (MPP) to inquire if any form of reasonable employment arrangements could

Around 1903, Patrick drove a similar type of horse and cart delivery wagon for a while.

be made for the young lad. This was about 1903 and the member of the Provincial Legislative Assembly was the Hon. William John Hanna who held the seat for Lambton County West for the Conservative Party from 1902 to 1918, and was the head of a successful local law firm.

This is how Patrick was introduced to Richard Vryling LeSueur, a prominent citizen and partner in Sarnia with the law firm, Hanna, McCarthy & LeSueur. Given the hearty recommendation of his senior partner, LeSueur took the young man under his wing, bringing him into the offices of their law firm and, in doing so, introduced young Patrick to the business of legal practice. Having a part-time job as an office clerk allowed Patrick not only to contribute to the family coffers but also to resume classes at the secondary school. There was no penalty applied for time missed, which was probably no more than a week or two in total.

Many years before Patrick came on the scene, LeSueur had himself been taken under the wing of Hanna, already a successful lawyer in Sarnia and a person of note who was so impressed with the young man that Hanna is said to have offered LeSueur a partnership upon his graduation if he would go to Osgoode Hall and study law. Accordingly, LeSueur graduated in 1903 and, as promised, became a junior partner in Hanna's law firm. LeSueur was to later become a well-known corporate and criminal lawyer

in Sarnia and across Canada, as well as president of Imperial Oil.
By 1904, the Sarnia City Directory indicated:

Hanna & LeSueur, Barristers, located at 145 ½ N. Front St.
P. Kerwin, clerk at 145½ N. Front St.
Gavin, John, shoemaker, at 223 N. Front St., and home as 112 Elgin St.
Front Street, 145½ N., LeSueur, Lawyer,
P. Kerwin, clerk Kerwin, Ellen [widow Patrick] lives 112 Elgin St.

Small, interesting items that might be seen as quaint by
today's standards were regularly included in local newspapers
like the *Sarnia Daily Observer*. Not only was there national and
international news, there were items such as the following that
reflected the local scene in May of 1905:

Got a bad fall

Patrick Kerwin, the young son of Mrs. Ellen Kerwin, met
with a mishap yesterday which caused him considerable
suffering. The lad was wheeling on the brick pavement on
Lochiel Street, and when turning the corner at Christina
Street the wheel slewed, and he fell heavily to the pavement.
The boy was almost stunned by the fall and complained of
severe pain in the side. He was taken to Homer Robertson's
drug store, where Dr. Bradley examined him, but found that
no bones were broken. The lad was taken to his home on
Elgin Street.[7]

Later in 1905, a notice in the newspaper in regard to
"Christmas Entertainment" read as follows: "Following is the
program to be given by the children of the Sunday school classes
of the Church of Our Lady of Mercy, Friday evening, Dec. 22nd, at
8 p.m." The notice then listed the many events on the evening's
agenda, including a Grand Chorus with the Church Choir, a
Highland Fling, a few readings, Physical Culture (Dumb Bell
Exercise), a Sleigh Song, Gypsy Dance and, at the start of Part II
of the entertainment, a "Duet, Instrumental...Patrick Kerwin and
Philis Kellett".[8] It is not known what instrument Miss Kellett
played, but it is assumed that Patrick played the piano.

While Patrick was growing up in his grandparents' household,
he attended high school, worked in the law office and put his
musical talents to work for pay and pleasure. He played the
trombone with Quinn's Band and Orchestra, who performed at

---

7 "Got a bad fall", *Sarnia Daily Observer*, May 3, 1905, with thanks to Patrick James Kerwin.
8 *Sarnia Daily Observer*, Dec. 20, 1905, with thanks to Randy Evans.

Patrick (centre) on trombone with members of Quinn's Band and Orchestra in front of old City Hall, Sarnia ON circa 1907.

concerts and marches. He switched to piano for out-of-town engagements when the orchestra's female pianist could not travel out of Sarnia — not even the twenty-five kilometres to Petrolia, Ontario, for example. At the time, it was not "the proper thing to do" for a woman to travel with a band.

According to my grandmother Georgina, and my mother Isobel, Patrick was an outstanding musician with a great facility for figuring out a song by ear or quickly sight-reading the music. He could have had a career in music but, considering the long view, a career in law was perhaps more suitable to his temperament and plans for a family.

Once high school was completed, in 1906, Patrick signed a clerkship contract for a paying job with R.V. LeSueur to become a student-at-law in the offices of Hanna, LeSueur & Price in Sarnia, Ontario. He registered with Osgoode Hall Law School as well. His mother had to sign as Patrick was a minor. A portion of the document reads (*italics* denote portion written by hand):

> Witness, that the said *Patrick Kerwin* of his own free will, (and with the consent and approbation of the said *Ellen Kerwin* testified by his execution of these presents) hath placed and bound himself, and by these presents doth place and bind himself clerk to the said *Richard Vryling LeSueur* to serve him from the day of the date hereof up to the date on which he shall be admitted as a student-at-law or entered as an articled clerk, whichever shall first happen in accordance

with the rules of the Law Society, and during and until the full end and term of *five* years from the date of his so being admitted or entered ....[9]

Patrick was promising to faithfully and diligently serve LeSueur as his clerk in the practice of a Solicitor. The three-page document goes on to have Patrick promise to keep secrets, not to steal and has R.V. LeSueur using "the utmost of his skill or knowledge" to teach and instruct his young clerk. Patrick became a "student-at-law", which was defined as "a law student who is undergoing training with a firm".

At that time there was an admissions test by The Law Society of Upper Canada before the student could embark upon his legal education. If the candidate was successful, they would become a student-at-law. Today in Ontario, at least two years of university is required before admission to law school. After a Bachelor of Laws (LL.B.) is obtained, articling is required, during which time the student is known as an articling student. This is then followed by the Bar Admission Course.

While working with LeSueur, Patrick was able to help his family financially as well as save towards the cost of his post-secondary education.

During Patrick's time with the firm, an advertisement placed in the local paper read as follows:

> HANNA and LeSUEUR
> Barristers, Solicitors, Notary Public
> Money to loan at lowest rates. Office — One
> Dillon Block, Front Street, Sarnia, On
> W.J. Hanna   V. LeSueur[10]

Another talent, otherwise unknown to the family about Patrick and his brother Vern, was that they were contributors to articles in the *Detroit News*. The Kerwin brothers contributed to a column written by C.C. Bradner, who worked as a reporter and later, with the newspaper's broadcast operation. Bradner was known as being a *raconteur* with a madcap wit. In a 1955 article in the *Detroit News* on this subject, reporter John C. Treen wrote:

> When the late C.C. Bradner had a column in the *Detroit News* of some 40 years ago called "Afterthoughts", two young brothers up at Sarnia, Ont., were frequent and witty contributors.

---

9 Family Archives. *See the originals reproduced at the end of this Chapter.*
10 *Sarnia Observer,* Aug. 3, 1907, 8, with thanks to Randy Evans.

They were Pat and Vern Kerwin, and Bradner thought so much of them he invited them down for a day of Detroit entertainment. It was a ripsnorter of a day, too, and the boys all but wrote the whole of Bradner's column for him.[11]

As witty as they might have been, the brothers were destined for careers outside the fields of entertainment or journalism. After finishing high school, Patrick's brother, Vern, was listed as being a brakeman and then a bookkeeper while living with his mother at 112 Elgin St. in the Gavin household.

The 1907/08 Sarnia City Point Edward Directory listed the following:

Gavin, John, shoemaker at 223 N. Front St., home at 112 Elgin St.
145½ Front Street, Hanna & LeSueur Co.
Kerwin Patrick, law student Hanna LeSueur & co. lvs 112 Elgin St.
Kerwin, Vernon, brakeman, home at 112 Elgin St.

After Patrick finished two years of working and studying law, he was ready to move on to the academic setting. Even though the contract with LeSueur had outlined five years of studying, it seems he was ready to depart and LeSueur was ready to let him go. The law school he was registered with when signing the contract with LeSueur was Osgoode Hall, located at 130 Queen Street West, Toronto, Ontario.

Unfortunately, Patrick's maternal grandfather, John Gavin, who had been a surrogate father to him, did not live to see his grandson go on to law school. Patrick and his family had lived with the Gavins for nearly ten years by this time and John Gavin was known as a kind, hard-working man who loved his family very much and was reputed to have treated them all well. Gavin died on June 12, 1908 at the age of 70.

With John Gavin celebrated and buried, Patrick went on to law school that autumn, with the continued notion that it was up to him to take care of his mother and siblings.

---

11 "Chief Justice of Canada Visits Detroit Brother", *Detroit News*, Oct. 30, 1955.

Clerkship Document, 1906

Articles of Agreement made (in duplicate) the
Twenty fifth day of *October* in the year of our Lord one
thousand *nine hundred and six*
BETWEEN *Ellen Kernin* of *the Town of Sarnia*
(the ~~father or~~ guardian) of the first Part,*
Patrick Kernin of the said Town of Sarnia
son of the said *party of the First part*
of the Second Part
And *Richard Vryling Le Sueur of the Town*
of *Sarnia, aforesaid* gentlemen, one of the Solicitors of the
Supreme Court of Judicature for Ontario, of the Third Part.

Witness, that the said *Patrick Kernin Ellen Kernin and*
of his own free will, (and with the consent and approbation of the said ~~Ellen Kernin and~~
testified by his execution of these presents,) hath placed and
bound, himself, and by these presents doth place and bind himself clerk to the said
Richard Vryling Le Sueur to serve him from the day
of the date hereof up to the day on which he shall be admitted as a student-at-law or entered as
an articled clerk, whichever shall first happen in accordance with the rules of the Law Society, and
during and until the full end and term of *five* years from the
day of his so being admitted or entered then next ensuing :

And the said *Ellen Kernin* doth
hereby for himself, his heirs, executors, and administrators, covenant with the said
Richard V Le Sueur . his executors, administrators, and assigns, that
the said *Patrick Kernin* shall and will well, faithfully and diligently serve the said *Richard V Le Sueur* as his
clerk in the practice or profession of a Solicitor of the Supreme Court of Judicature for Ontario
from the date hereof, during and until the end of the hereinbefore mentioned term.

And that the said *Patrick Kernin* shall not, at
any time, during such term, cancel, obliterate, injure, spoil, destroy, waste, embezzle, spend or
make away with any of the books, papers, writings, documents, moneys, stamps, chattels, or other
property of the said *Richard Vryling Le Sueur* his executors, administrators,
or assigns, or of his partner or partners, or of any of his clients or employers :

And that in case the said *Patrick Kernin* shall act
contrary to the last mentioned covenant, or if the said *Richard Vryling Le Sueur*
his executors, administrators, or assigns, or his partner or partners, shall sustain or suffer any loss
or damage by the misbehaviour, neglect, or improper conduct of the said *Patrick*
Kernin the said *Ellen Kernin Richard V. Le Sueur*
his heirs, executors, or administrators, shall indemnify the said *Richard V. Le Sueur*
and make good and reimburse him the amount of value thereof :

*Where a person about to be articled has attained his majority, his father or guardian is not a necessary party to the
instrument.

Clerkship Document 1 of 3.

And further, that the said _Patrick Kerwin_ will at all times keep the secret of the said _Richard U. Le Sueur_ and his partner or partners, and will at all times during said term rapidly and cheerfully obey and execute his or their lawful and reasonable commands, and shall not depart or absent himself from the service or employ of the said _Richard U. Le Sueur_ at any time during the said term without his consent first obtained, and shall from time to time, and at all times during the said term, conduct himself with all due diligence, honesty and propriety:

And the said _Patrick Kerwin_ doth hereby covenant with the said _Richard U. Le Sueur_ his executors, administrators, and assigns, that he the said _Patrick Kerwin_ will truly, honestly, and diligently serve the said _Richard U. Le Sueur_ at all times, during the said term, as a faithful clerk ought to do, in all things whatsoever, in the manner above specified.

In Consideration whereof and of _the sum of one dollar_ paid by the said _Patrick Kerwin_ (the receipt whereof the said _Richard U. Le Sueur_ doth hereby acknowledge) the said _Richard U. Le Sueur_ for himself, his heirs, executors, and administrators, doth hereby covenant with the said _Patrick Kerwin_ that the said _Richard U. Le Sueur_ will accept and take the said _Patrick Kerwin_ as his clerk;

And also that the said _Richard U. Le Sueur_ will by the best ways or means he may or can, and to the utmost of his skill or knowledge, teach and instruct, or cause to be taught and instructed, the said _Patrick Kerwin_ in the said practise or profession of a Solicitor of the Supreme Court of Judicature for Ontario, which the said _Richard U. Le Sueur_ now doth, or shall at any time hereafter during the said term use or practice:

And also will at the expiration of the said term use his best means and endeavours, at the request, cost and charges of the said _Patrick Kerwin_ and _Ellen Kerwin_ or either of them, to cause and procure him the said _Patrick Kerwin_ to be admitted as a Solicitor of the Supreme Court of Judicature for Ontario, provided the said _Patrick Kerwin_ shall have well, faithfully, and diligently served his said intended clerkship:

In Witness whereof the parties to these presents have hereunto set their hands and seals, the day and year first above mentioned.

Signed, Sealed and Delivered
BY THE WITHIN NAMED PARTIES,
IN THE PRESENCE OF

A. McKinley

Ellen Kerwin
R. U. Le Sueur
Patrick Kerwin

Clerkship Document 2 of 3.

AFFIDAVIT OF EXECUTION

Province of Ontario.

NTY OF *Lambton*

J. Anthony Ignatius McKinley

of the *Town* of *Sarnia*

in the County of *Lambton*

To Wit : *Student - at - Law* make oath and say :

1. THAT I was personally present, and did see the within Instrument and Duplicate thereof duly signed, sealed and executed by *Ellen Kerwin* *her* *and Patrick Kerwin* the parti*es* thereto :

2. THAT the said Instrument and Duplicate were executed at *the Town of Sarnia*

3. THAT I know the said part *ies*

4. THAT I am a subscribing witness to the said Instrument and Duplicate,

5. THAT the said Instrument and Duplicate were executed as aforesaid on the *Twenty fifth* day of *October* 19*06*

Sworn before me, at *Town of Sarnia*

in the County of *Lambton*

this *25th* day of *October*

in the year of Lord 19*06*

A. J. McKinley

William H. Rice

A Commissioner for taking affidavits in H. C. J., etc.

Clerkship Document 3 of 3.

Disraeli is reported to have described the legal mind as chiefly displaying itself in illustrating the obvious, explaining the evident, and expatiating on the commonplace.

—Justice Patrick Kerwin in an address to The Lawyers' Club
Toronto, November 13, 1952

Chapter 3

Law School
Toronto

In 1908 Patrick moved to Toronto to attend law school; the city's population was more than 300,000, quite a change from the town of less than 20,000 people this young man had known. By the late 19th century, Toronto had become an economic hub and one of the main destinations for immigrants seeking a new life in Canada.

The law school Patrick attended was built and operated by the Law Society of Upper Canada. The main function of the Society, established in 1797, was to ensure that all persons who practiced law in Ontario were competent, followed proper procedures and behaved ethically.[12]

Building of the school began in 1828 when the Law Society of Upper Canada spent £1,000 to purchase a six-acre plot from the Attorney General of Upper Canada, John Beverley Robinson, for the purpose of building permanent quarters. The property was just outside of what was then the Town of York on Lot Street, later renamed Queen Street. The original building was completed in 1832 and named after William Osgoode (1754-1824), the first Chief Justice of the province.

The Law Society agreed to house the Superior Courts of Justice for the province at Osgoode Hall in 1846. Osgoode Hall has been seen as the centre of legal life in Ontario since the original building was completed. In 1857, architects Cumberland and Storm added a "lordly classical portico that unified the structure, and a magnificent, vaulted library within — thus creating one of the finest edifices in Toronto in that day or this".[13]

In 1874 the Law Society transferred the central and west portions of the building to the government, freeing itself from its obligations as landlord to the courts. Today, the Law Society of Upper Canada and Government of Ontario remain co-owners of Osgoode Hall. 'Old Osgoode Hall' remains the headquarters of the

---

12 Mandate broadened in May 2007 to regulate providers of all legal services, including independent paralegals.
13 J.M.S. Careles, *Toronto to 1918 - An Illustrated History* (Lorimer, 1984), 89.

Law Society of Upper Canada, and houses the Court of Appeal of Ontario. The law school was relocated in 1969 to the campus of York University and named New Osgoode Hall. The school is reputed to have the largest law library in the Commonwealth.

During Patrick's time at Osgoode Hall, from the fall of 1908 to spring 1911, he attended classes at the location on the corner of Queen Street and University Avenue, now in the heart of downtown Toronto.

~

At the time, formal law school training was seen as supplementary to the education would-be lawyers received in law offices as articling clerks. The lectures at the school were most often delivered by practicing lawyers rather than by formal law professors. The wonderfully ornate courtrooms in Osgoode Hall included a few rows of plain-looking benches at the back for students who were obliged to attend anytime the Court of Appeal was in session. In this prestigious school, Patrick not only learned

King Street, Toronto, circa 1909.

a great deal as a student in the classroom, but also in court. His classes included: contracts, equity, practice, torts, real property, common law, criminal law, constitutional law, commercial law and company law. The courtroom brought forward whatever subject was on the docket.

The faculty members of Osgoode Hall Law School when Patrick attended included the following professors.[14] John D. Falconbridge: called to the Bar of Ontario in 1899; appointed a part-time lecturer at Osgoode Hall Law School in 1909 and served as Dean from 1923 to 1948; reputed to be the country's leading scholar of commercial law. John King: lawyer in Berlin (now Kitchener), Ontario, father of future Prime Minister, Mackenzie King; in 1893 accepted a part-time lectureship at Osgoode Hall; respected writer whose work included literary articles for the *Toronto Globe*, historical and biographical essays, and books on his legal specialty — defamation and criminal libel. A.H. Marsh: noted lawyer, writer and lecturer. N.W. Hoyles: Principal of Osgoode Hall Law School; a Newfoundlander turned Toronto lawyer and long-time head of Osgoode Hall Law School; later declared that the admission of women to the school was the greatest achievement of his time there. E.N. Armour: lawyer, educator, journalist, poet; taught real-property law and constitutional law while continuing his private practice and legal writing; he taught that *The British North America Act, 1867*, established the central government's authority over the provinces. J. McGregor Young: Professor of Constitutional and International Law. J. Shirley Denison: prominent Toronto lawyer; Treasurer of the Law Society of Upper Canada from 1944 to 1947; known for his great interest and contribution to the work of the Society; under the terms of his will, the residue of his estate passed to the Law Society for the relief of indigent Barristers and Solicitors and their families.

Until the 1950's, legal training in English Canada was dominated by an overwhelming emphasis on practical training, largely in law offices where aspiring students observed and participated in the daily activities of practitioners of law and learned the mechanics of legal practice. The philosophy of such an education was expressed by one commentator in 1923:

> There is a tendency in many, in this utilitarian age in which we live, even amongst those aspiring to practise one or other learned professions, to despise all learning that does not appear directly to be of assistance in making money.[15]

---

14 Courtesy of Paul Leatherdale, Archivist, The Law Society of Upper Canada, Osgoode Hall, June 12, 2012.
15 P. Home, "Legal Education in Ontario", *Canadian Bar Review 1*, (1923), 685-6.

~

No records were located in regard to Patrick's living arrangements from 1908 to 1909, but in 1910 the Toronto City Directory showed him residing at #1-243 McCaul Street [16] (just south of the University of Toronto) and articling with F.E. Hodgins, King's Counsel (K.C.). Hodgins was a partner with the firm of Hodgins, Heighington & Bastedo (59 Victoria Street) and later appointed to a seat on the Appeal Board of Ontario. The home where Patrick lodged is no longer in existence and there is now a small park behind a large building in that location.

For his last semester, from the fall of 1910 until graduation in 1911, Patrick resided at #1-374 Berkeley[17], a beautiful and well-kept Victorian-style duplex that still stands near the corner of Carlton and Parliament Streets. While living at this residence, Patrick articled for W.M. Douglas, a prominent Toronto lawyer. Law school, and his other activities, were only a streetcar ride away.

While attending school in Toronto, Patrick articled with the two Toronto barristers and solicitors already noted and, when back in Sarnia for the summers, he continued to article with R.V. LeSueur. It was in this Sarnia law firm that he was fortunate enough to meet Henry Howitt, Q.C., who would make a significant difference in Patrick's life in years to come. According to the Canadian Law Lists, Howitt practiced in Sarnia with the firm of Hanna, LeSueur & Howitt in 1910 and 1911.[18]

As a student attending Osgoode Hall, and in spite of having articled in law offices, Patrick needed extra funds to pay the bills as his family was not able to assist with continuing educational costs. His musical talents proved useful, and he was hired as a pianist for the picture shows in film halls. Films at the time were sometimes called photoplays, moving pictures, or a number of other descriptions as the industry grew. In the pre-dialogue era the films were not called 'silent movies', as this term only came into common usage upon the arrival of the sound era. Films at the time had live musical accompaniment to capture or enhance the mood of the action up on the screen. While some theatres had small orchestras, they were costly to keep up. Luckily for Patrick,

---

16 Toronto Archives, Toronto City Directory, Reel 57.
17 Ibid., Reel 58.
18 Courtesy of Paul Leatherdale, Archivist, June 7, 2012.

Auditorium Theatre, Queen St. West, Toronto, circa 1910.
commons.wikimedia.org/wiki/File:Auditorium_Theatre_in_Toronto.jpg.

the piano was the instrument of choice for moving picture accompaniment.

This new form of entertainment was inexpensive to attend and was considered a lower class activity by many. As this was not the type of occupation any 'respectable' young man would be involved with, his piano accompaniment job was all very hush-hush with only his closest friends and family knowing what he did to make ends meet.

During the time leading up to the sound era, films were shot and projected by a hand-cranked process, which meant that films were seen at a 'frames-per-second' rate that differs from that of the sound films. Some films could be as short as a minute or two, with the vast majority being up to ten minutes, depending on the subject matter. The length of time a film lasted also depended on how fast it was hand-cranked; if the projectionist cranked too fast, the film would end sooner than expected and vice-versa, and Patrick would have to adjust his piano accompaniment accordingly.

At the time, an enormous amount of film was being produced, much more than today, if that is at all conceivable. Most films of the period did not have sheet music written for them. They may have come from the distributor with cue sheets as to the type of music to be played, but not many would have provided this kind of information or direction for the musical accompaniment.

Patrick had to rely on his knowledge of popular music, classical music and his ability to improvise. He most likely had some set pieces, which he would use regularly for different moods of films. Additionally, he would not have had much, if any, time to prepare for new programmes nor would he have had the chance to pre-screen the films to be played as the slate of films changed on a regular basis, with popular ones being held over.

A story his daughter related of these times involved her father improvising or reading the music. He memorized what to play for the films and then repeated it numerous times. This allowed Patrick to put his law textbooks up on the piano so he could study while he played along with the action in the film — an excellent example of multitasking.

At the start of the industry, moving picture displays were often used as part of a vaudeville slate, mixed in with the live performers. The first permanent movie theatre in Toronto was the Theatorium at 183 Yonge Street near Queen Street. It was opened by John C. Griffin in March 1906.[19] Venues that are still in existence in Toronto, such as Massey Hall and the Royal Alexandra Theatre, showed films during the early years of the movie industry. It was a very exciting time in film history, and Patrick was involved on the leading edge of this evolving art form, even though he could not tell anyone about it at the time.

The clothing required for a young man at that time invariably was a suit, of which Patrick was rumoured to have only two at the time, along with starched collars. If one was worn or in need of cleaning or repair, the other was used. A suit from Eaton's would cost from five to ten dollars, depending on the cut and material.

The cost of getting around to school, law offices, theatres and home on the streetcar was two cents during the day and five cents for the night fare, when returning home from a late movie show.

While attending law school, Patrick met a young lady attending university for her teacher's degree. Her name was Isobel (Belle) Mace, and she invited him for tea at the Mace family home on Elm Avenue in the Rosedale area of Toronto. Though things did not work out between Belle and Patrick, he did strike up a friendship with Belle's next-older sister, Georgina, or Georgie to

---

19 Peter Morris, Embattled Shadows – A History of Canadian Cinema 1895 - 1939 (McGill-Queen's, 1978), 21.

Young Patrick and Georgina in the early days of their courtship, circa 1910.

those who knew her. "These two were destined to marry", Belle was to say later.

At Osgoode Hall Law School, some of Patrick's fellow students observed that, although he was not a particularly brilliant student in their opinion, he made up for this by hard, plodding work. "He had to slog like hell", an intimate said. "While his classmates at Osgoode were out having a good time, he kept his nose to the books."[20]

All this hard work was not in vain, for Patrick graduated at the top of his class in the Class of 1911. Other notable Osgoode Hall graduates of the Class of 1911 included Frank J. Hughes (Justice in the Supreme Court of Canada); J.E. Maden (Judge of the United Counties of Lennox and Addington); James Parker (Judge of the County of York); H.H. Davis (Appellate Division of

20 "Sketch 1142", *CP Biographical Service,* Sep. 30, 1959, 1.

P. Kerwin's Osgoode Hall Graduation photo, 1911.

Supreme Court of Ontario). In addition, there were sixteen other graduates in 1911 who became honoured with King's Counsel (K.C) designations while many other graduates went on to hold prominent positions in both legal and business circles.

According to family lore, Patrick was offered several positions with prominent Toronto firms upon graduating. However, his daughter recalled her father saying that he felt more comfortable practicing in a smaller community or as "a big fish in a small pond".

In summing up his time in Toronto, the *Fortnightly Law Journal* described Patrick as having "...studied with some of the foremost members of the profession in the Province".[21]

Upon graduation from Osgoode Hall and admission to the bar, Patrick briefly moved back to Sarnia to work with the firm of Hanna, LeSueur & Howitt. There his friend, Henry Howitt, a native of Guelph, suggested Patrick go to Guelph where he knew of a job opportunity with a law firm. Howitt himself was to join his uncle's firm in Guelph in the near future. Patrick accompanied Howitt to the 'Royal City', as Guelph is known, and was interviewed in 1911. It all went well and he joined the firm of Guthrie & Guthrie (Donald Guthrie and his son, Hugh Guthrie). Patrick's life as a practicing lawyer was about to begin in earnest in a city that was new to him.

---

21 *Fortnightly Law Journal*, Sep. 1935, 5.

I have always thought that
"The Law Society of Upper Canada"
is a full-blooded, richly endowed phrase
that cried out to be relished and
rolled around the tongue.

—Justice Patrick Kerwin in an address to graduating students,
Osgoode Hall, Toronto, June 29, 1950

Chapter 4

Start of a Career
Guelph

Disputes can be anything from a minor disagreement between two persons all the way to, and including, a full-fledged war involving millions. It can be a struggle resulting from incompatible or opposing needs regarding a singular event.

Conflict is a basic component of human interaction and an element we encounter that affects or drives us all at one time or another. Many disagreements need to be formally resolved in such a manner that we can all live and progress in safety, to ensure a functioning society. In order for this to happen, there is a process and a place for resolving disputes in our current way of life, in the hands of the men and women who act as our legal representatives and judges in our courts, within a system for the peaceable determination of disputes. Representing one side of these disputes would be the newly-graduated Patrick, now employed with the law firm, Guthrie & Guthrie in Guelph, Ontario.

In the spring of 1911, just after graduating from law school, Patrick, at the age of twenty-one, arrived in Guelph to start his career. There he discovered a thriving community with railroads, schools, a seminary and a population of over 32,000 inhabitants in the electoral district of Wellington South. Patrick quickly and purposefully tied himself to the community in full by joining various organizations and clubs in the city.

During his employment with Guthrie & Guthrie, the Law Society of Upper Canada certified that P. Kerwin of Guelph was duly admitted as a Solicitor of the Supreme Court Judicature for Ontario on December 7, 1911. The document confirmed that he was now on the:

> ...Rolls of said Court as one of the Solicitors thereof; He has this day paid the fees mentioned hereunder; This Certificate for year commencing with the first day of Michaelmas Term, 1911, is issued pursuant to the Revised Statutes of Ontario, 1897, Chapter 174.

The fees referred to above were $2.00 for the Bar, and $15.00 for the Solicitor's fee. The total of $17.00 was paid in full and the document was signed by the Secretary of the Law Society of Upper Canada.

Another document from the High Court of Justice, which had $0.54 worth of stamps on it (perhaps sent registered mail), read as follows (Family Archives):

> The High Court of Justice
>
> This is to certify that (Patrick Kerwin) of the (Town) of (Sarnia) in the county of (Lambton) was on the (20th) day of (December) in the year of Our Lord, one thousand nine hundred and (eleven) and in the (second) year of the Reign of His Majesty King Edward the seventh (name Edward being stroked out and GEORGE written in; seventh stroked out and fifth written in), duly sworn in and enrolled as a Solicitor of the Supreme Court of Judicature of Ontario, on the fiat of the Honourable Mr. Justice Middleton.
> Given under the hand of the Registrar and the Seal of said Court this (26th) day of (December),
> A.D. 1911.
> Signed <illegible> by the Registrar of the High Court of Justice for Ontario.

The date the certificate was signed showed that the Registrar was hard at work doing paperwork on Boxing Day, 1911.

Information gathered from the law firm's ledger[22] show that, in January of 1911, the salary drawn by the senior partner, Donald Guthrie, was $25.00 per week, whereas the junior partner, Hugh Guthrie, was paid $15.00 per week. Patrick's first appearance in the firm's account ledger is shown as March 11, 1911 when he paid $5.00 to the firm. Later, the firm issued a cheque on March 18, 1911 for that very same amount. The entry does not specify whom the amount was paid to but a reference to "fees" is noted. The next entry concerning Patrick in the ledger was made on May 13, 1911 when he was paid $50.00 as two weeks salary — an interesting amount as it is more than the junior partner's (Hugh Guthrie) salary at the time.

---

22 The Law Society of Upper Canada Archives, Guthrie, Guthrie & Kerwin Ledger.

As time passed, there are entries in the ledger showing amounts issued by cheque to Mrs. E. Kerwin (Patrick's mother) ranging from $15.00 to $25.00 — certainly much more than Patrick could have provided if he were still driving a horse and cart to deliver meat for a living.

By May 1913, the firm became known as Guthrie, Guthrie & Kerwin — quite an achievement for a young, twenty-three-year-old, up-and-coming lawyer whose salary was now set at $35.00 per week. Things had always been busy at the firm since Hugh Guthrie was occupied as an elected member of the Canadian House of Commons as of the year 1900,

County Solicitors Building, Guelph Ontario, Patrick's place of work (Photo by S.G. McKenna, 2012).

and the senior partner, Donald Guthrie, had additional duties as the City Solicitor for Guelph and also the Solicitor for Wellington County. The ledger also showed a number of times when Patrick asked for, and received, advances on his salary, especially in the spring of 1914, which is not surprising as this was just prior to his wedding in June of that same year.

The law firm that Patrick was now a partner in handled a wide range of cases, including Bankruptcy and Insolvency, Civil matters, Contracts, Creditors and Debtors Law, Divorce (listed as "Damages for Alienation of Wife's Affections"), Criminal, Damages, Employment, Municipal, Real Property, Natural Resources, Tort Law and Civil Liability, Wills, Estates and Trust Law, to name the main fields covered by the law office.

Results of the wide range of cases varied — sometimes in favour of his client(s), sometimes not. Examples include:

1914; *Guelph Worsted Spinning Co. v. Guelph* — flood damage to the company's property and buildings, Kerwin et al for the City. The hearings were in Guelph and Toronto with Judge Middleton finding in favour of the company.

1914; *Scrimger v. Town of Galt* — Municipal Corporations, Kerwin for the Plaintiff, Judgment in plaintiff's favour with costs.

1915; *City of Berlin v. Anderson* — Assessment and Taxes, case heard in Waterloo; Kerwin for defendant, action dismissed with costs.

1915; *Burrows v. Grand Trunk R.W. Co. and the City of Guelph* — Negligence of Railway Company and City Corporation; I. F. Hellmuth, K.C., and P. Kerwin, for the defendant city corporation; dismissed against City of Guelph without costs, Grand Trunk liable.

1916; *Creditors of Parkin Elevator Co. Limited v. Parkin Elevator Co. Limited* — Appeal by creditor in winding up the company; Kerwin for appellant; appeal allowed.

1917; *Mahoney v. Guelph (City)*; Negligence of Engineer — Injury to Member of Board; I. F. Hellmuth, K.C., and P. Kerwin, for the defendant city corporation; Action dismissed. No order as to costs.

1920; *R. v. Kaplan* — *Ontario Temperance Act*, Conviction for "Having or Giving" alcoholic beverages; Kerwin, for the defendant; Conviction quashed.

The lawyer, I. F. Hellmuth (Isadore Frederick, known by his second name) worked with Patrick's firm on a number of cases. This Canadian-born, Cambridge-educated lawyer had a practice in Toronto while he worked in conjunction with Guthrie & Kerwin.

Patrick's maternal grandmother, Catherine (Welton) Gavin, died in Sarnia on December 30, 1913. Patrick, of course, went to Sarnia for her funeral. This was the woman whose home he had lived in after his father's death and a person he loved very much. Her will left everything to her daughter, Ellen (Gavin) Kerwin, and named Patrick as Executor. Patrick's mother Ellen now officially ran the household on Elgin Avenue, as she had unofficially been doing for a number of years.

~

Donald and Hugh Guthrie, the father and son law partners, Patrick's employers and partners, influenced him greatly. An undated business card for the firm reads as follows:

Guthrie, Guthrie & Kerwin
Barristers, Solicitors, Notaries, etc.
Douglas Street
GUELPH, Ontario
Solicitors for City of Guelph, county of Wellington:
Wellington Mutual Insurance Company

Guelph Courthouse 1910, where Patrick argued many cases. (Wellington County Museum & Archives, wcmaonline.on.ca 01-2011).

Donald Guthrie, senior partner in the law firm at the time Patrick joined the practice, was born in Edinburgh, Scotland in 1840. At the age of 13, Donald and his two sisters travelled with their parents to New York City intending to join their Uncle Patrick McGregor, a barrister, who had left Scotland a few years previously and had done well. Unfortunately, as was common in the sea voyages of the day, there were many deaths due to cholera and the Guthrie children lost their parents during the trip to this disease. Once in the USA, Donald clerked in New York law offices, but after about one year, moved to Kingston in Canada West (as Ontario was then known) with his family, as his uncle had secured a position as a professor at Queen's University in that city.

Donald studied law in Toronto and, upon graduation from Osgoode Hall, moved to Guelph and took a position as managing clerk in the law offices of Fergusson and Kingsmill (A.J. Fergusson-Blair being his cousin). [23] In late 1863 a Guelph newspaper published the following announcement (Family Archives):

23 Hilary Stead, *Guelph – A People's Heritage 1827-2002* (City of Guelph, 2002), 38.

> Upon the retirement of the Hon. A.J. Fergusson-Blair (son of the founder of Fergus ON), of Fergusson & Kingsmill; business will be continued at the same office (Solicitor's Building) by John J. Kingsmill and Donald Guthrie under the name of Kingsmill & Guthrie.

Fergusson left to take care of his family's inherited Scottish estate in 1863. Kingsmill was appointed a judge of Bruce County shortly after Donald Guthrie joined the firm. By 1869, the law firm was in his name only.

Donald Guthrie was solicitor for City of Guelph and some neighbouring towns and counties from 1868 and was known as an expert in municipal law. Adding to his already busy schedule, he became president of the Guelph Gas Company after helping to organize it, and in 1870, upon its inception, became President of the Light, Heat and Power Corporation.

By 1870, the firm was known as Guthrie, Watt and Cutten. In 1882, Cutten retired, and in 1888 Hugh Guthrie, Donald's son, joined the practice. Watt retired in 1906. The firm was then known as Guthrie & Guthrie.

In 1876 the Liberal Party nominated Guthrie who was elected as representative of the Wellington South riding in the House of Commons. In 1882, for business reasons, he declined to run but he later ran in the Provincial election of 1886. Although this was difficult for him as he suffered from deafness from 1884 onward, he held that seat until 1894 when he retired. In 1895 he was appointed Inspector of Registry Offices for the Province of Ontario.

Donald Guthrie was married in 1863 to Eliza Margaret MacVicar and they had seven children: four boys and three daughters.

Hugh Guthrie was born in Guelph on August 13, 1866, the eldest son of Donald Guthrie, K.C., and was educated at the Guelph Collegiate Institute and Osgoode Hall, Toronto. He was called to the Bar in February 1888 and joined Guthrie and Watt. He married Henrietta Scarfe in January 1888 and they had three sons and one daughter. Hugh Guthrie brought Patrick into the firm in 1911.

Hugh Guthrie ran as a Liberal in the federal election of 1900 for the riding of Wellington South and won a seat in Parliament. During World War I, Prime Minister Borden, a Conservative member, put together the Unionist government made up of both Liberals and Conservatives as well as one Independent and one Labour member. Hugh Guthrie agreed to join and became the Solicitor General of Canada in this government on October 4, 1917. With the dissolution of the Unionist coalition in 1921, Hugh Guthrie did not rejoin the

Liberals but rather sat with the Conservatives for the rest of his parliamentary career. He also held the posts of Minister of Militia and Defence, Acting Minister of Justice and Acting Minister of National Defence (for a period all Cabinet ministers, other than the Prime Minister, were called acting as noted below), Minister of National Defence, temporary leader of the Conservative Party, Minister of Justice and, in 1926, Leader of the Opposition. In his political career he served as a minister in the governments of Prime Ministers Borden, Meighen, and Bennett.

After being defeated in his bid for re-election in 1935, Hugh Guthrie accepted the post of Chief Commissioner on the Board of Railway Commissioners and served in that position until his death.

Until 1931, Canada followed the rules set out in England to guard against abuse and influence stating, "... no person can hold an office of profit or emolument under the Crown and remain a member of the House of Commons." This meant that a Cabinet Minister could not receive a salary and hold their seat in the House of Commons. The only way a member could do so was if the constituency elected the member while he or she was already holding office of a salaried Minister. Otherwise an extra election would be necessary. In 1926, Prime Minister Meighen created the 'Acting Ministry', where the persons named to a portfolio in Cabinet were not the heads of the departments but were acting heads, and, as such, received no salary.

After Donald Guthrie's death in 1915, the firm was later renamed Guthrie & Kerwin. Thus, only a few years after Patrick had joined the law practice, he had become a full partner. The document included below deals with Patrick becoming a partner in Guthrie, Guthrie & Kerwin with only Hugh and Patrick as partners prior to the name change noted above. The document also mentions Patrick acting as an Examiner of Law School (at Osgoode Hall).

When Hugh Guthrie was appointed a minister of the Federal Government of 1917, Patrick became the senior partner in the Guelph law firm of Guthrie & Kerwin. When Hugh Guthrie was named a member of the Federal Cabinet in 1918, Patrick became the head of the firm and required another lawyer to help with the ongoing workload. He hired R. B. Hungerford who became a valued business partner and good friend. In later years, Hungerford took over the firm. Upon Guthrie's rise to the Cabinet, he had to resign the posts of City Solicitor for Guelph and Prosecutor for Wellington

Hugh Guthrie, Esq., and P. Kerwin, Esq., hereby agree as of January 1st 1916, to practise law together as partners under the name, firm and style of Guthrie, Guthrie & Kerwin; all debts of the firm of Guthrie, Guthrie & Kerwin, down to January 1st 1916 and all debts of Guthrie & Guthrie, or Guthrie , Watt & Guthrie, or Guthrie & Watt, to be assumed and paid or arranged for by the said Hugh Guthrie. All accounts owing to any of the above firms for services rendered prior to January 1st 1916 to belong to the said Hugh Guthrie so far as the said P. Kerwin is concerned. All books and assets of any of the above firms as of December 31st 1915 to belong to the said Hugh Guthrie so far as the said P. Kerwin is concerned. All books and assets purchased by the new firm since January 1st 1916 to be owned by the said Hugh Guthrie and P. Kerwin in equal shares. All net profits of the new firm to be divided as follows;-

The first $4000.00 equally; all over $4000.00 two-thirds to the said Hugh Guthrie and one-third to the said P. Kerwin.

Any sum to be received from time to time by Hugh Guthrie as Parliamentary indemnity to be retained by him without accounting to the partnership; the same arrangement to apply to anything to be received by P. Kerwin as Examiner of Law School.

Partnership,determined at end of any year on either party giving three months previous notice.

Dated 29ᵗʰ Feby 1916.

H Guthrie

P. Kerwin

Law Practice Agreement between H. Guthrie and P. Kerwin, Feb. 19, 1916.

County. These tasks were taken over by Patrick — who now had very busy days as part of a burgeoning career for a young professional who had yet to reach thirty years of age.

IT IS AGREED between Hugh Guthrie and Patrick Kerwin, both of the City of Guelph, Ontario, that the said Hugh Guthrie shall have no interest in the firm of Guthrie, Guthrie, & Kerwin, other than as Solicitor for the City of Guelph and the County of Wellington.

Guelph, January 1st.,1918.

H Guthrie

P Kerwin

Dissolution of Law Practice Partnership between H. Guthrie and P. Kerwin, Jan. 1, 1918.

Shortly before Patrick was to leave Guthrie & Kerwin, a letter was received at the law firm's office from the Ontario Government dated August 30, 1932. The letterhead noted it had been sent by the 'Department of the Provincial Secretary, Office of the Minister, Department of Game and Fisheries'. The letter was addressed to 'P. Kerwin, Esq., K.C., Messrs. Guthrie & Kerwin, Guelph, Ont.' and was written by George Challies, the Provincial Secretary and Registrar (1931 to 1934). The subject matter was in response to a query Patrick had sent asking about the history, make-up and provincial electoral information for the South Wellington district. The information noted the communities within the district, others added at later dates, and outlined the members of the Parliament of Upper Canada, then the Province of Canada, and, finally, the Province of Ontario who had represented the area. The information covered the time span from 1821 to the date of the letter. It is interesting to note what subjects captured Patrick's imagination at the time. One name stood out amongst the many and it was that of Donald Guthrie who, in 1887, sat as the Member from South Wellington for the sixth and seventh sittings of Parliament for the Province of Ontario. This, of course, was well before Patrick's time with the law firm.

Speaking of Patrick's responsibilities in the practice, the *Fort-nightly Law Journal* wrote:

> ...during the entire period his partner [Guthrie]
> occupied a seat in the House of Commons, necessitating
> his absence at Ottawa for a great portion of the year.
>
> In these absences the handling of the firm's extensive
> practice devolved upon the future Judge...this period of
> twenty-one years was one of great professional activity for
> young Kerwin, during which he was engaged frequently at
> the assizes as representative of the Attorney-General of
> Ontario. His firm were also solicitors for both the City of
> Guelph and the County of Wellington, in addition to
> several townships of the latter. This entailed an extensive
> municipal practice. The partnership also acted as local
> solicitors for one of the leading banks and for two of the
> hospitals. On his admission to the Bar and for several
> years afterwards, Mr. Kerwin acted as one of the examiners
> of the law school. He also — for about five years — acted as
> Deputy of the Inspector of Registry Offices, and as such
> visited many parts of the Province...At the time of his
> appointment to the Ontario Bench, Mr. Kerwin was a
> member of the Parole Board of the Province. This old
> established business, founded by his partner's father, had
> its ramifications extending far beyond the confines of the
> city, throughout the whole county. At almost every spring
> and fall term of the Court, Mr. Kerwin appeared either on
> the civil or criminal side — or on both.[24]

---

24 *Fortnightly Law Journal*, Sep. 16, 1935, 5.

Every lawyer knows that no system of law worthy of the name, whether it be cast in the form of a code or not, can be a mere collection of mechanical rules. By the law, a lawyer means the law in operation, the law in action; the law as it is commonly said is a living organism, within limits, of course, the power to adapt itself to changing circumstances.

—Justice Lyman Duff, 1915

Chapter 5

Family and Career
Guelph

During Patrick's time in Toronto he had become acquainted with Georgina (Georgie) Mace. As time went by, Georgina and Patrick's relationship became serious and, once he was well established in Guelph, they decided to marry.

On June 2, 1914, Patrick Grandcourt Kerwin married Mary Margaret Georgina Mace at Our Lady of Lourdes Church, located at 520 Sherbourne Street in Toronto.

A newspaper clipping at the time described their wedding:

Kerwin — Mace

The church of Our Lady Lourdes at half-past nine o'clock this morning was the scene of a pretty June wedding. When the marriage was solemnized of Georgie, daughter of the late George Mace and Mrs. Mace of Elm Avenue to Mr. Patrick F. [sic] Kerwin, the Rev. Father Canning performed the ceremony, the church being decorated with palms and white flowers. The bride, who was given away by her brother, Mr. Frank Mace, wore a gown of ivory satin with old point lace and pearls and tulle lace veil with sprays of orange blossoms, and she carried a shower of lilies of the valley and orchids. Miss Isabel [sic] Mace was her sister's bridesmaid, in buttercup satin with overdress of chiffon and a hat to match and she carried American beauty roses. Mr. (Vern) Kerwin attended his brother and the ushers were Mr. Harry Hefferman and Mr. A. McKinley. Mrs. Mace held a reception at her home in Elm Avenue, when she was wearing black silk and lace, with a bouquet of lilies of the valley. Mr. and Mrs. Kerwin left later for Winnipeg, the bride travelling in a mahogany cloth suit and a black and white hat. On their return they will reside in Guelph.[25]

---

25 "Kerwin — Mace", uncredited newspaper article, 1914, Georgina Kerwin's collection.

Mrs. George A. Mace
requests the honour of your presence
at the marriage of her daughter
Georgina Margaret
to
Mr. Patrick Grandcourt Kerwin
on Tuesday morning, June the second
nineteen hundred and fourteen
at half past nine o'clock
Our Lady of Lourdes Church
Toronto

Kerwin and Mace wedding invitation, 1914.

Patrick and Georgie on their wedding day at her mother's home, June 1914.

The Ontario Marriage Certificate showed the bride's parents' names (George and Bridget); Patrick's age (25); marriage date and location. However, it gave the bride's age as 24, but, having been born on June 4, 1886, she was actually just two days shy of her twenty-eighth birthday. This ruse of hiding how old she truly was kept going for many years as it was the norm for the groom to be older than the bride. Perhaps Patrick never knew her real age, or, more likely, it simply was not discussed as it did not really make any difference. Also incorrect was the groom's birthplace, listed as Guelph (that's where he then lived and worked but he was born in Sarnia), and his mother's name was misspelled as "Given" whereas it should have read "Gavin".

For their honeymoon, the newlyweds took the train to Winnipeg, Manitoba, where Patrick managed to coordinate time away with his new bride, and a meeting with several members of the Canadian Bar Association. There was no official meeting of the Association on record for that period but, when inquiries were made within the family, it was said that Patrick was combining a dose of practicality with the honeymoon.

Gladys Moran, a cousin of Patrick, and Frank Mace, brother of Georgina, met at the Kerwin-Mace wedding. They later married.

Georgina's grandfather, 'Squire' William Mace, was born in Todenham, Gloucestershire, England in 1803 and later moved to a farm near Sydenham, Ontario, in the early 1840s where he

Wedding reception at Mrs. Mace's home in Rosedale. L-R: Vern Kerwin, Patrick Kerwin, Georgina Mace, Isobel (Belle) Mace. June 1914.

The wedding party's official photograph: bride and groom at the far right. To the bride's right is Donald Guthrie (Patrick's employer); to the groom's right is the best man and, again to the right stands the maid of honour. The mothers of the bride and groom are sitting on the left, clad in darker clothing. (Mrs. Mace sits in the chair, 2nd from left, and Mrs. Gavin sits in the far left chair with her daughter, Frances Kerwin, sitting on arm of chair. Hugh Guthrie is standing in the middle with the top hat on. 1914.

raised his family. He later sold the farm and moved into the town of Sydenham proper, where he was a distiller and brewer.

George Mace (born 1850), Georgina's father, is reputed to have run off as a young man to California in order to seek his fortune in the latter part of that state's gold rush. He left with twenty-five dollars and pair of new boots and made it back a few years later with only the boots. He married Bridget Ryan and they began a family. Living on a farm in Exeter, Ontario, George was more interested in breeding horses than farming and was reputed to not be doing very well financially. The family moved to Ottawa when he changed careers. The Mace family lived in Ottawa for about four years, and were living in a double house located behind the University of Ottawa's Tabaret Hall when their daughter, Georgina (the author's maternal grandmother), was born. When she was still a youngster, the family moved to Toronto and lived in the neighbourhood of Rosedale, so-named as a tribute to the abundance of wild roses that graced the hillsides of the Sheriff William Jarvis estate. The home was bought from a family with the surname of Massey. Many years later, Georgina Kerwin spoke to Governor General Massey and asked him if her father might have purchased the home from a relative of his. Governor General Massey, who was not able to confirm this replied courteously, "There were many branches to the family".

~

At the end of the summer of 1914, the year the First World War broke out, Patrick, now a recently married man, felt a personal responsibility to do his part and went to enlist along with others caught up in the patriotic fervour. The story our family heard was that when Patrick met with the army recruiter, a person he knew well, the recruiter sent the young lawyer on his way with the advice, "Go home and be with your wife. You're just married and, anyway, there are plenty of volunteers and it'll all probably be over by Christmas." The recruiter was correct in that there were plenty of volunteers for the first Canadian contingent to go overseas and fight for King and country, but was wholly incorrect about how long the war would last. The next year, as the war continued, the Kerwins welcomed their first child.

The Kerwin home on Park Avenue in Guelph with original owners, Mr. and Mrs. Keleher pictured, circa 1894.

Those who did go overseas included Patrick's classmates: Norman Towers, called to the Bar at the same time as Patrick; Stewart Cowan, schoolmate with Patrick in Sarnia as well as Osgoode Hall and articled in Sarnia; William Hanna, articled in his father's law firm, Hanna and LeSueur (as did Patrick). However, all of these classmates died in World War I — a sobering experience for the young father and lawyer.[26]

Prior to buying their own home in Guelph, Patrick and Georgina lived at 55 Kirkland Street, the home where their first child, Mary Eleanor Isobel Kerwin, was born on June 16, 1915.

The home they purchased was a large, two-storey house at 17 Park Avenue, bought in 1916 from the widow of James Keleher, who was moving from the large home to live with one of her daughters. The story goes that Mrs. Keleher could not take everything with her, so she left a number of items for the new owners. One of these items was a crystal carafe and a set of matching heavy drinking glasses with the letters 'E.E.K' inscribed upon them, which ended up in the home of Patrick's daughter, Isobel. For years our family wondered *which* Kerwin 'E.E.K' was. When finally asked, my mother (Isobel) explained that the letter "K" was for Keleher, then went on to tell how Mrs. Keleher not only

26 Research by Randy Evans.

left behind these drinking glasses, but also a bust of Byron, a horse-hair couch and a number of other items throughout the home.

The horse-hair couch was very slippery, my mother recalled, and she and her siblings had great fun jumping up on the couch and sliding off onto the floor of their lovely home on Park Avenue.

The 1917 City of Guelph Directory indicated street, alphabetical businesses and other miscellaneous information for the price of only $3.00. This directory, issued in September of 1917 as a corrected version of the original 1917 version issued earlier that year, noted:

> Guthrie, Guthrie & Kerwin (Hugh Guthrie, MP, P Kerwin),
>   barristers & solicitors, 15 Douglas
> Guthrie, Hugh, PM (Guthrie, Guthrie & Kerwin), h 49 Edinburgh s
> Hattin, Viola, stenog Guthrie, Guthrie & Kerwin, 330 Eramosa rd
> Kerwin, Patrick, (Guthrie, Guthrie & Kerwin), h 71 Park av

A 1920 unnamed newspaper clipping saved by Georgina reported the death of her mother, Bridget (Ryan) Mace in Toronto at the age of seventy-three. The Kerwins took the train to Toronto for the funeral, leaving the children with a minder during the time away. Georgina's father, George Mace, had died in 1911, a few years prior to her marriage.

At Patrick and Georgina's home on Park Avenue in Guelph, the sound of children playing and laughing became the norm with the addition of three more children: Patrick, George and Philip.

By 1924, the Municipal tax rolls of Guelph (with population of approximately 16,000) showed Patrick still residing at 71 Park Avenue with the home's estimated worth set at $7,700. His age was listed as 36 and he was shown as a British Subject (Canadian citizenship did not come until after WWII). He was also listed as the owner of the home and his occupation that of a barrister. The number of persons in residence was indicated as six: husband, wife and four children (with young Phil only a year old by then).[27] The Kerwins could afford to have a maid regularly help Georgina run the household, a young woman of whom my mother (Isobel) spoke fondly.

We were told that our grandmother picked wild blueberries in the nearby cemetery when the children were young. It is said she liked the blueberries there very much and it was always quiet as no one else seemed to want to pick in that environment.

---

27 *Guelph Municipal Tax Roll*, (City of Guelph, 1924).

Isobel, Phil, George and Pat Kerwin, circa 1924.

In 1924, Patrick's brother, Vernon, married his fiancée, Rose Hanlon. Vern and Rose had met in Detroit, Michigan and fell in love while both working in the advertising field. Mr. and Mrs. Vernon Kerwin had no children and remained in their adopted city the rest of their lives with Vern climbing the ladder in the probation office for the Wayne County Circuit Court. At the time of Vern's retirement in 1964, he had become the Chief Probation Officer, which included the administration of the County offices.

Also during Patrick's years in Guelph, his sister, Frances, announced her marriage to George Beatty in June of 1930. The wedding notice reported:

A quiet wedding was solemnized Saturday morning, June 21, 1930, at the parish house of Our Lady of Mercy church, when Frances Ellen, daughter of Mrs. Kerwin and the late Patrick Kerwin [Patrick Sr.] of Sarnia, became the bride of George Albert Beatty, son of Mrs. Beatty and the late William Beatty, of Sarnia. The Rt. Rev. Monsignor J.T. Aylward performed the ceremony. The bride's attendant was Mrs. Vernon Kerwin, of Detroit, and the groom was supported by Vernon Kerwin...out of town guests included Mrs. Katherine Moran, of Mason City, Iowa; Mr. and Mrs. Patrick Kerwin and family, Guelph; Mr. and Mrs. F.G. Mace, Ottawa; Mr. and Mrs. Vernon Kerwin, Detroit; Mr. and Mrs. William Sproule, Oil Springs.[28]

---

28 *Sarnia Canadian Observer,* June 5, 1930, 5.

Patrick's workplace was located in the Solicitor's Building on the south side at 15 Douglas Street in downtown Guelph. Patrick walked to and from work as the family did not own a car for many years. Instead, they would rent a vehicle when required (business or holidays) and Georgina had the groceries delivered.

While visiting Guelph in researching Patrick's life, I retraced his steps by taking a walk from his office in the Solicitor's Building, located just a short block from the Speed River, to the family home on Park Avenue. This comfortable amble on a summer's eve through the neighbourhoods took only 15 minutes to complete. It felt quite special to be 'walking in his footsteps' along the tree-lined route he had taken almost every day during the twenty-one years he practiced law in Guelph.

The Solicitor's Building, constructed in 1863, is the historic centre of the legal profession in the city. While the building still stands, it is no longer used as a law office.

By 1869, the County purchased the building and took over its maintenance and it was said that, although the building was strikingly attractive from the outside, it was often a cold, damp, unpleasant workplace. In the 1890s, a firm was hired to dig a basement beneath the building and install a then state-of-the-art coal-burning hot-water boiler, and add radiators throughout the building. Around the same time, the building was fitted with gas lighting and, with city water pipes being laid along Douglas Street, the building was also fitted with plumbing. In 1911, the same year Patrick was hired, the Solicitor's Building was wired for electric light.[29]

Documents show that, in 1922, Mr. P. Kerwin requested that the County pay half the cost of a new linoleum floor for his office. The County considered paying half of the "repairs to Guthrie & Kerwin's offices, as agreed with Mr. Kerwin", but later the County amended their report and decided not to pay any of it. Finally, in 1927, the floors in the offices of Guthrie & Kerwin were "repaired and covered with battleship linoleum" with no mention being made of who ended up with the bill for these improvements.[30]

Douglas Street was known by residents of Guelph as "little Wall Street" in times gone by, as most of the city's law firms at one time or another had offices on the street and "considerable wealth lurked behind the not very artistic facades of the old building lines and artery". [31]

---

29 Elysia DeLaurentis, Archives, Wellington County Museum and Archives, Fergus, ON.
30 Ibid.
31 *Guardian* (Guelph), Nov. 21, 1962.

In a 1954 speech to those assembled at an Osgoode Hall dinner, Patrick spoke of his time in Guelph:

> Many years ago, John Galt, a famous Scotsman with The Canada Company, founded Guelph and when, in 1927, the Oath anniversary of that event was celebrated, even the Irish and English together with all other sections of the community joined with Galt's countrymen in celebrating the occasion. You must understand that most of the lawyers offices were on Douglas Street — banners were unfurled and flags erected and it was the suggestion of the then young practitioner that over the entrance to Douglas Street should be erected a banner bearing the inscription: *Abandon hope all ye who enter here.*[32]

Directly across the street from Patrick's office was the Priory Club, a private establishment to which he, and many of the city's power brokers, belonged. The Club was a place where Patrick could have lunch, relax and enjoy a few hands of bridge or cribbage, card games he enjoyed and played throughout his life. The building still exists but not as a private club. A book published by the Guelph Historical Society noted that:

> The elite men's club, the Priory Club of Guelph Ltd., occupied a club house at 18 Douglas Street, furnished with a billiard table and a bar with wine and spirits. It was open from 9:00 am to midnight every day except Sundays, when it opened at noon. Politics and religious questions of every kind were positively excluded from discussion.[33]

Patrick was a member of St. Patrick's Benevolent Society, which was a service organization that raised money for poor and needy Catholic families. In 1917, he was the secretary of the Society. Another membership he held was with the Knights of Columbus and he was voted Grand Knight in 1915. He always retained his membership in this club, "evidence that Guelph had a firm place in his heart" according to a newspaper article.[34] He and his wife were also members of the local golf club even though only he played.

Patrick and his family worshipped at the Church of Our Lady Immaculate; built from 1876 to 1888, it was the third Catholic Church to be built on the site, succeeding the original St. Patrick's,

---

32 Chief Justice Kerwin, Osgoode Hall, Toronto ON, Nov. 20, 1954.
33 *Guelph: Perspectives on a century of change 1900-2000* (Guelph Historical Society), 17.
34 *Guelph Mercury*, Feb. 4, 1963.

Isobel, Georgie, Phil, Patrick, Pat Jr. and George on Lake Huron holiday, circa 1926.

which had burned down, and St. Bartholomew's, which had been demolished to make room for a grander building.

In Guelph, Patrick mostly kept to family and a small circle of friends. In the family home he played quite often on a grand piano, and, as time went on, his children also learned to play.

Long-time friends of Patrick and Georgina were Jack and Grace Baker whom they came to know while living in Guelph. A.W. (Jack) Baker was a professor at the Ontario Agricultural College and went on to become head of the Department of Entomology and Zoology. The Kerwins would have Jack and Grace with a few other friends to their home on Park Avenue to play cards and, later, to sing songs with Patrick at the piano. Apparently, if you hummed Patrick a few lines from a popular song of the day, he quickly had the gist of the tune and, in a short time, the whole room would be singing along. The older Kerwin children covertly listened from the top of the stairs as their parents and friends had fun "singing their hearts out", as Isobel recalled. For the children, this brief bit of parental observation lasted only until they were noticed and promptly sent scurrying back to bed.

The friendship with the Bakers lasted the rest of Patrick's life. The Kerwins had an open invitation to the Bakers' cottage each summer at Cedarhurst Beach on Lake Simcoe near Beaverton, Ontario.

Patrick's preference was to keep a low profile socially and stay out of the public eye, preferring family activities, quiet time and work. However, as a noted resident, and as was the custom of the time, one's social activities were often published in the local newspaper whether it be for husband or wife. For example, reported in the "Social, Personals and Clubs" section of the *Guelph Mercury* was a description of a meeting of the Guelph Golf and Country Club's annual reception and tea. The 1932 article had a long list of those attending and a detailed description of the decorations noting "the tea table was particularly attractive, with a huge centre of mauve and pink snapdragons, gerbera, spirea and baby's breath. Mrs. P. Kerwin and Mrs. F. R. Ramsey poured tea."[35]

In May of 1932, Patrick and Georgina attended a school play in Toronto starring their daughter, Isobel, in a lead role. They had made the decision to send their daughter to Loretto Abbey, a boarding school, as they felt she would get a better secondary school education there. They attended the play during Isobel's high school graduation year.

The *Guelph Mercury* reported:

> A number from Guelph motored to Toronto last evening to attend the presentation of "The Slave Maid of Israel", which was given by the students of Loretto Abbey, Amour Heights, in which Miss Isabel [*sic*] Kerwin, of this city, took the leading part. The Premier of Ontario and Mrs. Henry lent their patronage, and guests and friends of the school from Guelph, London, Belleville and other cities were present for the occasion. The choruses were composed of the students of the school, and orchestral music was provided by some members of the Toronto Symphony Orchestra. Mr. and Mrs. P. Kerwin were among those from Guelph who attended the play.[36]

Patrick liked to holiday each summer with his family for a few weeks in a rented cottage on Lake Huron. As it was not all that far from Guelph, he would sometimes return for business and would then drive back a couple of days later to join the fun. As well, it was a good place for him to play a few quiet games of golf in a relaxing atmosphere.

The children would sometime bring friends with them to the cottage for companionship and to avoid boredom or the predictable spats with siblings. In a note to Isobel after Patrick's death, her friend Dodo recalled how much fun it had been that summer so many years ago and also how much she had enjoyed learning the game of bridge with Patrick, recalling his "gentle smile and teasing wit" (Family Archives).

---

35 *Guelph Mercury*, "Social, Personals and Clubs", May 25, 1932.
36 Ibid.

Isobel and Patrick on the beach, circa 1931.

By the early 1930s, three of the Kerwin children were teenagers; Patrick's daughter was a young woman and his sons were old enough to question and challenge their parents' reasoning on many subjects. Patrick had purchased a car so the children could learn to drive. And, as Georgina did not drive, it soon became the eldest child's (Isobel) duty to ferry her mother around Guelph and area for errands. Isobel recalled being drafted to drive her mother and friends to auctions, flea markets and estate sales as the ladies hunted for bargains. Some of these purchases ended up in the Kerwin home, and later in Isobel's home, often with no idea of the origin of the items. These were just some of the memories passed on by my mother. As well, even in her 90s, Isobel recalled that the telephone number at their home on Park Avenue was "697", and her father's work number was "24".

~

During Patrick's time with the law firm, the text of an advertisement to be inserted in a newspaper was confused by the typesetter with an advertisement of a laundry establishment such that it read: "Guthrie & Kerwin, Barristers, Solicitors, etc. Goods called for and delivered." In a 1954 speech given at Osgoode Hall, Patrick commented on this incident by noting, "I daresay more was promised in that notice than any lawyer could ever hope to sign, seal or deliver."[37]

In 1928, Patrick was named King's Counsel for the Province of Ontario. This is a title bestowed upon lawyers when it is thought that they had made an exceptional contribution to their profession. The practice of these appointments ceased in Ontario in 1985, and the Federal Government ceased the practice in 1993 with no substitute designation of this type implemented.

In Ontario, the Lieutenant Governor may appoint a Crown Attorney for each county and district. At times, extra help is required

---

37 Chief Justice Kerwin, Osgoode Hall, Toronto ON, Nov. 20, 1954.

in this capacity. The Deputy Attorney General may appoint a member of the bar of Ontario to act as Crown Attorney or assistant Crown Attorney, as the case may be. Patrick fulfilled these duties as a respected member of the bar when requested to do so.

Another duty Patrick took on was to be an exam invigilator at Osgoode Hall in the rooms in which he himself had taken the very same challenge. He would ride the train to Toronto for the day and be back home by dinner time as Guelph was but a short trip and there were many trains to choose from.

In early 1932, Patrick was named to the Parole Board for the County, adding to his already substantial duties. In traveling for this additional job, Patrick claimed at year end the princely sum of $240 in 'Allowance and Expenses' to complete the tasks at hand.[38]

Patrick was happily settled into his life in Guelph and his career as a respected and busy lawyer in the city.

~

The Guelph Incident

In early June of 1918, Patrick, still a young lawyer, was called from the comfort of his home to deal with an issue that required immediate attention at the Jesuit Novitiate just north of Guelph. Father Bourque dialled RE-697 at 9:30 pm from the Novitiate to tell his lawyer that they were being raided by the Military Police. The issue at hand dealt with residents of the Novitiate and some government officials who had misinterpreted the *Military Service Act (MSA)* that had passed into law in June of the previous year. At the outset of World War 1 in July 1914 most Canadians thought the conflict would be a short one. Unfortunately, everyone was greatly and sadly mistaken. As the war progressed, getting men to enlist was becoming much more difficult; indeed recruiting across Canada had come to a near standstill by the end of 1916. Conscription seemed to be the only solution, but the government of Sir Robert Borden was reluctant to go down that road, as it was a widely unpopular and contentious proposal.

On July 24, 1917, Parliament passed the *Military Service Act (MSA)*, which came into force August 29 of that year. The *Act* read: "All the male inhabitants of Canada, of the age of eighteen years and upwards, and under sixty, not exempt or disqualified by law, and being British subjects, shall be liable to service in the Militia."[39]

---

38 *Allowances and Expenses for Parole Board, Public Accounts of the Province of Ontario for the Year Ending 31st October 1932-33*, (Province of Ontario).
39 The *Military Service Act*, Ottawa: The King's Printer, 1917.

Prime Minister Borden realized that the conscription issue might split the country and decided a coalition government committed to conscription would be in the best interests of the country. He announced the composition of what he called the Union government on October 12, 1917. The general election, held on December 17 of that year resulted in a slim majority for the Unionists. Patrick's law partner, Hugh Guthrie, having sat as a Liberal with Wilfrid Laurier's caucus for 17 years, joined the new Unionist government as a result of the 'Conscription Crisis of 1917'.

The first draftees under the *MSA* were called up in January 1918, and there were hundreds of defaulters. The responsibility for the apprehension of defaulters under the *MSA* was assigned to the Dominion Police who were placed under the control of the Department of Militia and Defence. Theirs was a difficult and thankless job.

In November 1917, the military representative for the Guelph area requested the men of the Novitiate to present themselves for medical inspection as a prerequisite to conscription. In the *Act*, all divinity students were exempted from compulsory service. This Novitiate's solicitor, twenty-eight year old Patrick, advised that members of recognized Religious Orders are, under Section 2 and the schedule to *Military Service Act*, excluded from the operation of the *MSA*.

This should have ended the matter but, due to prompting by a group of militant anti-Catholics in the Guelph area, it did not. With ill-will and bad feelings growing over the winter, there were now rumours of some that were willing and ready to burn down the Jesuit house because it was thought German spies were being hidden in the buildings. By June of 1918, the Assistant Provost Marshal for London ON, received a memo which stated that there were several young men at the Jesuit Novitiate in Guelph trying to escape military service. A deputy Assistant Provost Marshal was ordered to proceed, investigate and search for men avoiding military service at the Novitiate's location.

The 'Guelph Incident', as I have termed it, began with a most extraordinary visit from the Dominion Police to the Jesuits' St. Stanislaus Novitiate on June 7, 1918. The Assistant Provost Marshal, along with a police inspector and nine men of the Dominion Police surrounded the Novitiate at 9:30 pm. The head of the Novitiate called their solicitor to deal with the government officials. Patrick rushed to see what he could do to clear up the issue.

Upon his arrival, Patrick found all the residents of the Novitiate lined up outside in the chilly evening weather only dressed in their nightclothes. They were each in turn being questioned by the person in charge of the raid. Patrick managed to calm the inquisitors down a bit, but it was difficult to maintain composure in face of the enthusiasm these men displayed for their task. Even the Minister of Justice, Charles J. Doherty, was telephoned, as his son, Marcus Doherty, was one of the young men studying to become a priest. The Minister advised the perpetrators that the raid was illegal, but did not attempt to intervene in any other manner.

Other calls were made which took until well after midnight and, as there was a definite chill in the night air that evening, Father Bourque invited Patrick, the provost marshal and his men inside to warm up with a cup of cocoa. The young men who had been paraded out of their dormitories were also allowed to return to the warmth indoors. The Dominion Police's operation had gone from a clandestine raid to disaster with a hint of farce.

In April 1919, at the instigation of the Rev. Kennedy H. Palmer and the Guelph Ministerial Association, along with Sir Sam Hughes, a Member of Parliament and known rabid anti-Catholic, specific charges were levelled in the House of Commons about the handling of the affair.[40] On Hughes' insistence, the government appointed a commission of investigation. Patrick represented the Novitiate during this investigation. The Royal Commission looking into this matter attracted front-page interest.

After hearing evidence presented by twenty-one witnesses, all the charges were rejected by the Royal Commission. The press offered favourable opinions on the Commission and its findings while certain anti-Catholic publications decried it all as a Jesuit attempt to dodge the draft. The commission felt that, "much that took place and [had] given rise to the matters investigated before us arose from the failure of those concerned to rightly understand the full effect of this statute."[41]

Patrick's involvement was in the heart of the matter and he felt that the correct version of the events that took place that evening at the Novitiate were outlined in the Commission's report. Dealing with the raid and representing the Novitiate for the enquiry stuck with him for quite a long time according to his daughter, who spoke of it often.

---

40 John D. Arnup, *Middleton: The Beloved Judge* (The Osgoode Society, 1988), 83.
41 *Middleton*, 83.

Students of law must be taught not merely what the professor knows, but they must be trained to think for themselves.

—Chief Justice Patrick Kerwin at the University of New Brunswick upon receiving an Honourary Doctor of Laws Degree, Fall Convocation, St. John, 1954

Chapter 6

The Ontario Court
Toronto

In 1932 Patrick was acting as the special Crown Prosecutor for the province during the fall session of the Ontario Superior Court in Hamilton, Ontario, when he received a telephone call at noon on September 27 that changed his and his family's lives. Patrick had just arrived in Hamilton the day before and was preparing for several criminal cases to be convened that afternoon when this important call notified him of his appointment as a Judge on the High Court of Justice of Ontario.

At the age of forty-two, just one month shy of his forty-third birthday, Patrick was the youngest person yet named to the Ontario bench. For twenty-one years prior, he had been practising law in Guelph and was the senior partner in the firm of Guthrie & Kerwin. The other partner on the nameplate of the firm was the Honourable Hugh Guthrie, then the Dominion Minister of Justice in the Bennett government. This relationship caused some unfavourable comments speculating about undue favouritism, as the Minister was chiefly responsible for the appointment. However, an editorial in the *Border Cities Star* newspaper (later to become the Windsor Star) at the time noted "...these comments came from those who did not know Patrick's ability and certainly they will be silenced wherever he appears on circuit".[42]

Patrick, upon hearing of his appointment to the Ontario Courts, was quoted as saying,

> Of course I cannot continue in this capacity [as special prosecutor] since my appointment and its ratification by the Governor General has been made public today. I will commence my duties at this afternoon's court as usual, but another Crown representative will be sent here this afternoon by Hon. W.H. Price, the attorney-general.[43]

---

42 *Border Cities Star*, Windsor, Sep. 1932, 3.
43 Unnamed newspaper article, 1933, Georgina Kerwin's collection.

P.C. 2122

Certified to be a true copy of a Minute of a Meeting
of the Committee of the Privy Council, approved
by the deputy of His Excellency the Governor
General on the 27th September, 1932.

The Committee of the Privy Council, on the recom-
mendation of the Minister of Justice, advise that
Patrick Kerwin, Esquire, of the City of Guelph in the
Province of Ontario, one of His Majesty's Counsel
learned in the law, be appointed a Judge of the High
Court of Justice for Ontario.

E.J. Lemaire,
Clerk of the Privy Council.

Letter from the Privy Council of Canada. Library and Archives Canada,
1932, Microfilm Reel M-1081:234.

The call appointing Patrick was not entirely out of the blue as
one must apply to become a Judge in the Ontario courts. Patrick
must have completed the required paperwork a while before,
perhaps at the suggestion of his law partner.

Upon receiving his letter from the Privy Council Office, Patrick
wrote to Prime Minister Bennett on September 29, 1932,
confirming that he had received the letter appointing him as
Judge of the High Court of Justice for Ontario.

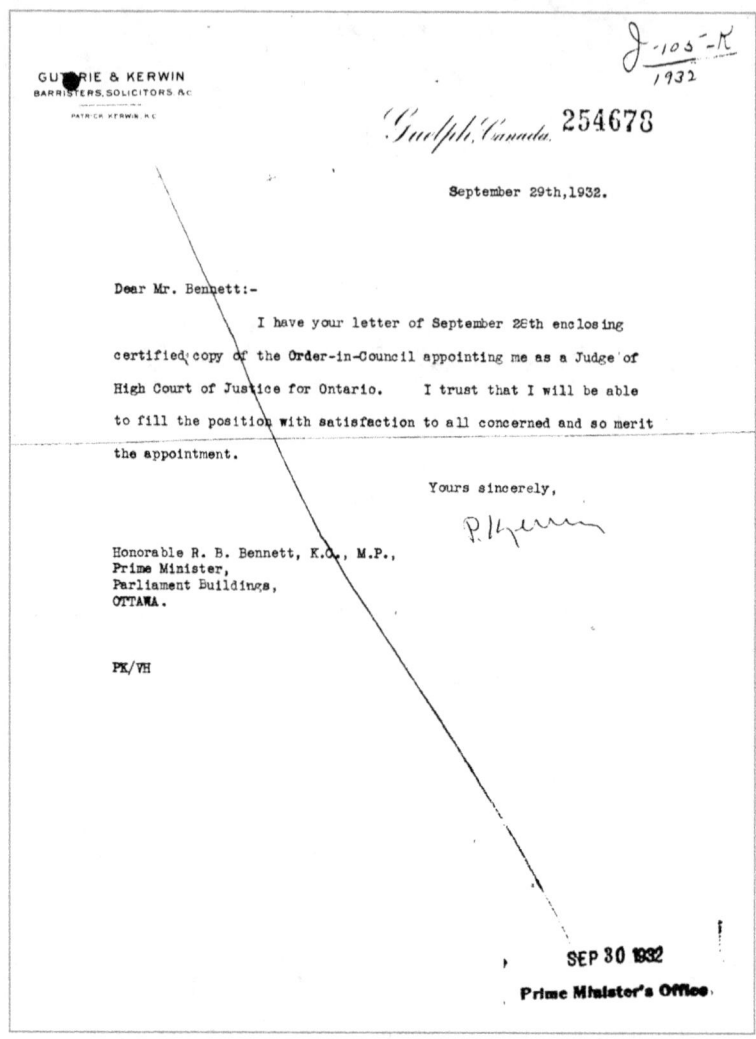

GU**RIE & KERWIN**
BARRISTERS, SOLICITORS &c

PATRICK KERWIN, K.C.

Guelph, Canada, 254678

September 29th, 1932.

Dear Mr. Bennett:-

    I have your letter of September 28th enclosing certified copy of the Order-in-Council appointing me as a Judge of High Court of Justice for Ontario.   I trust that I will be able to fill the position with satisfaction to all concerned and so merit the appointment.

                      Yours sincerely,

                      P. Kerwin

Honorable R. B. Bennett, K.C., M.P.,
Prime Minister,
Parliament Buildings,
OTTAWA.

PK/VH

SEP 30 1932
Prime Minister's Office

Letter to Bennett. Library and Archives Canada, 1932, Microfilm Reel M-1081:234.

    Patrick Grandcourt Kerwin was sworn in on October 14, 1932 as a judge of the High Court Division of the Supreme Court of Ontario at Osgoode Hall in Toronto, in one of the courtrooms where he had sat as a student while attending classes just over twenty years before.

    The swearing-in ceremony was performed in the presence of eleven members of Ontario's highest Court, including Sir William Mulock, Chief Justice of Ontario (who presided) and Chief Justice Latchford of the Appellate Court. Edmund Harley, senior registrar of the Supreme Court, read the commission under the great seal of Canada, appointing the new justice. Mr. Justice Kerwin then took successively the oath of allegiance and the oath of office. After being formally welcomed by W. N. Tilley, K.C., Treasurer of the Law Society, Patrick responded,

> I realize the honour and dignity are great. I also realize that the duties and obligations are great. I hope to fulfill them properly, and in doing so I shall require the collaboration of members of the bench and bar. I hope the same consideration will be shown to me as those previously sworn into this high office.[44]

The ceremony concluded and the members of the bench came forward to congratulate the newest justice and shake his hand.

In Guelph, Patrick's appointment to the Ontario bench necessitated naming replacements as City Solicitor for Guelph and as County Solicitor for Wellington County, both positions he had occupied for some time. Additionally, Patrick's elevation to the bench created an opening on the Ontario Parole Board to which Patrick had only been appointed earlier in 1932.

~

The Supreme Court of Ontario is not one court but a collection of several divisions dealing with a variety of types of law. These courts exercised both civil and criminal jurisdiction through its two branches, the Court of Appeal and the High Court of Justice. The 1924 *Act* which established it provided that the Supreme Court of Ontario should consist of nineteen judges to be appointed as provided by *The British North America Act*, that is, by the Governor General (in effect the Federal Government).[45]

The High Court of Justice was the superior court centrally based in Toronto. The justices traveled each spring and autumn throughout Ontario's many counties and districts to hear criminal and civil cases at sittings known as the Assizes. The Court had jurisdiction over all summary and indictable offenses and types of law including, but not limited to: murder, manslaughter, treason, fraud, and theft. It was a court of both Equity and Common Law and was the highest trial court in Ontario for all criminal and civil matters. The High Court of Justice of Ontario

---

44 Unnamed newspaper article, 1933, Georgina Kerwin's collection.
45 Margaret Banks, "Evolution of the Ontario Courts 1788-1981", Vol. II, in *Essays in the History of Canadian Law* (1983), 494.

has since gone through various incarnations and now that workload is part of the Superior Court of Justice of Ontario. The Superior Court of Justice continues as the Court of record with jurisdiction in all civil and criminal matters. Its seat is at historic Osgoode Hall in Toronto, and the court has sessions in fifty-one cities across the province.

> Judges play many roles. They interpret the law, assess the evidence presented, and control how hearings and trials unfold in their courtrooms. Most important of all, judges are impartial decision-makers in the pursuit of justice. We have what is known as an adversarial system of justice — legal cases are contests between opposing sides, which ensures that evidence and legal arguments will be fully and forcefully presented. The judge, however, remains above the fray, providing an independent and impartial assessment of the facts and how the law applies to those facts.[46]

~

Mondt Trial

In November of 1932, Patrick travelled to Barrie, Ontario, to preside over a manslaughter trial of some note. This case involved a famous wrestler and promoter, Joe 'Toots' Mondt.

> In the summer of 1932, Mondt, and his brother, Ralph Mondt, ... were driving on Highway 24 just east of Collingwood, [in] a 16-cylinder Cadillac sports car ... [He] collided with a car driven by J. Edward Burnie of Toronto. Burnie's passenger, 21-year-old Theresa Luccioni, was killed instantly. [The coroner concluded] that Mondt had been driving too quickly [and he was charged with manslaughter].
> Mondt ... was represented by prominent Toronto lawyer, D. Lally McCarthy, later the Treasurer of the Law Society of Upper Canada and the son of one of the founders of the law firm that evolved into McCarthy Tétrault, now one of Canada's largest.[47]

Mondt testified that he was only driving at 35 to 40 miles an hour and that it was Burnie who swerved over the line and into his car. The jury was not impressed. The initial charge of manslaughter was dismissed but the jury found Mondt guilty of criminal negligence after deliberating for four hours. In the end,

---

46 "The Role of the Judge", www.cscja-acjcs.ca/role_of_judge-en.asp?l=5. Accessed Dec. 2017.

47 www.garywill.com/toronto/mondt.htm Accessed Dec. 2010.

Mondt was sentenced to one year in the Ontario reformatory (a prison for adults) at Guelph. According to local newspapers at the time, the Judge, Patrick Kerwin, had suggested an acquittal in his charge to the jury.

McCarthy immediately filed an appeal and Mondt ended up only spending one night in jail, later to be released on $20,000 bail (approximately $300,000 plus in today's dollars). The appeal was heard and the Court of Appeal ruled in Mondt's favour after which he faced a barrage of civil suits.

Larocque & Lavictoire Trials

In December of that same year, the new Ontario Justice Kerwin travelled to L'Orignal, Ontario, where he presided over a murder trial. Two men were accused of killing a young helper named Bergeron on their farm on whose life they had arranged and placed insurance. The accused were William J. Larocque, age 57, a married farmer, and Emmanuel Lavictoire, age 51, a married gardener. The story indicated that these two had partnered up to murder people for life insurance. In January 1932 they stabbed Leo Bergeron in Larocque's barn with pitchforks. They then released a horse to make it look like Bergeron got trampled. Later, a bloody pitchfork handle was found by the police in the rafters of the barn. It is also thought this pair murdered another man, Athanase Lamarche, in 1930. The accused were found guilty of Bergeron's murder.[48]

In his charge to the Jury, Justice Kerwin (transcript of evidence denoting him as 'His Lordship') began with:

> Gentlemen of the Jury, the accused are charged with having murdered Leo Bergeron on March 18th, 1932. That is a serious charge. The trial that has been progressing here in L'Orignal, for some eight days, is serious and of great importance to the accused, and of great importance to all of the inhabitants of these United Counties. You have listened with a great deal of patience to all the evidence that, in a case of this kind, had necessarily to be introduced. All of it, of course, has not the same weight; all of it has not the same bearing, but the Crown considers, from its point of view of present evidence in connection with the charge against the accused, that all of it should be presented for your consideration.[49]

---

48 *Ottawa Journal*, Dec. 16, 1932, 16.
49 Supreme Court of Ontario Official Court Report, p.1109, Library and Archives Canada RG-13, vol. 1584 (1, 2, 3), file CC390; 1932.

The Jury came back after deliberating for a few hours with a verdict of guilty. It was at this time that Justice Kerwin sentenced both accused to hang.

The *Ottawa Journal* wrote,

> It was Mr. Justice Kerwin's first time to preside over a murder case in an Assize court since his recent appointment to the Bench and he was visibly affected as he passed the double death sentence at the conclusion of the lengthy trial.[50]

In a letter dated December 23, 1932, Justice Kerwin forwarded a letter to the Secretary of State with the Jury's recommendation for mercy in both cases. From there the recommendation would be presented to the Privy Council by the Governor General for consideration. On March 11, 1933, the Governor General wrote that he was, "unable to order any interference with the sentence of the court".[51] The sentence was to stand.

According to Patrick's eldest child, Isobel, having to sentence Larocque and Lavictoire to death weighed heavily upon her father. She said they had spoken about it in his study at home and she felt it troubled her father a great deal. On the other hand, Patrick's second son, George, a young teenager at the time, asked his father how he could do this — hang these men? Patrick listened to his son's anguish in dealing with this matter and calmly replied, "I did not hang them, George; the law did."

Beyak & Hoff Trials

In 1933, Ontario Justice Kerwin presided over two murder trials in the town of Sandwich, now part of the city of Windsor, Ontario. The Crown Counsel (prosecutor) was Sir Alfred Morine, K.C., assisted by his son, A. Neville Morine. The first of the two trials Patrick presided over was that of Mr. Peter Melvin Beyak (aka Buick), who was employed as a machinist. Mr. Beyak was accused of killing his common-law wife, Jessie Nehbereski, after striking her with a meat cleaver during a quarrel. The second trial was that of Mr. Jacob Hoff, a Windsor fish peddler accused of killing his wife, Katie, with a revolver.[52]

In describing the trial of Mr. Beyak, in an undated newspaper clipping kept by Patrick's wife taken from The *Detroit Free Press*, the reporter described the judge in the following manner:

---

50 *Ottawa Journal,* Dec. 16, 1932, 5.
51 Library and Archives Canada, RG13, vol.1578, 442.
52 *Detroit News,* Oct. 1933.

Not a detail escaped the attention of the pleasant-faced, intellectually keen judge. His soft, musical voice betrays his Celtic origins. With his silk gown and starched collar and white tie he might have passed for a bishop in another setting. He spoke easily and fluently and his desire to be fair, to see that the accused man had every opportunity to present his case always was in evidence. "Don't lead the witness", he cautioned the prosecutor several times.[53]

Another American newspaper reporter, Sherman R. Miller, was quite surprised how a Canadian court proceeded and made several observations:

The first thing that is impressed upon the American spectator is isolation of the prisoner. He is placed in a box, about six feet by three feet, and must sit on a bench directly facing the judge. He sits upright, in full view of the jury, with his back to the audience, and facing the backs of his attorneys. It seems strange...not to see him sprawling on the counsel table, squirming around to grin at friends and mumbling behind his hand into the ear of his lawyer.

The barristers, attired in their black gowns and white wing collars, carry with them the dignity of their proud positions. They do not glare across the table at each other or pound their fists or wave their arms about wildly. In fact, they do not shout at all. Neither do they question the decisions of the judge, or ask him to adjourn while they look up citations to thrust at him.

And, as for the judge, his actions are nothing short of astonishing. He sits quietly, facing the person who is addressing him. He listens intently and does not seem to be afflicted with any nervous condition which would make him leave the bench to take a stroll about the court or cause him to change his position in the chair every five minutes.

And further, he answers the lawyers in the same courteous tone with which they address him. It is very disappointing to find that no one seems to be mad at anyone else.

Furthermore he seems to be astonishingly expert at his business. An attorney gets halfway through a question, which might be a leading one.

"Just a moment please, Mr. Crown Attorney," interrupts the judge in a quiet tone. "I think that perhaps you are attempting to establish a question the answer to which might be misconstrued by the jury. Please refrain from continuing that line of questioning."

---

53 "Swift Justice Dooms Slayer", *Detroit Free Press,* Georgina Kerwin's collection.

"Very good, My Lord," the attorney answers in the same tone.

And the judge, he only seems, wonder of wonders, to be interested in having the jury return a fair and unbiased verdict.

"Murder," he says, "under our law simply means to cause the death of a person. The onus is on the Crown to prove this. Whatever has happened, you must remember that the woman is dead, and that this man is responsible for her death. Do not be swayed by sympathy for the defendant, but balance such sympathy with sympathy for the country and for your fellow man. You must decide merely whether the defendant was through some action deprived of his self-control. If this is true, find a verdict of manslaughter. If you decided otherwise in your deliberations, the verdict must be murder."

That's all. The jury goes out. Another case is started. The jury comes in two hours and half later.

"Guilty of manslaughter," is the verdict.

It is after 6 o'clock. Everybody goes home. The day's work is over. As one American at the trial said as he turned to leave, "These trials in Canada aren't any fun, but good lord, they certainly don't fool around, do they?" The bailiff at the door overhears the remark and scratches his head. He is probably still trying to figure out what the visiting American meant.[54]

This visiting newspaper reporter from the United States was struck not only with the civility of the court in Ontario but also wondered why there were no lawyers "yelling at each other, strutting like roosters" to prove a point.

Based on the evidence brought forward, which included the police report, fingerprints, photos, statement of the accused and a coroner's inquest, Peter Beyak was found guilty and, according to the law of the land, was sentenced to death by the presiding judge with no recommendation for mercy. The execution took place on December 6, 1933.

In the second case tried that same week in Sandwich, Ontario, Jacob Hoff had pleaded not guilty of shooting his wife even though he declared he shot her because she had admitted misconduct with a roomer who lived in their home. Hoff was almost blind from the effect of the shot which he fired into his own head after shooting his wife. In the end, this prisoner was found guilty of manslaughter and sentenced to life imprisonment.

---

54 Sherman R. Miller ,"An American Sees Our Courts", Georgina Kerwin's collection.

The *Border Cities Star* said of the judge in these trials:

> The courtesy, fairness and expeditiousness with which Mr. Justice Kerwin has been handling the Supreme Court docket on his first visit to Sandwich has made a deep impression on the Bar and the Press of the Border Cities.
>
> It is particularly noticeable that while His Lordship is never ruffled, he conducts his court with firmness, not hesitating to set down a barrister who oversteps the rules of evidence, as some are prone to do, and yet always taking such action in a way that makes any hard feeling impossible. The Border Cities and Essex County will always be glad to welcome Mr. Justice Kerwin.[55]

Working in Toronto and travelling across the province, Patrick found himself dealing with numerous types of law in the cases he heard; estates, trusts, wills, criminal offences, divorces, alimony judgments, foreclosures, liability, intellectual property, negligence, and much more. Some of the cities in which he heard cases were: Stratford, Sandwich, Kitchener, Hamilton, Guelph, Sarnia, Toronto, Ottawa, Cornwall, Welland, London, Sault Ste. Marie, Haileybury, Orillia and many more.

In hearing a case in Toronto involving a disputed will, Roy Kellock was the lawyer representing the executors. Kellock was later to become Justice Kerwin's colleague on the Supreme Court of Canada. Another interesting trial was in Sarnia where the lawyer for the defendants was N. L. LeSueur, the son of the man for whom Patrick worked as a young man. Regrettably for N.L. LeSueur, the case did not go the way he would have preferred.

Fortunately for Justice Kerwin, he heard many cases in Weekly Court in Toronto during his time on the Bench in Ontario. This meant he could go home after a long day's work and spend time with his family rather than in a hotel in another community.

---

55 *Border Cities Star,* Georgina Kerwin's collection.

Contrary to the opinion of Mr. Bumble,
the law is not "an ass, an idiot" and however
imperfect it may appear to a disappointed
litigant, its object is to regulate the transactions
of, and the relationships among, various
members of the human race.

—Chief Justice Patrick Kerwin at the University of New Brunswick
upon receiving an Honourary Doctor of Laws Degree,
Fall Convocation, St. John, 1954

Chapter 7

Life as a High Court Justice
Toronto

The appointment to the bench in the High Court of Ontario meant that Patrick and his family needed to relocate from Guelph to Ontario's capital city, Toronto, which was a rapidly growing city with a population of just over 800,000. The move was somewhat sad, as the Kerwins were well liked in Guelph and it was the city where their children were born. A local newspaper at the time reported, "It is considered likely that the Kerwin family will find it necessary to move to Toronto and their departure will be keenly regretted in social circles".[56]

Patrick would have to retire as a member of the Priory Club, the Guelph Golf and Country Club, the Wellington Law Association and the charities he had belonged to and supported over the years. He remained a member of the Guelph chapter of the Knights of Columbus. At the time the appointment was announced, Guelph Crown Attorney J. M. Kearns was quoted as saying:

> He will carry to his new duties a wide experience derived from a large practice. In criminal law, he has acted as Crown Prosecutor in connection with many very important cases, and he has been both city and county solicitor. His genial manner and approachability assure that the members of the Bar practicing before him will receive an attentive and sympathetic hearing.
> The members of the profession in Guelph regret very much that Mr. Kerwin and his family will leave Guelph, but they rejoice in the fact that he has been so highly honoured.[57]

Guelph Magistrate Fred Watt commented on his long-time colleague and friend, saying:

> Mr. Kerwin has appeared frequently in this court and has always been welcome... Sir John A. Macdonald [when] asked what were the qualifications of a judge said, "He should be a

---

56 Unnamed newspaper article, Georgina Kerwin's collection.
57 Ibid., 1933.

gentleman, and if he knows the law, so much the better."
Mr. Kerwin amply fills the first requirement and he has much
more than a little knowledge of the law. All the members of
the Bar and all his friends congratulate him upon the honour
which he has received.[58]

The newspapers in Patrick's hometown of Sarnia reported the
appointment and included a short and sensible quote from his
mother on this subject; "I was very much pleased to hear of my
son's appointment." [59] I am sure my great-grandmother was indeed
fiercely proud of her eldest son's most recent accomplishment.

At a dinner held at the Guelph Golf and Country Club, friends
and associates honoured their friend and newly appointed judge.
The sentiments of the gathering were expressed in an address
delivered by J. Godfrey Smith, chairman for the evening:

> We have gathered here this evening in honor of the recently
> appointed Mr. Justice Kerwin, who as Pat Kerwin has for the past
> twenty-one years been our friend and associate. It was with great
> pleasure that we congratulated him upon his appointment to the
> Supreme Court of Ontario.
>
> He is vice-president of this club and has been a director for the
> past five years. His services have been given freely, and I can
> assure you they have been appreciated and we regret exceedingly
> that he will be unable to fill the post of president of this club next
> year... For many years Pat has served in the community in many
> important capacities. His splendid ability, his high principles, his
> delightful and considerate personal qualities have been given to
> these services and have won the admiration of his many friends.[60]

At this dinner, Patrick was presented with a gift of 'handsome'
cut glass and Georgina was presented with a Sheffield tray.

This appointment also marked the end of his long partnership
with Hugh Guthrie, which had lasted twenty-one years. During
this entire period, Guthrie occupied a seat in the House of
Commons, necessitating his absence from Guelph for a great
portion of each year. During these absences the handling of the
firm's extensive practice had devolved upon Patrick.[61]

---

58 Unnamed newspaper article, Georgina Kerwin's collection.
59 Ibid., Sep. 1933.
60 J. Godfrey Smith, Address to the Guelph Golf and Country Club, 1933. Georgina Kerwin's
collection
61 "Supreme Court of Canada Judges - the Hon. Patrick Kerwin", *Fortnightly Law Journal*,
Sep. 16, 1935, 55.

BARRISTER HONORED

Long regarded as one of the most outstanding members of the legal fraternity in this city, Patrick Kerwin, K.C., has been appointed a justice of the Supreme Court of Ontario, and his friends, not only of the Bar, but in his many other associations, will join in rejoicing at the high honor which has been accorded him.

Mr. Kerwin takes to his new post all the qualities which have made him successful in his chosen profession. His wide experience includes not only criminal law, his knowledge of which was recognized in his frequent appointments as special Crown Prosecutor, but in matters municipal he is an outstanding authority.

It is a singular compliment that a man of Mr. Kerwin's comparative youth should be elevated to so prominent a position. He will be the youngest judge on the Ontario Bench, but there is not the slightest doubt that he will maintain to the fullest degree the highest traditions of the Canadian judiciary.

Guelph Newspaper article, 1932.

~

With his appointment to the court confirmed, it was time for Patrick, his wife and family to find a home in Toronto. Their children, Isobel (17), Patrick (15), George (13) and Phil (9) needed to be enrolled in appropriate schools near to wherever they were to reside.

As Patrick was familiarizing himself with his new post, the rest of his family went house shopping. On this subject, Patrick deferred to his wife's most sensible judgment. Many of the family homes within their price range at the time would be considered large in today's terms. They sought a home with four bedrooms (at least) and room enough for a study for Patrick to use when working at home. They combed the areas in and around "northern" Toronto for the right house. One of the main criteria used as they surveyed home after home was whether or not George (the tallest member of the family at well over six feet) could fit in the bathtub. While house hunting, their first foothold in Toronto was a large apartment rented by the month on Avenue Road, just north of Bloor Street. Soon the family moved to a rental home on Welland Avenue in the Moore Park area of Toronto (near Yonge Street & St. Clair Avenue). Eventually they found a more suitable and permanent residence large enough for the family's needs at 88 South Drive, in the Rosedale section of Toronto. This home was just a short block from where Georgina's parents had lived on Elm Avenue and where she had grown up. Patrick and his wife decided to rent rather than purchase a home. In the long run, the home in Guelph was the last and only home they were to own, as the Kerwin family lived in rented residences from then on.

One excellent reason to rent is that, when something goes wrong in the home, the landlord is often responsible for fixing it. This was not only convenient for the family as Patrick was often away, travelling far and wide from county to county as a Justice for the Province of Ontario, it was also practical in that apparently Patrick could not put a nail in straight to save his life. His wife, Georgina, was the "Mr. Fix-it" in the home as Isobel remembered. Her mother had an old, firm, wooden peach basket containing the essential tools to do small jobs around the house (hammer, wrench, nails, pictures hooks, etc.). It was also said that her husband did not know about it but perhaps in reality he did not want to.

One family tale has the Kerwins enjoying breakfast together one morning in their home on South Drive when Patrick told his wife that a certain lamp in the living room was broken and he felt that, in its present state, it was dangerous and could start a fire. Patrick advised Georgina that she would need to call an electrician to have it fixed that very day. She calmly agreed, saying, "Yes dear", and that she would get it looked at right away. After Patrick had gone to work, she only had to change the light bulb to make it functional.

While Patrick travelled across the Province of Ontario, his wife was left at home for long stretches of time to run their home, take care of the children and pay the bills. Fortunately, Georgina was very much up to the task and, according to all, did a splendid job. But she did miss her husband a great deal.

The 1935 Toronto City Directory showed the following for Patrick's employment and residence:

> Kerwin, Patrick Hon., Justice Appellate Division, Supreme Court of Ontario, Osgoode Hall, Res.: 88 South Drive.[62]

Living in this section of town was fortuitous for Isobel in that her best friend from boarding school, Mary German, and her family, lived just around the corner. Many years later I listened to them reminisce about those days and Mary recalled with an identifiable laugh that, when dining with the Kerwins, Isobel's father, at the end of the meal, would push back his chair and declare that he was "sufficiently suffonsified", thereby notifying one and all that he had had enough to eat, thank you very much.

An old family friend, Ann German (Mary's sister), remembered Justice Kerwin as a wonderful person with a gentle sense of humour; he was a strict father but was not a mean or vindictive person in any way. She said her own father, Jack German, a lawyer in Toronto, thought Patrick was a great judge, which apparently was a very rare thing for him to say of any judge. Ann also noted that Georgina ruled the house firmly but when Patrick did not want to go along, even she could not make him change his mind.[63]

Just prior to moving from Guelph, Isobel had finished high school at the boarding school in Toronto and had come back home to live with her family. Her parents then thought it would be a good idea to send their eldest daughter to a 'business' school of sorts for young ladies which was, in reality, a secretarial school. Within a few days, Isobel came home vowing to never return, having firmly decided this was not for her. She advised her

62 Toronto Archives, Toronto City Directory, reference M1 9216.
63 Interview with Ann German, Toronto ON, June 24, 2010.

parents the teachers were "backwards" in their thinking and fervently declared she knew more than they did. Soon after the family re-located to Toronto, Isobel was determined to attend the University of Toronto. This plan was decidedly against her mother's wishes, as Georgina thought it was high time for her daughter to be thinking of marriage, not schoolwork. Upon hearing his daughter plead her case on this matter in his study at home, Patrick overturned his wife's decision and offered Isobel the use of the money they had set aside for her marriage to now be used for her university education. As my mother remarked, her father would always listen to a cogent, clear argument. This decision also reflected Patrick's views on the value of education, and was consistent with his views on fairness and equity. She happily enrolled in the University of Toronto, attending St. Michael's College, where she worked hard to earn an Honours Degree in English, a degree which would serve her well in years to come.

Patrick's son, Patrick Kilroy was an excellent student with a flair for card games. He completed high school in Toronto and, later, earned an undergraduate degree in Political Science and Economics from the University of Toronto. From there he elected to follow in his father's footsteps in the field of law and attended Osgoode Hall. Patrick and Georgina chose the middle name, Kilroy, for their eldest son as a tribute to the priest who married them in Toronto. As Georgina was Anglican and wanted to marry a Catholic, there could have been problems were it not for Father Kilroy, who smoothed the process. Much to their relief, the priest agreed to marry the two without much fuss at all.

The second son, George, was, in his own words, "a tolerable" student but was active in athletics during high school, playing football for the school. In later years his mother admitted that she hoped George would attend university but, after surviving the Second World War, George started work with what she referred to as "a little company called IBM". It turned out that George did very well in his career with this "little company" and others, so his mother need not have worried about his future and ability to provide for a family.

The youngest, Phil, was the *wunderkind* of the family. He was a quick learner with a unique and inquisitive mind. Reading and understanding most of the books in the family library, young Phil excelled in all subjects. He managed to graduate from high school by the age of fourteen but was held back by "the Sisters", as the story goes, because they thought he was too young to attend university. So, with his fate decided for the next year, Phil repeated grade 13 in high school taking courses that piqued his interest such as Greek, which, according to Isobel, he learned very well. He was off to the University of Toronto the next year and, again, excelled. The periodical published by the Students' Administrative Council at the University wrote of Philip that he studied, "English Language and Literature. Cultivated an enthusiasm for Chaucer and an aversion to Milton".[64]

~

Back in the courtroom, Patrick was quoted in a newspaper article where the title describes it all by stating "No Place for Handshaking". The incident outlined in the piece occurred during a five-minute recess in proceedings of the Supreme Court of Ontario held one day in the city of Welland. When a witness shook hands with a juror, both were immediately censured by Mr. Justice Kerwin who said, "This is not permissible and I trust it will not occur again in this or any other court". This unacceptable behaviour occurred during the civil action of John Clapton, Niagara Falls, on behalf of his daughter, Ethel, for $5,000 damages against Albert N. Lindsay, of St. Catharines and Samuel Marcuso, of Niagara Falls, for injuries the child received while playing when struck by a car driven by Lindsay. The article goes on to explain that, even if many might have regarded the incident as quite ordinary, it was pointed out by Justice Kerwin that the court jurors are expected to avoid contact with those interested in actions upon which they are to return a verdict.[65]

Nearly two decades later, Patrick spoke briefly of his time as a judge in the Ontario Courts. In a 1954 speech given at an Osgoode Hall dinner he told those assembled, "Here I spent in weekly court, in chambers, and in writing judgments what was left of three years after commercial travelling trips to almost every county and district centre in the province."[66]

64 *Torontonensis,* University of Toronto, 1944, 29.
65 "No Place for Handshaking", uncredited newspaper article, Georgina Kerwin's collection.
66 Chief Justice Kerwin, Osgoode Hall Dinner, Nov. 20, 1954, 1.

It is thought by some that law (including equity) has certain fixed rules permitting of no exceptions and suffering no easing of their rigours. What is overlooked is that law is made for mankind and not mankind for law.

—Chief Justice Patrick Kerwin in an address at Osgoode Hall, Toronto 1954

Chapter 8

The Supreme Court of Canada
Ottawa

On July 20, 1935 R. B. Bennett, the Prime Minister and head of the Conservative government of 1930-35, appointed Patrick to the Supreme Court of Canada on the advice of the Minister of Justice, the Hon. Hugh Guthrie. This represented the thirty-fourth appointment to the Supreme Court of Canada since its establishment in 1876, and the fourteenth from the Province of Ontario.[67] Patrick filled the position vacated almost a year earlier on the retirement of Justice Frank Hughes. There had been speculation that Justice Minister Guthrie himself would be appointed or that a Western man, Judge A. A. Dysart of Winnipeg, might be chosen to fill the vacancy.

In January of that same year, one newspaper article considered the issue of who might replace Justice Hughes in this manner:

> Resignation of Mr. Justice Frank Joseph Hughes from the bench of the Supreme Court of Canada, is expected to become effective within the next five days. No decision had been reached as to his successor but it is believed one will be named at once because of the heavy calendar awaiting attention of the court which opens on February fifth.
>
> Mr. Justice Hughes is resigning for personal reasons. He was appointed March 17, 1933, from the Ontario Supreme Court. There is already one vacancy on the Supreme Court bench, and pending permanent appointments it might be necessary to temporarily appoint an "ad hoc" judge to assist at the February sittings.
>
> Mr. Justice P. Kerwin of the Ontario Supreme Court, and Mr. Justice A. A. Dysart of Winnipeg, have been prominently mentioned as likely appointees to the Supreme Court of Canada. Mr. Justice Dysart has also been mentioned as a possible chairman of the board of railway commissioners. This position has now been vacant a year and a question was asked in the House of Commons yesterday with respect to the delay in filling it. A statement may be given in the House to-morrow relative to the appointment.[68]

---

67 "Supreme Court", *Fortnightly Law Journal*, 55.
68 "Mr. Justice Kerwin May Go To Ottawa", Georgina Kerwin's collection.

Frank J. Hughes, whom Patrick replaced, was also a Catholic from Ontario. Justice Hughes had only been on the court for two years when he decided that he would rather return to the other side of the bench and the practice of law. Hughes' resignation opened up a place on the Court for another Ontario Catholic. Patrick's province, religion, and, one might suspect, the influence of Hugh Guthrie, all worked in his favour. The issues of geography and religion were just two of the staples of Canadian judicial selection.

In an undated article from Patrick's hometown of Sarnia, the announcement of his appointment to the Supreme Court noted that he was "better known to Sarnians as Pat", then went on to add, "his courtesy and fairness have brought him much commend-ation."[69] On this same subject, a prominent lawyer of Toronto said, "He will be very much missed as a trial judge. If one were asked, 'what were the predominant qualities of the new Judge,' the answer would no doubt be, 'expedition, courtesy and patience'."[70]

The *Fortnightly Law Journal* wrote of Patrick:

> ...his extensive experience at numerous assizes was undoubtedly of assistance to the new Judge, in his trial work. His Lordship has a pleasing and democratic manner. His Irish ancestry is no doubt responsible for this in a large measure. He is no poseur, neither does he cultivate any slavish adherence to indurate tradition. In his short career on the Bench he has won for himself the reputation of being hard working and conscientious; fair and impartial; able and well equipped; courteous to counsel and abundantly fair to witnesses. He has gained a lasting place in the esteem and affection of the profession throughout the Province.[71]

In an undated clipping from the *Toronto Telegram*, an editorial spoke of Patrick's appointment to the Supreme Court:

> Regarded as one of the most outstanding members of the Supreme Court of Ontario, the Honourable Mr. Justice Patrick Kerwin has been appointed a Justice of the Supreme Court of Canada, and his friends, not only of the Bar, but in his many other associations will join in rejoicing at the high honour which has been accorded him ... It is a singular compliment that a man of Justice Kerwin's comparative youth should be elevated to so prominent a position. He will be the youngest Judge on the Bench of the Supreme Court of

---

69 Unnamed newspaper article, Georgina Kerwin's collection.
70 "Supreme Court", *Fortnightly Law Journal*, 56.
71 Ibid.

Canada, but there is not the slightest doubt that he will maintain to the fullest degree the highest traditions of the Canadian Judiciary.[72]

The following was published in the *Canada Gazette* following a meeting of the Committee of the Privy Council on July 20, 1935:

> The Committee of the Privy Council, on the recommendation of the Minister of Justice, advise that the Honourable Patrick Kerwin, a Judge of the High Court of Justice for Ontario, be appointed a Puisne Justice of the Supreme Court of Canada. Signed by the Assistant Clerk of the Privy Council [73]

At the time of Patrick's appointment the Supreme Court of Canada was comprised of the Chief Justice and six Puisne Justices. The Oxford dictionary gives the definition of puisne as, "Adjective, Law. Applied to an inferior or junior judge in the superior courts of common law".[74] Thus, puisne, pronounced 'puny', simply means lesser or ranked after the Chief Justice. In this context, its definition is that of an associate member of the court.

The court that Patrick joined was led by Chief Justice Lyman Duff. The associate Justices were: T. Rinfret, J. Lamont, L. Cannon, O. Crocket, and H. Davis.

> Sir Lyman P. Duff (1865-1955) was the eighth Chief Justice of the Supreme Court of Canada. In 1906, at the age of forty-one, he was appointed a Judge of the Supreme Court of Canada, becoming the youngest person thus far appointed to the Court, and he would serve longer than anyone else. He became Chief Justice in 1933.[75]

In 1918 he was made an Imperial Privy Councillor, and for 25 years thereafter, he also sat every year with the Judicial Committee of the Imperial Privy Council in London, England, hearing Appeals from all parts of the British Empire. Frequently, Sir Lyman was chosen to write the judgments of their Lordships. As to his reputation, several newspapers and magazines of the time compared Duff to the most distinguished judicial luminaries in the world, while others judged him to have the best legal mind in the modern history of Canada.

---

72 "Editorial", *Toronto Telegram,* Georgina Kerwin's collection.
73 Library and Archives Canada, File R188-39-8-E via Access to Information, July 3, 2013.
74 *Oxford English Dictionary, Compact Edition,* Vol. II (Oxford University Press, 1971), 2353.
75 David Ricardo Williams, *Duff: A Life in the Law* (University of British Columbia Press, 1984), 66.

Duff very much liked to control the flow of events in his courtroom, and tended to discourage his colleagues from putting too many questions to lawyers. Yet, it was said that he was not aloof — his door was open to colleagues who might want advice.[76]

When Patrick joined the court, there were three annual sittings, the first — the January term — ran from the fourth Tuesday of January through to Easter; the second started on the fourth Tuesday in April and ran to the end of June; the last term began on the first Tuesday of October and continued until just before Christmas. The judges could take holidays between June and October once all their outstanding judgments were completed. All seven judges, except in case of illness or serious circumstance, sat on the constitutional cases and murder appeals, as well as important cases involving new legislation. In all other matters that came before it, five judges formed the court.[77]

In an article published in the April 1936 issue of *MacLean's Magazine*, the authors addressed the subject of the number of Justices on the Court:

By an Act of Parliament in 1896, the Supreme Court was to "consist of a chief justice, to be called the Chief Justice of Canada, and five puisne [associate] judges, who shall be appointed by the Governor-in-Council by letters patent under the Great Seal". However, with six judges debating a case, deadlocks were apt to occur, so in 1927 an amendment was added providing for the appointment of a seventh judge. This greatly facilitated the rendering of judgments.[78]

In the same *MacLean's Magazine* article on the court, Patrick was described in the following manner:

We see an able jurist whose decisions have been considered logical and just, and at the same time we see a lovable and human character, a man still reminding us of a boy; a witty, courteous, friendly gentleman whose wide variety of cases has given him a deep understanding of and sympathy with his fellow men, and who will give great effectiveness to the body whose roster his appointment has now completed.[79]

---

76 Williams, *Duff: A Life*, 167.
77 "Supreme Court", *Fortnightly Law Journal*, 55.
78 Madge MacBeth and Leslie T. White, "The Seven Justices of the Red Robes", *Maclean's Magazine*, Apr. 1936, 26.
79 Ibid., 47.

Once he was living in Ottawa, Patrick immediately began to learn French. These lessons went on for quite a number of years and, eventually, he was able to hear and read cases in that language. This effort was much appreciated by his colleagues and those pleading cases in French.

In the opinion of Messrs. Snell and Vaughan[80], the Court was often exploited, using the Justices to deal with labour arbitrations and other assorted tasks. This was due to the Court itself being viewed as a subordinate institution to the Privy Council in England. For example, in 1934, Chief Justice Duff agreed to act as sole Commissioner of a federal Royal Commission to inquire into allegations regarding the manner in which former Prime Minister Meighen had discharged his duties as Commissioner of the Ontario Hydro-Electric Power Commission. In the fall of 1935, Justice Davis acted as the sole commissioner to investigate the Long-shoremen's industrial dispute on the Vancouver waterfront. There were many more disputes dealt with by the Justices of the Court, including in 1941, when Patrick was named a joint chairman of two conciliation boards dealing with Canadian railway employees' application for a cost-of-living bonus. The investigation dealt with the dispute between the Canadian National Railway and its employees, who were members of the Canadian Brotherhood of Railway Employees.

In 1946, while Puisne Judge at the Supreme Court, Justice Taschereau co-chaired with Justice Kellock the Royal Commission on Spying Activities in Canada, put in place following the "Gouzenko Affair".[81]

~

Early in 1939, Prime Minister Mackenzie King invited King George VI and Queen Elizabeth (later to become known as the 'Queen Mother') to come to Canada, and to his immense gratification, they accepted. The Royal couple were welcomed by crowds wherever they went. At Prime Minister King's request, the Queen dedicated the cornerstone of the new Supreme Court building on May 20, 1939, in the presence of a large audience that included the Prime Minister and all seven of the Supreme Court Justices. Speaking in both French and English, the Queen remarked,

---

80 James G. Snell and Frederick Vaughan, *The Supreme Court of Canada – History of the Institution* (University of Toronto Press: 1985), 158.
81 Ibid.

It is fitting that on these heights above the Ottawa —
surely one of the noblest situations in the world — you
should add to the imposing group of buildings which house
your Parliament and the executive branch of government, a
worthy home for your Supreme Court. Henceforth, on these
river-side cliffs, there will stand in this beautiful Capital, a
group of public buildings unsurpassed as a symbol of the
free and democratic institutions which are our greatest
heritage.[82]

The Queen then remarked,

Perhaps it is not inappropriate that this task [laying the
cornerstone] should be performed by a woman; for a
woman's position in civilized society has depended upon the
growth of law. [83]

This tour included King George dedicating the recently
completed National War Memorial. After the dedication, he and
his entourage walked to Parliament where the King granted
assent to a number of bills in the Senate, with the Justices of the
Court also in attendance. It was an exciting time since King George
VI was the first reigning monarch to set foot on Canadian soil.

At the opening of Parliament or at other formal government
functions where the Justices of the Supreme Court were in
attendance in the Senate, they would sit on a round woolsack.
The history of the seat lies deep in British tradition from a time
when the Lord Chancellor once dispensed justice from such a
throne. When the number of Justices was increased from seven to
nine, the appropriate number of comfortable chairs later replaced
this sack for official occasions, as the original woolsack would
have been too crowded. Patrick recalled, "It was never a comfortable
seat anyway."[84] The wool sack remains standard seating in the
House of Lords in Great Britain.

~

82 Snell and Vaughan, *The Supreme Court*, 177.
83 https://todayinottawashistory.wordpress.com/tag/parliament-hill/, Accessed June 22, 2017.
84 Irene Corbally Kuhn, "Personality Panel - Supreme Court Veteran", *Manitoba Ensign*, June 6, 1953, 45.

King George VI, Queen Elizabeth (future Queen Mother), and Patrick (bottom left, looking away from the throne) with the other Justices of the Court sitting on the woolsack, 1939.

Since the beginning of the Canada superior court, a final

appeal against a judgment of the Supreme Court of Canada could be made to the Judicial Committee of the Privy Council of the United Kingdom. This was not formally constituted as a court — initially it was not staffed by judges and its members did not even need to be lawyers — although over time, it evolved into something virtually indistinguishable from a court. The Committee was not part of the regular English court system which dates back to the sixteenth century. Essentially, it was an outgrowth of the British imperial experience, a mechanism for handling legal appeals from 'territories' that were held by the Crown which were not considered part of Britain, and which were therefore not subject to the regular courts or the governance of the British Parliament. In 1895, the British Government made provision for senior justices from Australia, South Africa, and Canada to serve on the Judicial Committee.[85]

In 1926 Lord Balfour, Britain's Foreign Minister, suggested that all Dominions be granted full autonomy with respect to their legislation, thus establishing equality among Britain and the individual Dominions. At the time this included the Dominion of Canada, the colony of Newfoundland, the Commonwealth of Australia, the Dominion of New Zealand, the Union of South Africa, and the Irish Free State.

The Statute of Westminster was to implement the declarations and resolutions set forth in the Reports of the Imperial Conferences held at Westminster in 1926 and 1930, and in 1935 the Judicial Committee of the Privy Council decided that the Canadian Parliament had the power to make the Supreme Court of Canada the final Court in criminal cases (civil appeals to Britain continued until 1949). This Statute proclaimed that, although the Dominions were to remain in allegiance with the Crown, each would be granted full legal autonomy. Britain and its now autonomous Dominions became known as the British Commonwealth of Nations.

Civil Appeals

Perhaps one of the most important constitutional cases that came up during Patrick's time as a Puisne Justice of the Supreme Court was its ruling on the Federal Government's request for the Court's opinion on the constitutional validity of a bill to abolish civil appeals to the Judicial Committee of the Privy Council in

---

85 Peter McCormick, *Supreme at Last – The Evolution of the Supreme Court of Canada* (Lorimer, 2000), 6-7.

London, England. The first bill on this topic was introduced to Parliament in 1938 and referred to the legislative competence of the Parliament of Canada to enact Bill No. 9, entitled "An Act to Amend the *Supreme Court Act*", [1940] S.C.R. 49.

In the debates in Parliament regarding this bill, the criticisms of the Privy Council that had been so severe in the debates of the previous years were missing; the sovereignty of Canada was stressed in current arguments and opposition was now all but silenced; the Minister of Justice, Ernest Lapointe, stated his entire agreement with the bill and announced that he would in the near future recommend it be referred to the Supreme Court for a ruling. As promised by the government of the day, the bill that would seek to abolish appeals to the Judicial Committee of the Privy Council in London was referred to the Supreme Court. The case was heard in the middle of June 1939 by six judges: Chief Justice Duff, Rinfret, Crocket, Davies, Kerwin, and Hudson. Noticeably absent at the hearing was the judge from the Province of Québec.[86]

---

86 Ian Bushnell, *The Captive Court - A Study of the Supreme Court of Canada* (McGill-Queen's Press, 1992), 261.

Members of the Supreme Court of Canada in the "old" Courthouse. Justice Kerwin sits third from the right, circa 1940.

There were those who had misgivings about the abolition of appeals to the Judicial Committee of the Privy Council in London. They wondered whether the Supreme Court of Canada was competent to have the last word in difficult constitutional and other cases. However, in the opinion of most Canadians, since becoming Canada's court of last resort, the assembly of learned judges on the Canadian Supreme Court had discharged their responsibilities in an impressive manner.

After examining the legality of the case amending the Supreme Court's jurisdiction, Patrick voted with the majority in an opinion handed down on January 19, 1940, that such a bill was within the powers of the Canadian Parliament (Crocket and Davis dissented). The Supreme Court's opinion was then referred to the Judicial Committee of the Privy Council by Ontario, New Brunswick and British Columbia. With approval by this Committee, the Supreme Court of Canada could become the court of last resort in Canada.

However, World War II had started between the dates of the hearing and the decision of the Supreme Court. Because of the possibility of an appearance of disloyalty if abolition of the appeal was advocated while the war was under way, the hearing before the Privy Council in London was delayed until after the war ended.[87]

During the war, Patrick and the other justices joined Canadian Parliamentarians and Senators to hear British Prime Minister Winston Churchill deliver his noted 'chicken and neck' speech. PM Churchill's words were a response to comments made by French Maréchal Philippe Pétain, of the Vichy French Government, who was convinced that Germany would successfully invade Britain as it had done France. PM Churchill stated: "When I warned them that Britain would fight on alone whatever they did, their generals told their Prime Minister and his divided Cabinet, 'In three weeks England will have her neck wrung like a chicken.' Some chicken! Some neck!"[88]

The reference case which dealt with the ending of appeals decided by the Supreme Court of Canada in 1940, was heard by the Judicial Committee of the Privy Council in London in late October 1946 before the large bench of seven judges. The judgment of the board was rendered in January 1947 and it confirmed the opinion of the Canadian Supreme Court that Ottawa did indeed have the power to end all appeals to London. The Lord Chancellor stated: "It is in fact a prime element in the self-government of the Dominion that it should be able to secure through its own courts of justice that the law should be one and the same for all its citizens."[89]

The provinces of Ontario, New Brunswick, and British Columbia had fought against recognizing the power of the Dominion (fearing the Court might become subservient to the Federal Government), while Québec, Manitoba, and Saskatchewan, as well as the Dominion Government itself, had supported the existence of the constitutional authority. Nova Scotia, Prince Edward Island, and Alberta had not taken part in the case.[90] One of Ottawa's main reasons for ending appeals to London was the anomaly of Canada using the court of another country as its final court of appeal. Dependence on the Privy Council in England, Justice Minister Stuart Garson told the House of Commons, was a "badge of colonialism"; independence from it would be "an important step toward complete nationhood for our country".[91]

---

87 Bushnell, *The Captive Court,* 261.

88 Winston Churchill, Speech to Canadian Parliament, Ottawa, Dec. 30, 1941.

89 "Abolition of Appeals to the Privy Council", The *Canadian Bar Review,* June-July 1950, 581.

90 Bushnell, The Captive Court, 273-274.

91 Gerald Waring, "Supreme Was Just A Word", Montreal Standard, Ottawa Bureau, Jan. 21, 1950.

Even after the long delay due to the war, implementation of the *Act* did not happen overnight, as the Federal Government had to draft and pass legislation. A Bill making the Supreme Court of Canada the final Court of Appeal was introduced by Prime Minister Mackenzie King in 1947 as a private member's bill during his last tenure as leader of the Government and of the Liberal Party. This effort was not successful. It was not until the summer of 1949 that the Liberal government of Prime Minister Louis St. Laurent introduced the bill which was eventually passed by Parliament. The abolition was characterized as part of the process of achieving full self-government, of complete nationhood. The Conservative opposition's contribution to the debate was to suggest that more study was needed owing to the importance that the British Privy Council had had as an interpreter of the constitution. The statute to abolish the appeal to the Privy Council and to make the judgments of the Supreme Court final and conclusive was given royal assent on December 10, 1949.[92] Finally, the Supreme Court of Canada became the court of last resort for all judgments in Canada.

Patrick was the Court's acknowledged expert on constitutional law and he played a leading role in this momentous decision. Shortly after the passage of the 1949 *Act*, he was quoted as saying,

> The court will, on all proper occasions, take the necessary steps in order to bring matters, as the occasion requires and as the march of circumstances demand, in line with what is proper for that time; because, as Shakespeare said: We must not only make a scarecrow of the law, setting it up to fear the birds of prey, and let it keep one shape, till custom make it their perch, and not their terror.[93]
>
> The *Act* was not retroactive — it applied only to actions commenced after the date of promulgation. This meant that for cases already in the system the right of appeal to London remained; the last Canadian appeal, *Ponoka-Calmar Oils v. Wakefield* [1952] S.C.R. 292, was decided by London in 1959.[94]

The *Supreme Court Act* passed by Parliament in December of 1949 stated that, "The Supreme Court shall have, hold and exercise exclusive ultimate appellate, civil and criminal jurisdiction within and for Canada; and the judgment of the court shall in all cases be final and conclusive."

---

92 Bushnell, The Captive Court, 274.
93 Unnamed newspaper article, Georgina Kerwin's collection.
94 McCormick, *Supreme at Last*, 6-7.

One of the many items in this *Act* also specified that judges should reside in the city of Ottawa or within an area of five miles. Also with this 1949 *Act*, the bench reached its current size of nine judges. The number of members reflected the increased number of cases and importance of the Court.

For Australia, it was not until 1975 that all appeals to the Privy Council in England were ended. For New Zealand, this occurred in 2002.

On the bench, the Chief Justice of Canada, or, in his or her absence, the senior Puisne Justice, presided from the centre chair with the other justices seated to his or her right and left by order of seniority of appointment. At sittings of the Court, the justices usually appeared in black silk robes but they wore their ceremonial robes of bright scarlet trimmed with Canadian white mink in court on special occasions and in the Senate at the opening of each new session of Parliament.

The Court considered requests for leave to appeal prior to any being accepted. A description of the Court's actual hearings were described as "taking only a day or two". Each session of the court, in February, April and October, lasted a few weeks and covered perhaps a dozen to 15 cases. But when the hearing was over, the judges' work was not ended; it had only just begun. The hard work was to research and write a judgment.

> In civil or criminal trials, the judgment settled a point of law and became binding thereafter on all lower courts for similar cases. In the constitutional cases, the judgment set the form and application of *The British North America Act*. It was delicate work to phrase a decision so that it could be applied correctly, without distortion or miscarriage of justice, to all similar issues for years to come.[95]

Between 1933 and 1949, the broader non-judicial functions of both the Court and its members expanded as constitutional controversies focused national attention on the institution. The Chief Justice was well known and highly respected. All in all, the stature and prestige of the Supreme Court were rising, as reflected in the changes in the institution's jurisdiction and even in its accommodation.

Citizenship

After World War II, Canadians believed that the war had truly confirmed Canada as a sovereign nation and they wanted the rest

---

95 "Seven Wise Men", *Maclean's Magazine*, Mar. 15, 1949, 66-67.

of the world to recognize the country's hard-won status. For that to happen, however, the remaining emblems of colonialism had to be removed and the symbols of independent nationhood substituted. Shortly after the war Paul Martin Sr., a senior Liberal Cabinet Minister, conceived of the idea of a separate Canadian citizenship after touring the military cemetery at Dieppe, France, where hundreds of Canadian troops had been killed only a few years before. Paul Martin Sr. noticed that the gravestones identified the dead as 'British subjects'. But to Martin, these brave young people were actually Canadians, either by birth or by migration to this country, and he felt it was only fitting that they be recognized as such. Martin decided to explore whether he could change this. Up until that point, Canadian nationals had been legally defined as British subjects, both in Canada and abroad.

When Martin introduced a citizenship bill to the House of Commons on October 22, 1945, he said,

> For the national unity of Canada and for the future and greatness of this country, it is felt to be of utmost importance that all of us, new Canadians or old, have a consciousness of a common purpose and common interests as Canadians; that all of us are able to say with pride and say with meaning: I am a Canadian citizen.[96]

The *Citizenship Act* was enacted on June 27, 1946, and came into force on January 1, 1947. It provided for the conferring of a common Canadian citizenship on all Canadians. With this legislation, Canada became the first Commonwealth country to create its own class of citizenship separate from that of Great Britain. Henceforth, Canadian citizenship could be acquired by immigrants who had been naturalized in Canada, non-Canadian British subjects who had lived in Canada for five or more years, and non-Canadian women who had married Canadian citizens and who had come to live in Canada.

In a moving and historic ceremony on the evening of January 6, 1947, in the Supreme Court of Canada chamber with all Justices in attendance, 26 individuals were presented with Canadian citizenship certificates. Among them were Prime Minister William Lyon Mackenzie King (certificate 0001), and Yousuf Karsh, the internationally acclaimed Armenian-born photographer. Others in attendance were: Naif Azar (Palestine), Jerzy Meier (Poland), Helen

---

96 www.cic.gc.ca/english/resources/publications/legacy/chap-5.asp Accessed Mar. 2017.

Sawicka (Poland), Louis Brodbeck (Switzerland), Joachim Hellmen (Germany), Jacko Hrushkowsky (Russia), Anton Justinik (Yugoslavia), Zigurd Larsen (Norway), Joseph Litvinchuk (Romania), Nestor Rakowitza (Romania), and Mrs. Labrosse (Scotland).[97]

Chief Justice Rinfret, along with all other Justices, including Patrick Kerwin sitting beside the Chief Justice, presided at this ceremony and, according to family lore, Patrick was proud and thrilled to have been part of this momentous change in Canadian life.

Canadian nationality was extended to the residents of Newfoundland when the British colony joined Canada as a province on April 1, 1949.

~

Noble et al. v. Alley

As a member of the Supreme Court, Patrick heard a landmark case in 1950 involving inherent discrimination (*Noble et al. v. Alley* [1951] S.C.R. 64 1950-11-20). On the shores of Lake Huron was the Beach O'Pines, a particularly nice community to spend a summer day in 1948 — providing one was a Caucasian and Christian. At the time, 'The Pines' found itself at the heart of a battle regarding discrimination that was thought to be legal. Annie Noble had purchased a lot in 1933. After fifteen years, she decided to sell to a man named Bernie Wolf. Everything seemed to be fine until Mr. Wolf's lawyer noted the following clause in the original deed:

> The lands ... shall never be sold, assigned, transferred, leased, rented ... to ... any person of the Jewish, Hebrew, Semitic, Negro or coloured race or blood, it being the intention and purpose ... to restrict the ownership ... and enjoyment ... to persons of the white or Caucasian race not excluded by this clause. [98]

Bernie Wolf was Jewish, a fact that did not trouble Annie Noble in the least. However, Wolf's lawyer was worried that the deed could cause his client some problems even if Ms. Noble had not signed the original agreement. To avoid any possible complications, they sought to have a judge nullify the restriction. However, instead of avoiding further complications, the buyer and seller found themselves immersed in them.

---

97 www.canadiana.ca/citm/imagepopups/pa129262_e.html Accessed Apr. 2015.
98 en.wikipedia.org/wiki/*Noble_v_Alley* Accessed June 2016.

Word spread in the community that a Jewish person was attempting to buy in 'The Pines'. Apparently, this would not do. They fought to have the restriction stand. Both the Ontario Supreme Court and the Court of Appeal found the restriction valid, and the case ended up at the Supreme Court of Canada.

The Court declared invalid the section of the agreement which required that owners, renters or occupiers of the property must be "persons of the white or Caucasian race ...". [99] The court decided that this restriction was unenforceable because it ran with the owner rather than with the land, contrary to common law covenant doctrine. Additionally, the Supreme Court ruled the covenant to be void for uncertainty because its racist language was unclear. The effect of the decision was to question the legal status of any existing discriminatory property covenant based on race or religion. The ruling reinforced efforts by advocacy groups such as the Canadian Jewish Congress to outlaw these institutionalized weapons of discrimination, efforts which led several provincial legislatures to outlaw them by the early 1950s. The Supreme Court's decision constituted an important step in the broader battle for human rights and against discrimination on racial and religious grounds in Canada.

~

By 1950, Canada's Supreme Court was led by Chief Justice Thibaudeau Rinfret, who had served for twenty-five years, first as a member and later as Chief Justice, and tended to show his impatience in court. Justice Robert Taschereau, the second justice from Québec, was noted for his insistence on precision from counsel. Patrick, from Ontario, who had been sitting in the Supreme Court since 1935, was the senior Puisne Justice and was known to be a kindly and able man. Roy Kellock, also from Ontario, was known for his industriousness and for the tenacity with which he held a viewpoint once arrived at. To all observers, Ivan Rand, the justice from the Maritimes, was marked by his intellectual ability and his probing questions. Respect for his repeated and penetrating queries in Court led him to be the justice most feared by counsel; one observer reported that Justice Rand "uses the word 'why' like a machine gun". [100] In 1944, the

---

99 scc-csc.lexum.com/scc-csc/scc-csc/en/item/3691/index.do Accessed June 2016.
100 I. N. Smith, "The Supreme Court of Canada – A Layman Takes a Look", *Ottawa Journal*, 1952, Georgina Kerwin's collection.

able J.W. Estey had come to the Supreme Court from the prairies. The most recently arrived justice was Charles Locke, "a rugged, solid man who listened impassively" to counsel.[101] Two more judges joined these seven justices in late December 1949, John Robert Cartwright and Joseph Honoré Gérald Fauteux (both of whom were to become Chief Justice).

In a 1952 booklet on the Supreme Court, the *Ottawa Journal*'s Associate Editor, Norman Smith wrote,

> Patrick Kerwin is senior of the Puisne Judges. Born Sarnia 1889, practiced law Guelph. In 1932 became judge Supreme Court of Ontario. July 1935 came to the Supreme Court. A twinkle in his eye belies the fact that he has much of the court's work on his hands. Some say Mr. Kerwin is the ablest judge of all. Was a Conservative appointment but Liberals know him to be shrewd jurist and able organizer. He is a Catholic.[102]

~

Saumur v. The City of Québec

Of the many cases heard by Patrick and the court, one of the most frequently cited decisions of the Rinfret Court is *Saumur v. The City of Québec*, [1953] 2 S.C.R. 299. The background was the long-standing unpopularity within Catholic Québec of the Jehovah's Witnesses, aggravated by the fact that the Witnesses saw themselves as having a religious duty to spread their views with persistence and energy — characteristically, by standing on street corners with copies of their periodical publications, as well as by door-to-door missions. Nor did it help that their views included unflattering opinions of the Catholic Church that were couched in flamboyant biblical terminology.[103]

The Québec Government especially did not like the pamphlet published by the Jehovah's Witnesses titled "Québec's Burning Hate for God and Christ and Freedom Is the Shame of all Canada". The pamphlet sharply criticized the Québec provincial government's suppression of the Witnesses and, in their opinion, the courts were doing nothing to prevent it.

Laurier Saumur was born a Catholic in the Province of Québec and later became an active member of the Jehovah's Witnesses, going door-to-door. At the time, police harassment of Witnesses

---

101 Ibid.
102 Ibid.
103 McCormick, *Supreme at Last*, 29.

was widespread in Québec, and Saumur had been arrested 103 times for distribution of Witness literature. He and a group of Jehovah's Witnesses decided to challenge head-on the Québec City municipal by-law that prohibited the distribution of literature in the streets without the written authorization of the city's Chief of Police, on the basis that it was outside the municipality's jurisdiction, and that it was religious and political censorship. The courts in Québec ruled that the by-law was valid.

The full bench of the Supreme Court of Canada heard the case to decide if this was an action dealing with Constitutional Law or that of a Municipal By-Law. The result was a 5–4 decision determining that the by-law was invalid. The Court held that the subject matter of the law was in relation to "speech" or "religion" which were both in the exclusive legislative jurisdiction of the Federal Government. The majority noted that the law had the effect of constituting the Chief of Police as censor, deciding whether certain literature was objectionable. The result, they observed, would be that the Chief of Police censored unpopular groups such as the Jehovah's Witnesses.

Two of the dissenting judges, Rinfret and Taschereau, saw the law primarily as related to the use of the streets; and only involved a police regulation aimed at the suppression of conditions likely to cause disorder within society. In their decision they wrote,

> The pith and substance of this general by-law is to control and regulate the usage of streets in regard to the distribution of pamphlets. Even if the motive of the City was to prevent the Jehovah's Witnesses from distributing their literature in the streets, that could never be a reason to render the by-law illegal or unconstitutional, since the City had the power to pass it: usage of the streets of a municipality being indisputably a question within the domain of the municipality and a local question.
>
> Freedom of worship is not a subject of legislation within the jurisdiction of Parliament. It is a civil right within the provinces. The provisions of the by-law are not covered by the preamble to s. 91 of the *B.N.A. Act*, nor have they the character of a criminal law. Furthermore, even if the right to distribute pamphlets was an act of worship, freedom of worship is not an absolute right but is subject to control by the province.[104]

The two other dissenting judges, Cartwright and Fauteux, wrote,

---

104 Supreme Court Judgments, (1953-10-06) 2 S.C.R. 299: 301-302.

It was within the competence of the Legislature to authorize the passing of this by-law under its power to legislate in relation to (1) the use of highways, since the legislative authority to permit, forbid or regulate their use for purposes other than that of passing and re-passing belongs to the provinces; and (2) police regulations and the suppression of conditions likely to cause disorder, since it is within the competence of the Legislature to prohibit or regulate the distribution in the streets of written matter having a tendency to insult or annoy the recipients thereof with the possible result of giving rise to disorder, and perhaps violence, in the streets. An Act of a provincial legislature in relation to matters assigned to it under the *B.N.A. Act* is not rendered invalid because it interferes to a limited extent with either the freedom of the press or the freedom of religion.[105]

The dissenting judges found no basis for Saumur's claim that it prevented the Jehovah's Witnesses from their religious practice.

Mr. Justice Kerwin held that the *Freedom of Worship Act* of Québec applied, and because of a conflict between the by-law and the *Act*, the by-law could not be applied to Saumur. The *Freedom of Worship Act* provided that:

...the free exercise and enjoyment of Religious Profession and Worship, without discrimination or preference, so as the same be not made an excuse for acts of licentiousness, or a justification of practices inconsistent with the peace and safety of the Province, is by the constitution and laws of this Province allowed to all Her Majesty's subjects within the same.[106]

Justice Kerwin wrote:

Whether or not the *Freedom of Worship Act* whenever originally enacted (it is now R.S.Q. 1941, c. 307) be taken to supersede the pre-Confederation Statute of 1852 (14-15 Vict., c. 175), the specific terms of the enactment providing for freedom of worship have not been abrogated. Even though it would appear from the evidence that Jehovah's Witnesses do not consider themselves as belonging to a religion, they are entitled to "the free exercise and enjoyment of [their] Religious Profession, and Worship" and have a legal right to attempt to spread their views by way of the printed and written word as well as orally; and their attacks on religion generally, and one in particular, as shown in the exhibits filed, do not bring them within the exception "so as the same be not made an excuse for

---

105 Ibid.
106 Bushnell, *The Captive Court*, 315-16.

licentiousness or a justification of practices inconsistent with the peace and safety of the Province", and their attacks are not "inconsistent with the peace and safety of the Province" even when they are directed particularly against the religion of most of the Province's residents. As the by-law may have its effect in other cases and under other circumstances, if not otherwise objectionable, it is not *ultra vires* [beyond the power of] the City of Québec, but since it is in conflict with the freedom of worship of the appellant, it should be declared that it does not extend so as to prohibit the appellant as a member of Jehovah's Witnesses from distributing in the streets any of the writings included in the exhibits.

Furthermore, since both the right to practice one's religion and the freedom of the press fall within "Civil Rights in the Province", the Legislature had the power to authorize the City to pass such by-law.[107]

Patrick's judgments directly reflected his judicial philosophy. He maintained that the reasons for judgment in a case should deal with the particular case, and principles of wide application should rarely be enunciated. In sum, there was only to be one resolution of the particular dispute and no judicial creativity.[108]

Subsequent to this decision being delivered, it was used to dismiss more than 1000 cases against Witnesses in the Province of Québec. It was only one of a series of cases the Supreme Court dealt with concerning the rights of Jehovah's Witnesses under the Duplessis government of Québec. Subsequent to the Saumur case was one case where Premier Duplessis was personally sued for revoking the liquor license of a Jehovah's Witness, *Roncarelli v. Duplessis* [1959] S.C.R. 121. In the end, Roncarelli won the case (see Chapter 11 for more details).

The Jehovah's Witnesses' publication, *Awake*, wrote about the decision with the banner for the article reading, "Jehovah's Witnesses Not Seditious". [109] The *Awake* article hailed Justice Kerwin's "integrity, impartiality and fearlessness".

~

It is incumbent on the Chief Justice of the Supreme Court to act as the Governor General's Deputy upon request from His or Her Excellency. If His or Her Excellency is temporarily absent from Canada for more than one month, dies, or is incapacitated while holding the position, the Chief Justice, by virtue of the

---

107 Supreme Court Judgments, (1953-10-06) 2 S.C.R. 299: 301.
108 Bushnell, *The Captive Court*, 317.
109 "Jehovah's Witnesses Not Seditious", *Awake* Vol XXXII Issue 5, Mar. 8, 1951, 3-7, 27-28.

Letters Patent constituting the office of Governor General, becomes what is termed the "Administrator of the Government of Canada" upon taking the oath of allegiance, and is thus responsible for the due execution of the office of Governor General prescribed by the Letters Patent. The Governor General may appoint others to be his/her Deputy, or in the case of the death, incapacity, or absence from Canada of the Chief Justice, the Senior Judge of the Supreme Court of Canada becomes Administrator.

Each time this is done, a Proclamation is signed, certified by the Deputy Registrar General of Canada, and issued in the *Canada Gazette* whereby the person acting on behalf of the Governor General is identified by name and position. Our family is fortunate to have a few copies of these Proclamations with respect to my grandfather that were sent to my mother, Isobel (Kerwin) McKenna in 1977 by Ken Campbell, former Executive Secretary to the Chief Justice.

Over the years, while the senior Justice on the Court and later, while Chief Justice, Patrick acted as the Administrator of Canada on behalf of the Governor General on numerous occasions. In this position, he provided Royal Assent to the bills at hand in the Senate and then either would adjourn the Senate or prorogue Parliament depending on the circumstances, received the credentials of new ambassadors, and performed a host of other duties related to the office.

In July of 1947, both the Governor General and the Chief Justice were away. Thus Patrick, as the senior Justice, was appointed to act for the Governor General during a special meeting of the Privy Council, when he shared the announcement of King George VI giving consent to the marriage of Princess Elizabeth to Lieut. Philip Mountbatten. Newspapers of the day reported,

> Mr. Justice Patrick Kerwin of the Supreme Court of Canada, acting as the deputy governor-general in the absence of Viscount Alexander, met with members of the council and read to them a message received from the King. [110]

In September 1949, both Governor General Viscount Alexander and Chief Justice Rinfret had left for Britain. A newspaper clipping reported:

Mr. Justice Kerwin Acting in Place of Alexander

---

110 Unnamed newspaper article, 1947, Georgina Kerwin's collection.

In a brief ceremony, the duties of the Governor General in
Canada Monday were vested temporarily in Mr. Justice Patrick
Kerwin of the Supreme Court of Canada. The 61-year-old justice,
native of Sarnia, Ont., became officially the "Administrator of the
Government of Canada" in the absence of Viscount Alexander,
now on his way to Britain for a two-month visit. Normally, when
the Governor General is absent for more than one month, the
Chief Justice of the Supreme Court of Canada acts in his place
as "administrator".

However, Mr. Chief Justice Thibaudeau Rinfret is in Britain,
and Mr. Justice Kerwin has taken over the duties as the next
senior justice. [111]

Patrick, again acting as Administrator of the Government of
Canada, presided over the opening of Canada's 21st Parliament
(second session) on September 15, 1949, with the Liberal leader
Louis St. Laurent as Prime Minister and the official opposition led
by George Drew of the Conservative Party. The *Journals of the
Senate of Canada* describe Patrick's involvement as follows:

After a while the Honourable Patrick Kerwin, a Judge of the
Supreme Court of Canada, in his capacity as Deputy Governor
General, having come and being seated at the foot of the Throne.

The Honourable the Speaker commanded the Gentleman
Usher of the Black Rod to proceed to the House of Commons and
acquaint the House that:

"It is the Honourable the Deputy Governor General's desire
that they attend him immediately in the Senate Chamber".

The House of Commons being come. [112]

In the index of this volume, Patrick's name is shown as,
"Kerwin, The Honourable Patrick — Deputy Governor General:
Informal Opening of Parliament". [113]

As to where Patrick sat in the Senate on behalf of the
Governor General, the phrase utilized in the *Journals*, 'seated at
the foot of the Throne', was explained to me as follows:

There are two thrones located in the Senate Chamber, one
is for the Queen or the Governor General and the other is for
the Queen's spouse or the Governor General's spouse. The
thrones are used primarily for official state events, such as
the opening of Parliament when the Speech from the Throne
is read. The Speaker's chair is normally located directly in

---

111 Ibid., 1949.
112 *Journals of the Senate of Canada*, Fourth Session of the Twenty-First Parliament,
1951, Library of Parliament, Volume XCIV, 222.
113 *Journals of the Senate of Canada*, Vol. XCI, Second Session, 1949, 17.

front of the two thrones on the same dais. However, it is removed when the Thrones are used for official state events.

On less ceremonial occasions, when the Governor General or a deputy of the Governor General comes to the Senate Chamber during the course of a sitting of the Senate (such as for a Royal Assent ceremony), the Speaker's chair is not removed from the Chamber. The Governor General, or a deputy, will sit in the Speaker's chair during the ceremony. When this occurs, the expression "… being seated at the foot of the Throne" is used to signify that they are seated in the Speaker's chair which is located directly in front of the Thrones and that he or she is not seated on the actual Throne. [114]

The *Journals of the Senate of Canada* also recorded numerous other times Patrick was called upon to act on behalf of the Governor General giving Royal Assent to bills at regular and special sessions of Parliament, proroguing Sessions of Parliament, and Opening Parliament.

In another task of a similar nature in June 1951, Patrick was appointed as the Administrator of the Government of Canada when Governor General Viscount Alexander and Chief Justice Rinfret were again away at the same time. In a series of letters between the Assistant Secretary of the Governor General and the Under Secretary of State, there was a discussion as to the actual time of day when he would assume the duties. The discussion revolved around what exact time the Governor General would depart Canadian waters beyond the Gulf of St. Lawrence.

A concern raised in respect to the timing of the swearing of the oaths of office was expressed by the Assistant Secretary of the Governor General in one letter stating:

> I gather that "the line" will be crossed some time before midnight on June 10th and that for a few hours the country will be without an administrator to act in the place of the Governor General. You will have noted that the third paragraph of Article VIII of the Letters Patent provides that the powers shall not be vested in the administrator until he has taken the required oaths. [115]

Then he went on to add,

---

114 Email to the author from Annie Joannette, Communications Officer, The Senate of Canada, Dec. 17, 2013.
115 Letter from the Assistant Secretary of the Governor General to the Under Secretary of State, Library and Archives of Canada, File RG6-A-1, item 1842 – 1951, May 1951.

> However, perhaps we should not worry about such possible "gaps" ... for it is the difficulty of drafting a provision that will cover all possible eventualities and classes of cases.[116]

This was resolved after the Under Secretary of State, C. Stein, spoke directly with the steamship company who estimated that "His Excellency's ship will be well out of the gulf of St. Lawrence by Monday the 11th June."[117] With that confirmed, the Governor General asked Patrick to act as Administrator from Monday June 11 until Wednesday, August 1 inclusive, with the oaths of office to be taken by Patrick at 4:15 p.m. on Monday, June 11, 1951, in his Chambers in the new Supreme Court Building.

An article in the *Ottawa Citizen* (June 1953) described acting on behalf of the Governor General as "double duty":

> Hon. Mr. Justice Patrick Kerwin, senior puisne justice of the Supreme Court of Canada, is carrying two top-ranking offices these days. He is both His Excellency the Administrator of Canada, during the absence of His Excellency the Governor-General on a month's vacation in the United Kingdom, and he is acting Chief Justice of Canada until Chief Justice Rinfret returns from his trip to attend the Coronation.
>
> Justice Kerwin was sworn in as Administrator at a brief ceremony in his Supreme Court chambers yesterday morning.[118]

A session of Parliament can end when the Governor General accepts the Prime Minister's advice to "prorogue" Parliament until the next session, which must, by law, come within a year. Prorogation brings the business of both the Senate and the House of Commons to an end. All pending legislation dies on the Order Paper and committee activity ceases, though all members and officials of the Government and both houses remain in office.

On June 26, 1954, Patrick was again acting for the Governor General and the Chief Justice when he was asked to prorogue Parliament by the government of Prime Minister Louis St. Laurent. A message was sent from the Honourable Patrick Kerwin, a Judge of the Supreme Court of Canada, acting as Deputy of His Excellency the Governor General, desiring the immediate attendance of the House in the Senate Chamber. The following letter from the Secretary to the Governor General to the Speaker of the House

---

116 Ibid.
117 Ibid.
118 "Double Role for Kerwin These Days", *Ottawa Citizen*, June 17, 1953, 11.

indicates the intention of Mr. Justice Kerwin as Administrator of Canada.

GOVERNMENT HOUSE
OTTAWA 2
OFFICE OF THE
SECRETARY TO THE GOVERNOR GENERAL

24th June 1954.

Sir,

I have the honour to inform you that the Honourable Mr. Justice Kerwin, acting as Deputy of His Excellency the Governor General, will proceed to the Senate Chamber at 6.00 p.m. on the 26th June, 1954, for the purpose of proroguing the First Session of the Twenty-Second Parliament.

I have the honour to be, Sir, Your obedient servant,

J. F. DELAUTE,

Secretary to the Governor-General (Administrative)
The Honourable Speaker of the House of Commons
Ottawa [119]

That was an eventful day for Patrick as one of his grandsons, the author of this book, was born that evening.

~

A newspaper article from May 1954 kept by Georgina speculated as to who would be selected as the new Chief Justice of the Supreme Court of Canada when Chief Justice Thibaudeau Rinfret turned 75, the required retirement age of members on the Court. In this article the author weighed in with the following:

On the evening of June 21, Prime Minister Louis St. Laurent will have an important telephone call to make. The next day will be the 75th birthday, and thus the automatic retirement date, of Thibaudeau Rinfret, Chief Justice of Canada's Supreme Court. On the eve of the Chief Justice's retirement, by long-established custom, the Prime Minister will call Rinfret's successor to tell him directly of his appointment to the country's highest judicial office.

---

119 *Journals of the House of Commons of Canada* Session, no. 83278-55. (1953-54).

Top favourite in the speculation is Ontario-born Patrick Kerwin, 64, a puisne [associate] judge on the nine-man court since 1935, and next in seniority to Rinfret. One factor, however, may work against Kerwin's appointment. Like Rinfret, Kerwin is a Roman Catholic, and only once in the court's history, in 1906, has one Catholic Chief Justice succeeded another. The normal course is to alternate between Catholic and Protestant. If that principle is followed and the new chief is named from the present court, 70-year-old Ivan Cleveland Rand, the ranking Protestant, may be chosen.

Another possibility is that the new Chief Justice will be an outsider. Finance Minister Douglas Abbot, a first-rate lawyer and a Protestant (Anglican), is known to be ready to quit the Cabinet. By law, three members of the nine-man court must come from Québec. Abbot was born in Lennoxville, Que., and would maintain the province's representation if he replaced Québec-born Thibaudeau Rinfret.[120]

In another uncredited newspaper article kept by Georgina titled, "Justice vs. Discrimination", the author characterized the topic of Justice Kerwin's religion as a non-issue in deciding who should be the next Chief Justice of Canada:

To discriminate against an individual on grounds of his religious conviction is generally admitted to be unworthy.

If a capable individual, whose achievements, character and professional eminence are above reproach, is to be denied his seniority, and thus in fact demoted, because he belongs to a particular faith, there can be no doubt that discrimination is being practiced.

Yet voices have been raised, advocating precisely this course in connection with one of Canada's most respected jurists. They want deserved preferment denied because he is a Catholic. We only hope that this prejudiced clamour referring to the Supreme Court Justice Patrick Kerwin, next in line as Chief Justice, will not influence the government's just choice.

Let there be no confusion on one point. We strongly believe that all sections and groups should be fairly represented in the affairs of our country. Here we are dealing with justice to capable men already in office.

Justice Kerwin has for several years discharged the duties of presiding over the court when Chief Justice Thibaudeau Rinfret was away. He has filled that role with distinction and ability. The legal profession has had ample proof to assure itself of his high judicial qualities in the many cases over which he has presided.

---

120 Unnamed newspaper article, 1954, Georgina Kerwin's collection.

There is more than merely the treatment of Justice Kerwin involved. There is a basic principle at stake.

Today the Supreme Court of Canada is the highest judicial authority in our land. We have reason to pride ourselves that the Bench in general and the Supreme Bench in particular has men serving society according to the highest standards of impartial judgeship.

Those who tried to find flaws in the conscientious administration of justice by expecting religious or sectional partialities, in the famous Jehovah Witness case, failed miserably. We were more in agreement with Justice Cartwright's conclusions than with those of Justice Kerwin, but we had no grounds for surprise to find either Protestant Justice Cartwright giving judgment against the Witnesses, or Justice Kerwin conscientiously coming to a different conclusion.

If we felt that a judge no longer was giving legal opinion, but acting as a member of a group, we would say that he was unfit for this high office.

What absolute nonsense to suggest that a Catholic can't succeed a Catholic, any more than that a Protestant can't succeed a Protestant, if he were fit and next in line. Seniority of course is only one qualification. But all other things being equal no one should be ruled out, as has been advocated in some journals, because of his religion.

To supersede Justice Kerwin with a political accommodation, by making the Chief Justice's dignity a political plum or a denominational pirouette, would harm the dignity of our judiciary. It would be even more serious than the infliction of an unmerited slight on the learned and deserving judge, "handicapped" by nothing but the religion he professes.[121]

On July 1, 1954, Justice Patrick G. Kerwin was named Chief Justice of the Supreme Court of Canada, a designation and title that was accepted as the right choice. As of that date he became known as Chief Justice of Canada by the legal community and society at large, and when acting on behalf of the Governor General, as recorded in the *Journals of the House of Commons of Canada*.

The person who named Patrick to the post was Prime Minister Louis St. Laurent, known prior to his political career as a "lawyer's lawyer". St. Laurent had come to politics at the behest of then Prime Minister Mackenzie King in 1941. From there, St. Laurent became leader of the Liberal Party and, in 1949, went on to win one of the largest electoral majorities to date.

---

121 "Justice vs. Discrimination", uncredited newspaper article, Georgina Kerwin's collection.

Dissents, Concurrences, and Decisions, by Judge
Reported Supreme Court Decisions, 1949-1954 [122]

Judge	Panels	Divided panels	Wrote Decision	Contributed to Decision	With majority	Concurrences	Dissents
					%		
Chief Justice Rinfret	220	156	8.6	35.9	46.2	32.1	21.8
Kerwin	277	206	23.8	59.9	47.1	35.9	17.0
Taschereau	264	185	15.9	39.4	51.4	33.5	15.1
Rand	270	205	15.2	67.8	26.8	60.0	13.2
Kellock	227	168	21.1	66.1	33.9	51.8	14.3
Estey	284	213	8.1	46.8	39.4	48.4	12.2
Locke	267	199	9.7	49.1	36.7	39.7	23.6
Cartwright	221	158	15.8	54.3	36.1	43.7	20.3
Fauteux	157	115	12.1	26.8	59.1	29.6	11.3

122 P. McCormick, *Supreme at Last*, 20.

I was very glad when
Right Reverend Father Hanley
suggested that I speak tonight
on the Supreme Court of Canada,
as it relieved me from the obligation
of choosing a subject.
If it transpires that it be found rather
dull and uninteresting,
part of the blame will be his.

—Chief Justice Kerwin in an address to the
Newman Club, Kingston, Ontario
January 16, 1957

Chapter 9

The Supreme Court and its Buildings
Ottawa

When the cornerstone of the current Supreme Court of Canada building was dedicated by Queen Elizabeth in 1939, she stated, "The location was a worthy home for our Supreme Court".[123] To get to this point, the Court had gone through times where it lacked a decent place to work and, in the initial years, it lacked respect as well.

The Supreme Court of Canada is our country's final Court of Appeal and serves Canadians by providing decisions on issues of public and legal importance. Its jurisdiction is derived mainly from the *Supreme Court Act*, as well as from a few other Acts of Parliament, such as the *Criminal Code*.

Prior to Confederation in 1867, courts of law thrived in the 18th century in Lower Canada, Upper Canada, (Québec and Ontario respectively) and in the Maritime colonies. In fact, the need for an organized system of courts in the land had been recognized long ago, appearing in a communiqué sent by Samuel de Champlain in August of 1610 in which his list of grievances from the people of New France to the King included the need for stronger courts.

In the constitutional conferences that led to the creation of Canada in 1867, there was little discussion about the Supreme Court. The Fathers of Confederation were content simply to provide for the possibility of creating such a court and let Parliament consider the idea later. Section 101 of *The British North America Act, 1867*, (renamed the *Constitution Act, 1867* in 1992) authorized Parliament to "provide for the Constitution, Maintenance, and Organization of a General Court of Appeal for Canada".[124]

Less than a year after Confederation in 1867, Sir John A. Macdonald, who was then both Prime Minister and Minister of Justice, took the initiative regarding the creation of a superior court. Some argued that a Supreme Court in Canada could hear

---

123 Uncredited newspaper clipping, Family Archives.
124 Chief Justice Kerwin, "Speech to the Newman Club", Kingston, ON, Jan. 16, 1957, 2.

112

only those cases arising out of the laws of the central government; the court could have no jurisdiction over provincial law. This view was unacceptable to Macdonald.[125]

Initial attempts to set up a general Court of Appeal by Macdonald's government in 1867 and 1870 were not realized as many argued *The British North America Act, 1867,* did not anticipate the creation of such a court. Numerous Members of Parliament opposed the project fearing the unknown consequences for provincial rights.

> The issue of creating the Court passed to the new Liberal government of Alexander Mackenzie who, in their first Speech from the Throne on March 27, 1875, indicated that a bill would be introduced to create the court.[126]

This government took up the issue in earnest, stating that a supreme court was "essential to our system of jurisprudence and to the settlement of constitutional questions".[127]

The Supreme Court Bill proposed establishing two courts with the one piece of legislation: a supreme court and an exchequer court. The Bill severed the Supreme Court's original jurisdiction in revenue matters; that area would now be the responsibility of the Exchequer Court.

The Exchequer Court would deal with such matters as patents, trademarks, Canadian tax matters, expropriations by and claims against Canada. The jurisdiction of the Supreme Court of Canada was to be strictly appellate in nature. The government of the day persuaded Parliament to vote for the establishment of a supreme court by arguing that it was needed to standardize Canadian law and to provide constitutional interpretations on issues that would affect the evolution of the new federation. The *Supreme Court Act* received royal assent on April 28, 1875, and was brought into force on September 17, 1875.

~

On November 8, five Puisne Justices were sworn into office, as was the first Chief Justice, the Hon. William Buell Richards, the former Chief Justice of the Ontario Court of Common Pleas. The first Registrar appointed was Robert Cassels whose office was

---

125 Snell and Vaughan, *The Supreme Court,* 3, 6.
126 Bushnell, *The Captive Court,* 13.
127 *The Supreme Court of Canada and its Justices 1875* (Dundurn, SCC & PWGSC, 2000), 12.

responsible for the administration of the Court. From there, arrangements for the Court's functioning were taken in hand; staff were appointed, law books were ordered, rules and procedures began to be considered and temporary accommodations were found.[128]

Partly at the suggestion of Governor General Dufferin, the justices adopted the stately scarlet and ermine robes of the English bench for "red letter days" and black robes for everyday.[129] Perhaps it is fortunate for all concerned that he did not suggest the Justices adopt the wigs as well.

The justices heard cases in the former reading room of the Senate while plans were being implemented to provide permanent quarters for the court; later the Court moved to the room just south of the (then) new library of Parliament. The Court officially sat for the first time on January 17, 1876, but did not have any cases to hear. The first case the Court heard, in April of that same year, was a reference from the Senate requesting the Court's opinion on a private bill. Having dealt with that, the Court next sat for one week in June of 1876, when it disposed of three cases. It was not convened again until the following January, when it began to hold regular sessions with a full agenda.

In 1876, Sir Alexander Mackenzie's Liberal administration was the first to recommend abolishing Canadian appeals to the Privy Council in London, England. The proposal did not survive the criticism of the Leader of the Opposition, Sir John A. Macdonald, and many members of Parliament. The last appeals to England were only abolished in 1949.

~

Sir John A. Macdonald's government, having been re-elected in 1878, demonstrated its basic commitment to the enduring presence of the Supreme Court by having plans drawn up in 1881 to refurbish a building formerly used as stables and workshops located at the northeast corner of Bank and Wellington Streets west of the West Block on Parliament Hill. The building was described as an attractive two-storey gabled stone structure in the parliament's gothic style of the day. The building's origins were said to be a source of embarrassment to the Court over the next fifty years and more.

---

128 Snell and Vaughan, *The Supreme Court*, 16-17.
129 Ibid., 16.

The first Supreme Court of Canada building — National Archives of Canada (National Archives of Canada, PA-51815) circa 1950.

Small as the original structure was, the Supreme Court was not given full use of the building; they shared it with an art gallery and the Exchequer Court. Space limitations and the condition of the building soon began to cause problems for all. There were numerous and on-going complaints about the unsuitable site, and the dreadful smell that permeated the building (remnants of its former life as a stable), and about the distance to the parliamentary library.

In 1887 a major report was forwarded to the Justice Department and the Public Works Department detailing the weaknesses of the courthouse. Some of their findings included: the courtroom was too small and the ceiling leaked; there was no room to dispose of chamber business such that motions, taxation, bills of costs, and other such items were dealt with by the justices within their own small offices; the lack of a library necessitated using the walls and window of the conference room for shelving space, thus causing frequent interruptions by readers to the justices' meetings; storage space for books had already been exhausted, and to store the official Reports the registrar was forced to resort to the attic, which could only be reached by a step ladder. The location of the rooms meant that the justices had no privacy as the corridor outside their offices was used as a public thoroughfare. In this

115

same report, the Chief Justice complained "of the discomfort, inconvenience and bad ventilation of his room, as well as of the general unsuitable nature and insufficiency of the accommodation provided for the Court and Judges".[130]

To appease the Court, in 1887 the art gallery was moved out of the building, but most of the space was required for the Exchequer Court. Two years later, plans were formulated for a proposed major extension to the Supreme Court building.

In 1890 a construction contract was signed for $10,765, a figure that grew to $30,457 by the completion of the contract. This paid for major additions to the existing structure: a basement and two additional storeys.

This almost doubled the size of the courthouse. The outside was finished in a style corresponding in material and detail to the existing structure. The judges' rooms were moved into the new section, and several old offices were knocked down to make room for a law library. Several other rooms were refurbished, and there were now stairs to the new attic, an upgrade from the ladder used prior to the renovation. The addition and the internal alterations slowed most of the complaints about the building for a time. Chief Justice Ritchie's basic criticism remained unresolved: the courthouse did not represent the high status that the Supreme Court deserved. But given the opinion of the public and the political leaders at this time, the physical representation of the Supreme Court of Canada was probably an accurate reflection of its position in the Canadian political structure.

The changes did not prevent the Registrar's complaint in 1897:

> ... nothing has been done to the Building. The walls in the new part, in which are situated the Judges' Chambers and officers' rooms, have never been whitewashed, or the cracks made from the settling of the building filled in. I think I am not using language at all too strong, when I say that the present condition of the building is filthy and quite unfit for the purpose for which it is used.[131]

Fire was a major concern as the building had no firewalls and was constructed partially of flammable materials. A number of sheds had been built against the back of the building, and there were assorted piles of lumber near or against the courthouse. Inadequate storage space inside the building resulted in dangerous

---

130 Snell and Vaughan, *The Supreme Court*, 49-50.
131 R. Cassels to E. L. Newcombe, SCC Letterbook 13, 200-2, 25 Feb. 1897.

stacking of materials. As well, sanitary conditions were an additional concern. Much of the furniture was moth-eaten, and the pests had begun to spread elsewhere in the building. In some of the justices' rooms, reported the Registrar in 1900:

> ...moths have so destroyed the chairs that a person's fist can be shoved through the covering at many points and the material which has been used in the upholstering is alive with these insects. The result is that the judges' robes have been in some cases ruined... The corridors and the rooms are constantly filled with bad odours, particularly in the morning, evidencing an unsanitary condition of the plumbing.[132]

Nevertheless, at the time of Lyman Duff's appointment to the Supreme Court in 1906, the interior of the courtroom was described in the following terms:

> The courtroom itself resembled a chapel: peaked beams formed the ceiling; the rich wood paneling of the walls, graced by carved scrolls with a floral motif, glowed with the patina of age. The judges from their dais peered at the counsel, who were seated according to rank. Behind the lawyers were low-backed pews ranged on both sides of a central aisle.[133]

In that same year the government held a national competition for two new buildings; one for the general department offices and the other to house the Supreme Court of Canada, the Exchequer's Court, and offices for the Department of Justice.[134] The buildings were to be located on the west side of Sussex Street, between Wellington and St. Patrick Streets (current location of the Chateau Laurier Hotel and Major's Hill Park). The buildings were to be long and narrow and included a pedestrian bridge over the Rideau Canal to link Parliament Hill with the new structures. However, as can sometimes happen with these competitions, things began to unravel and the plan was never realized. The Court would have to stay in their current quarters for quite a while longer.

To deal with a couple of issues inside the Court, in 1927 the government of the day (under Prime Minister Mackenzie King) initiated two amendments to the *Supreme Court Act*. The first

---

132 Cameron to E. L. Newcombe, SCC Letterbook, 1900-01, 3, E. R., 29 May 1900.
133 Williams, *Duff: A Life*, 66.
134 Janet Wright, *Crown Assets – The Architecture of the Department of Public Works, 1867-1967* (University of Toronto Press, 1997).

finally increased the number of permanent members of the Court to seven, thus eliminating the possibility of a tie vote when the full bench sat. The second amendment was to establish compulsory retirement at age seventy-five which applied not just to future members but to all current members of the Supreme Court.[135]

An April 1936 *Maclean's Magazine* article described the Justices' place of work as "the shoddy little building". The author went on to describe the work of the Court:

> The Supreme Court of Canada is a place of peace and quiet thought where robed judges work meticulously through statutes, exhibits and arguments presented by the lawyers. The Supreme Court is a place of investigation of the law where judges and lawyers face each other in close quarters and the argument on a point(s) in law or the legality of earlier trial is the rule of the day, not witnesses or passionate pleas made by the prosecutor and defense, as can happen in lower courts.
>
> On an average day in the Court, with an eye on the clock, the Registrar of the Supreme Court starts the proceeding by calling for "order", and the two massive doors open at the back of the chamber. From this doorway the Chief Justice and his "brothers" — as they call each other, — enter and the Justices take their assigned seats at the bench with the Chief Justice in the middle. The seats they sit on are red-leather upholstered chairs with high pointed backs that look extremely rigid and gothic — they also look comfortable, unlike the benches the public use at the other end of the courtroom. The slightly curved bench, or table, behind which they all sit, is raised several feet above the rest of the court to provide ample view of those arguing in front of them.
>
> Black is the usual colour worn by the Justices in the form of a silk gown over a white shirt with hanging white tabs on the chest. The scarlet, ermine-trimmed, robes are worn for official occasions such as the opening of Parliament and, in the past, whenever a criminal case is heard involving capital punishment.
>
> The appellant, also garbed in a black gown, brings forth their argument with citations along the way to show that history is on their side in this case. The responding counsel gets their chance to speak and works hard to discredit the appellant's case. Meanwhile, the Justices bring questions, points of law and interruptions to the fore in dealing with weak statements, repetition or ill-considered arguments.
>
> The Supreme Court of Canada! Truly a term to conjure with. The highest tribunal in the country. It awes one. Even the shoddy little building cannot rob the institution of that peculiar reverence one automatically feels.[136]

---

135 Snell and Vaughan, *The Supreme Court,* 125.
136 MacBeth and White, "The Seven Justices", 1936, 26.

Upon being named to the Court, Justice Rand spoke about his first experiences in the building he was to work in:

> ...if you wish to enter, you will find a door over which has been sculpted in the stone the words 'Judges Entrance', but which is used by everybody. Then you enter a dingy hall and go up to the first floor by a shaky staircase which leads you into a corridor, on each side of which you have something that might be styled 'Monks' Cells,' and that is where the Justices of the Supreme Court of Canada elaborate their judgments. The courtroom had the appearance of a small chapel, with seats very much like church pews. The judges' chairs were Gothic in character.

In fact, the courthouse was a national disgrace: the plumbing was bad; the place smelled; it was poorly lit and ventilated; and rodents and insects resided there. Many of the books and records were decomposing in the damp air. It was also a firetrap, and, in 1935, an inspector's report recommended that the building be condemned. [137]

After a number of false starts, real progress on a new Supreme Court of Canada building began to take place upon the return to office of the King government in 1935. In that same year, officials from the department of Pensions and National Health had made a room-by-room, brick-by-brick survey of the old Supreme Court structure. Their report included the following description:

> The building is antiquated, the rooms are small, ceilings are low, and the lighting and the ventilation very poor. This is particularly true of the rooms that are occupied by the Judges, which are considered the worst features of the building. These are comparable to old fashioned bedrooms in an old-time hotel, and there is no doubt that constant and prolonged occupancy of these rooms will have a deleterious effect upon the health of the occupants. [138]

After this examination the old courthouse building was, in the words of the inspectors, "condemned as being injurious to the health of the occupants and totally inadequate for the purpose for which it is used". [139]

Ernest Cormier of Montreal was selected for the prestigious task of designing the new courthouse. Cormier was a noted architect

---

137 William Kaplan, *Canadian Maverick - The Life and Times of Ivan C. Rand* (2009), 97.
138 Williams, *Duff: A Life*, 205.
139 *Report re: Building Occupied by Supreme Court of Canada*, vol.4328, File 2994-1-C, Public Archives (PAC RG11).

who had designed the Québec Court of Appeal building in Montreal, the Government Printing Bureau in Hull, and the University of Montreal, to name but a few of his commissions.

The new Supreme Court of Canada building was to be situated just west of the Parliament Buildings on a bluff high above the Ottawa River and set back from the often active Wellington Street by a deep stretch of lawn. This building would provide a dignified setting worthy of the country's highest tribunal.

The location at the top of a cliff overlooking the Ottawa River had, at one time, been a thriving upper-town neighbourhood that included notable homes and mansions aplenty. In 1918 the government designated the area the parliamentary district and began expropriating residents and businesses with the last home demolished in 1938. Gone was the appropriately named Cliff Street as well as homes of all types, various buildings and businesses such as: the Canadian Bank Note Company, the Perley Home for Incurables, the Capital Brewing Co., Home for Friendless Women, and the Ottawa Curling Club.

> This new Supreme Court of Canada building was one of the most outstanding products of the Federal Government's building programme of the 1930s. A massive granite building built in the minimalist classical style, it housed the Supreme Court chambers, two courtrooms for the Exchequer Court and general office space. In Cormier's work, classicism was expressed not in terms of a vocabulary of details but in terms of a set of underlying principles of order, symmetry and balance. This building also played an important part in defining a new architectural image that would shape federal buildings in Ottawa in the postwar period.[140]

With this new building almost completed, the Justices and staff of the Court keenly anticipated moving to the new structure, but there was one catch in the whole affair: completion of this new building was approved by the government on condition that the space be assigned to the burgeoning war-related bureaucracy for the duration of World War II. Thus it was employees of National War Services, National Revenue and National Defence who occupied the Supreme Court building for the new building's first years. The judges and staff of the Supreme Court had to wait, yet again, to be housed in a suitable and safe location.

---

140 Wright, *Crown Assets*, 36.

It was not until January 1946 that the Supreme Court of Canada was finally able to move into its new quarters, located at 301 Wellington Street in Ottawa. In early February 1946, the Justices of the Supreme Court of Canada heard their first case in their new building.

But the Supreme Court building was still not complete. Firstly, the building was largely unfurnished; any furniture brought over from the old courthouse was old and decrepit. Ernest Cormier applied to the government in 1945 for authority to design new furnishings. This went on for a number of years and even in 1950, Cormier was still ordering coat hooks, wardrobes, tables, furniture, book shelving, rugs, armchairs and much more to completely erase the image of the previous building.

Furthermore, as various war-services agencies had occupied third-floor offices for three years, numerous repairs were required. It was not until 1947 that Cormier was able to begin repairing damage done by the previous occupants, improve lighting, and design furniture suitable to the building. Shortly after the Justices occupied their new building, it became evident that the library was both poorly located and designed. Access to it from the courtroom was difficult and caused a good deal of inconvenience. It was decided to move the library to the third floor, making use of space originally designed for storage.

At the time of the move to the new building, Chief Justice Rinfret had hoped to draw public attention to the Court's new position through a formal opening of the building, or a reception, or a dinner, but the government claimed that it could find no funds to cover the expenses. After discussing the matter, the cabinet decided not to ask Parliament for the money because it might give rise to a controversial debate over the Court. Justice Kerwin commented,

> They [the cabinet ministers] decided that they could not ask for a vote in Parliament in the estimates to cover such expenses as they were afraid that that would give rise to many difficulties, and possibly some unpleasantness.[141]

In a 1956 address, Chief Justice Kerwin had these comments to share as he spoke about the Supreme Court:

> Accommodation is supplied for the Members of the Court and the necessary staff and also a library of about 135,000 volumes, which should be a source of pride to every Canadian

---

141 "Dinner to celebrate new courthouse", PAC, L. St. Laurent Papers, vol. 118.

The plaque where the old Supreme Court Building was located at Bank and Wellington (Photo by Stephen G. McKenna 2014).

and as to which I give a few details. There are to be found copies of all the statutes of Canada and of every province and of Great Britain and of Ireland and from the various countries of the Commonwealth, the reports of decisions of the Supreme Court of Canada and the Exchequer Court and of all the Provincial Courts. There is a comprehensive collection of reports of the Courts of Great Britain, Ireland, Scotland and the Commonwealth countries. There is a separate division comprising nearly 40,000 volumes and containing reports of every State in the United States of America. There are practically all the legal textbooks published in Great Britain and Canada and a great number from every part of the Commonwealth and from the United States, as well as about 15,000 law Treaties and reports from France and Belgium. In addition there is a precious collection of rare law books and folios of the sixteenth, seventeenth and eighteenth centuries pertaining to the common law and the law of France, the latter of which, particularly, are of great importance in considering the civil code of the Province of Québec. The Library contains a number of biographies and autobiographies of men known to the law, as well as volumes of a more general nature.[142]

---

142 Chief Justice Kerwin, "Speech to Canadian Club", May 11, 1955, 8.

The old Supreme Court building was torn down in 1956 to make room for a parking lot behind the West Block on Parliament Hill. A plaque was installed to mark the place of the Court's previous home which reads: "This wall is built of stone formerly in the building which housed the Supreme Court of Canada, 1881-1945. It was erected for use of government workshops in 1873 and demolished in 1956."

~

For the first seventy-five years of its history, the Supreme Court of Canada was not truly supreme. It was possible to appeal decisions of the Court to the Judicial Committee of the Privy Council, which meant that those in England could overrule the Supreme Court; similarly, the Canadian Court was bound to accept and apply precedents established by the Judicial Committee. Furthermore, appeals could go directly from provincial superior courts to the Judicial Committee without being heard by the Supreme Court. All of these factors seriously undermined the stature and authority of the Court.

A bill brought to Parliament in 1949 called for the Federal Government to eliminate all appeals to the British Privy Council. As of 1933, all criminal appeals had been made the domain of the Supreme Court of Canada, but many felt the time had come to sever the lingering umbilical cord in regard to civil appeals. The Honourable Stuart Sinclair Garson, the Minister of Justice and Attorney General of Canada from 1948 to 1957, and Member of Parliament for the riding of Marquette, Manitoba, spoke on this issue on September 20, 1949 in Parliament:

> The bill which is now before us will strip off these badges by abolishing appeals to the Privy Council. In that sense it represents an important step towards complete nationhood for our country, to create in the Supreme Court of Canada exclusive, ultimate appellate civil and criminal jurisdiction within and for Canada and by abolishing appeals to the Privy Council and by making the judgments of the Supreme Court final and conclusive in all cases.[143]

In 1949, Prime Minister Louis St. Laurent, who in his career prior to being in politics had appeared as counsel in many Supreme Court cases, ended the practice of appeals in Canadian civil

---

143 *House of Commons, Debates, 21st Parliament, 1st Session*, ed., Sep. 20, 1949 Vol. (Canada, Parliament, 1949).

matters to the Judicial Committee of the Privy Council of Great Britain, thus making the Supreme Court of Canada the highest avenue of legal appeal available to Canadians. The same year, the Financial Post carried this front-page editorial on the Court:

> Parliament and our Supreme Court are our two key institutions. The value and strength of our Supreme Court, the contribution which it makes to our national stability and unity, depends on the reputation of integrity, skill and wisdom which it wins for itself.
>
> Canada's national stature has done a lot of growing in recent decades. The Supreme Court ought to make sure growth of its statutes keeps pace.
>
> The Supreme Court's place in men's minds, its value to the strength and development of this nation, depends solely on the skill, patience and objectivity with which its members hear each and all of the cases before them; on the depth and quality of human understanding reflected in their judgments.
>
> In 1949, as part of the transition to the final court of appeal, the number of judges was increased from seven to nine [the two "extra" were John Robert Cartwright from Ontario, and Gerald Fauteux from Québec] which is the present total on the bench. Of the nine, three must be from Québec and tradition dictates that three others are from Ontario, two are from the West, and one is from Atlantic Canada.[144]

~

The Supreme Court of Canada now receives between 550 and 650 applications for leave to appeal every year and hears around 80 appeals.

In front of the Court's building today, the Canadian flag flies from two staffs; the staff to the west is hoisted daily by Supreme Court staff, the eastern flag flies only when the court is sitting. Two 3-metre high bronze statues stand next to the building's front steps: *Veritas* (Truth) on the west side and *Justitia* (Justice) on the east, sculpted by Toronto artist Walter B. Allward, the creator, sculptor and architect of the Canadian National Vimy Monument at Vimy Ridge in France. These works from the early 1920's were created to form a huge memorial to King Edward VII and were to be stored until its completion. However, with the outbreak of the First World War in 1914, and the statues completed, the memorial project was put on hold. Unfortunately, *Veritas* and *Justitia* were

---

144 *Financial Post*, May 4, 1949, 1.

forgotten for almost 50 years. In 1969 they were discovered and rumours say they were found either in government storage or in crates buried under the Court's parking lot. They were erected on their present site in 1970. At the rear of the building, a fountain and a terrace overlook the Ottawa River.

The imposing structure contains a grand entrance hall, the Supreme Court's main courtroom, the judges' offices, library and conference room, the offices of administrative staff, the Court's library and two courtrooms used by the Federal Court of Canada. The building was described by *Maclean's Magazine* as, "probably the finest public building in Canada".[145]

On the subject of the Supreme Court of Canada, in an address to the Continuing Legal Education Society of Nova Scotia on October 2, 1981, the Right Honourable Chief Justice Bora Laskin, P.C. stated,

> Although its early days were perilous, with its survival not certain, it has surmounted many challenges to its jurisdiction and has, I venture to say, earned the stability and confidence which it now reflects in its work. It has come out from the shadow of the Judicial Committee of the Privy Council, in political recognition that an independent nation must have its own independent final court. The players change, of course, but the institution lives on.[146]

---

145 "Seven Wise Men", *Maclean's Magazine*, 8.
146 Rt. Hon. Bora Laskin, "Address to the Continuing Legal Education Society of Nova Scotia", Oct. 2, 1981.

*Canada today has a legal system
in which its people could take
great satisfaction.
Law* [is] *not an exact science,
but no stone would be left unturned
... with the best possible determination
of the rights of man.*

—Chief Justice Patrick Kerwin as quoted in the *Sarnia
Daily Observer*, October 25, 1957, 20

Chapter 10

Life as a Puisne Judge
Ottawa

By the time the Kerwins arrived in 1935, Ottawa was a city of over 120,000 people with a mix of English and French spoken everywhere, and English being the predominant language of business.

It must have been a special moment for Patrick when he first came with his wife by train to Ottawa as a newly appointed Justice of the Supreme Court of Canada. In 1935, the railroad tracks ran along the east side of the historic Rideau Canal where Colonel By Drive is now located in Ottawa. What the Kerwins saw from their window was an unobstructed view of the Parliament Buildings as the train came around that final curve heading into downtown toward the train station. Today, high-rise office towers and condominiums block much of the view of the Parliament Buildings in the capital city.

A shining star amongst train stations, the Grand Trunk Central Station was opened in 1912. With arched coffered ceiling in the waiting room and connected to the Chateau Laurier Hotel by an underground pedestrian tunnel, the structure's classical revival design was based on the, then, recently-built Washington DC Union Station. By the time Patrick and Georgina came to Ottawa the station had been renamed Union Station and was where royalty, soldiers, celebrities, and regular folk arrived in town.

They spent their first few nights at the Chateau Laurier Hotel. Then, as new residents of Canada's capital, they moved to the Roxborough Apartments on the corner of Elgin Street and Laurier Avenue (now the site of Confederation Park) until they found a house.

Life in Ottawa was busy for the Kerwin family. Having just moved to Toronto in 1932 from Guelph, here yet again was another move to a different city and a family home was needed. The Kerwins decided to rent rather than own their own home and they eventually settled in a large house on Wilbrod Street at the southwest corner of Charlotte Street, in the Sandy Hill area of Ottawa. This district held a number of foreign embassies, consulates, large

Supreme Court of Canada as seen from the Ottawa River.(S. McKenna, 2014).

homes for successful citizens of Ottawa, a university and numerous low-rise apartment buildings.

Once in Ottawa, Patrick joined The Rideau Club, located at that time directly across from Parliament Hill, where he had lunch most days. A family story has it that when he arrived home at the end of the day to sit down with his family for dinner, his comment would sometimes be, much to his wife's dismay, "Oh, this is what I had for lunch." He nevertheless ate what he was served at dinner. Another funny story tells of Patrick's dislike for liver, but how much he liked his wife's venison, as she relabelled liver whenever she served it.

~

In October of 1935, Mackenzie King and the Liberal Party returned to power after defeating R. B. Bennett's Conservative government. As Prime Minister King lived only a few blocks away from the Kerwins, the Prime Minister would often run into George Kerwin as the student walked to high school. The Prime Minister, never one to shy away from soliciting votes for the next election, would greet young George, shake his hand and encourage him to vote Liberal. It seemed the Prime Minister did not realize that this tall young man was not only too young to vote (even though George reminded him every time) but was the same person he met day after day. This often made my mother laugh as she was never fond of King anyway due to what she and her mother considered to be his treatment of her father in his early years on the Supreme Court bench. It was not a Liberal or Conservative issue, she just did not like the man and thought him peculiar, even before the diaries of the former Prime Minister became public.

At the Opening of the Third Session of the 18th Parliament in 1938, a newspaper article described the pomp and pageantry of it all, including what everyone was wearing. As Patrick would be sitting with the rest of the Supreme Court Justices on the woolsack, his wife and daughter attended the ceremony. The newspaper described their outfits as follows:

> Mrs. Patrick Kerwin, wife of Mr. Justice Kerwin, wore a
> pretty model of wine shade crepe Romaine with draped skirt.
> Miss Isobel Kerwin, daughter of Mr. Justice and Mrs. Kerwin,
> was in Buttercup shade with the bodice of satin and a yellow
> tulle skirt.[147]

A story told by Isobel about her father in his early years as a Justice of the Supreme Court had Patrick doing some special work (the task itself is not known) for the then Prime Minister, Mackenzie King:

> One particularly hot and nasty summer, the Prime Minister
> asked the relatively new Justice of the Supreme Court to work
> on a 'special job' for him. The request came just prior to the
> Court's summer recess so this meant my father would not be
> able to take a vacation that year. Not one to complain, he
> worked long and hard all those humid summer months on the
> task at hand. One problem was the heat during that particular
> summer season; it was hotter and more humid that year than
> usual with your grandfather not having the benefit of air
> conditioning in the old Supreme Court building, which, really,
> wasn't a very nice place to begin with. Being exposed to the
> intense heat and bad odours in that building for prolonged
> periods caused health problems that plagued him for the rest
> of his life. Even more galling, when my father met with the
> Prime Minister at the start of the fall session that year, the
> Prime Minister said that they were not "doing that anymore"
> and they were to drop the whole matter. Since we only lived
> two blocks from the PM's home, it would have been nice to tell
> the Justice that information before he worked the summer and
> suffered from heat stroke a number of times, don't you think?

---

147 *Ottawa Journal*, Jan. 27, 1938, 19.

On this same topic, Patrick's wife, Georgina, would not elaborate, but she did not take kindly to hearing Prime Minister King's name mentioned. She would tersely state her opinion on this subject saying, "the building made him sick" in her later years and put the blame squarely on the shoulders of Prime Minister King.

While Patrick was busy with his new career in the Supreme Court, his wife, Georgina, was kept busy with the numerous social activities and obligations of the wife of a prominent citizen. A selection of undated newspaper clippings from her collection included the following (Family Archives).

On Wilbrod Street:
Mr. Justice and Mrs. Patrick Kerwin have taken up residence at 490 Wilbrod Street, corner of Charlotte Street.

Ottawa Social Notes (Special to The *Gazette*):
Ottawa, November 26. — Mrs. Patrick Kerwin received this afternoon, for the first time since coming to Ottawa, at her residence, 490 Wilbrod Street. Mrs. Kerwin wore a gown of rust and silver crepe. Presiding at the tea table, which was decorated with bronze and gold chrysanthemums, were Miss Duff, Mrs. F. A. Anglin and Mrs. E. R. Angers, and assisting were Mrs. E H. Coleman, Mrs. C. A. Gray, Mrs. Mace [her sister-in-law], Mrs. E. T. B. Pennefather.

For the Sewing Group:
Mrs. Patrick Kerwin entertained at luncheon at the Royal Ottawa Golf Club on Wednesday. Covers were laid for 24, the guests being members of the sewing group at Government House, to which Mrs. Kerwin belongs.

GOVERNMENT HOUSE, OTTAWA.
The Governor General and the Princess Alice gave a dinner party on Wednesday evening, to which the following were invited: The Hon. T. A. and Mrs. Crerar, Colonel the Hon. C. W. and Mrs. Gibson, the Rt. Hon. Arthur and Mrs. Meighen, the Hon. Mr. Justice and Mrs. Kerwin, Vice-Admiral A. E. Evans, the Mayor of Ottawa and Mrs. Lewis, Colonel H. M. Bankhead, Mr. and Mrs. W. R. MacDonald, Mr. and Mrs. A. R Adamson, Mr. and Mrs. R. L. Blackburn, Colonel and Mrs. A. E. Dubuc, Lt. Colonel and Mrs. J. D. Fraser, Mr. and Mrs. C. A. Gray, Mr. and Mrs. Gordon Gale.

MRS. KERWIN IS TEA HOSTESS
Welcomes Many Guests at Her Home, 490 Wilbrod Street.
Entertaining at the tea hour on Thursday, Mrs. Patrick Kerwin, wife of Mr. Justice Kerwin, welcomed many guests at

her home, 490 Wilbrod Street. The hostess wore a charming costume of rust shade threaded with gold.

Mrs. A. B. Hudson, Mrs. Hugh D. Scully, Mrs. Thibaudeau Rinfret, Mrs. O. S. Crocket, Mrs. E. R. Angers and Mrs. D'Arcy Scott presided at the tea table, which was effective with deep rose tulips and small yellow genesta. Yellow tapers were also used on the table. Mrs. J. S. Girven, Mrs. Wilfrid Scott and Miss Isobel Kerwin assisted in the tearoom.

There are numerous articles in the family archives describing the many events, dinners, balls, galas, etc., the Kerwins attended in which Mrs. Kerwin's clothing was creatively and comprehensively described. And, of course, one could never wear the same ensemble twice so she had a generous wardrobe that she culled on a regular basis, often giving away many fine gowns and dresses.

In his teenage years George, the second son, showed a propensity for instigating what he considered as 'fun' while their parents were away. He decided to have a party at the house one weekend evening and it was a loud and successful party. The neighbours called the police and George, being the polite and savvy person he was, invited them in for drinks, which they accepted. All was well by the time his parents arrived back home for Sunday dinner. Just as George was thinking he had gotten away with it, his father stood to carve the roast and, as he did, his foot knocked an empty beer bottle over that had been hiding beside the leg of the dinner table. Explanations were made and words were had with young George at that point.

In 1937, Justice Patrick Kerwin was awarded the honourary degree of Doctor of Laws by the University of Ottawa. The Doctor of Laws degree, *honoris causa* (LLD), when awarded by a law school, is considered an earned degree and this may be the cause of some errors noted in Patrick's history with some people stating he had attended the University of Ottawa as a student. Actually he had attended the University ceremony to receive the degree. As well, he acted as a Regent for the University Board.

On September 23, 1941, Patrick's mother, Mrs. Ellen (Gavin) Kerwin, died. It was reported that Mrs. Ellen Kerwin had been staying with her daughter and son-in-law at their house at 337 Confederation Street in Sarnia as she had been in poor health for some months. The newspaper announcement noted that "... her husband, who died in 1898, was a Great Lakes captain and operated several tugs and boats". Listed as surviving relatives were "Mr. Justice Kerwin of Ottawa, Vernon L. Kerwin of the Probation Department of the Wayne County Circuit Court, Detroit,

Mrs. Beatty of this city and a sister, Mrs. Kate Moran of Mason City, Iowa".[148]

Isobel recalled an incident during the war when she was sent over to visit the neighbours to borrow a cup of sugar as her mother was midway through a recipe and short on that item. Sugar was, of course, in short supply but Georgina was preparing to host a special guest. As it turned out, their neighbour was the home of the High Commissioner of Australia, whose wife would help Mrs. Kerwin out in her time of need; she too understood the challenges of hosting properly in times of shortage.

While living with her parents in Ottawa on Wilbrod Street, Isobel announced her engagement to John Joseph McKenna, son of Lieutenant-Colonel J. A. McKenna and Julia (Moran[149]) McKenna of Ottawa. Isobel and John were married on November 29 1941. An item appeared in the Social and Personal Activities column in a local newspaper that read,

> Mr. Justice and Mrs. Patrick Kerwin entertained at dinner on Saturday evening at the Royal Ottawa Golf Club for out-of-town guests attending the McKenna-Kerwin wedding.[150]

As Patrick and his wife were members of this Club, the venue was used for a number of social occasions and celebrations as well as an occasional game of golf for Patrick.

The newly-married couple soon moved to Canadian Forces Base Petawawa, a base that John's father, Lieutenant-Colonel Andrew McKenna (known as "the Colonel" to everyone), as a member of the Royal Canadian Engineers, helped build many years earlier. John McKenna was a lawyer attached to the Judge Advocate General's office in Petawawa, Ontario, early during the war, and later went overseas with an Artillery Regiment.

When Isobel and John first arrived in Petawawa, the young bride plugged in the short-wave radio — a wedding gift from her brothers. As soon as the radio warmed up, she heard a disturbing news report and went in to tell the others assembled in the small living room. None of them believed she had heard correctly and, at Isobel's urging, they came to the next room to listen to the radio to hear the news. It was December 7, 1941, the day the Japanese bombed Pearl Harbour.

Other tales of their time in Petawawa include the newlywed bride trying to bake a pie during the winter at Base Petawawa on

---

148 *Sarnia Observer,* Sep. 24, 1941, 3.
149 No relation to the Kate Moran of Mason City, Iowa.
150 "Social and Personal Activities", *Ottawa Citizen,* Dec. 1, 1941, 18.

the wood stove (which was also their only source of heat), and failing dramatically when her husband found it impossible to cut the dessert even with the sharpest of knives. Isobel and John were living in what was, in reality, a summer cottage.

Shortly thereafter, John McKenna was sent overseas and Isobel moved back with her parents in Ottawa. During this time, the Kerwins' only daughter did her part for the war effort by driving ambulances for the returning wounded in Ottawa. Her tasks were mostly to take injured soldiers from the downtown train station to a convalescent home set up by a religious order on what was then the edge of town (now known as the Alta Vista area). She

Justice and Mrs. Kerwin visit their daughter and son-in-law in Petawawa ON, 1942.

later worked for Censorship during war time. Upon John's return from overseas at the end of the war, they briefly lived with Justice and Mrs. Kerwin on the somewhat renovated third floor of the house on Wilbrod Street prior to moving to the city of Eastview, part of the Ottawa area, and later to the family home I knew in the Alta Vista area. Isobel and John had seven children, five boys and two girls.

In April of 1943, Patrick's eldest son, Patrick Kilroy Kerwin, married Mary Gertrude Doyle of St. Catharines. The reception was in Welland House, at the corner of Ontario and King Streets (now a Brock University student residence) in St. Catharines. Son Patrick had earned a degree in Political Science and Economics from the University of Toronto, where he was a member of the Phi Delta Phi fraternity. Then, following in his father's footsteps, the younger Patrick attended Osgoode Hall to study law. He articled at the St. Catharines firm of Fleming and Harris, where he continued to practice after being called to the bar in 1941. Indeed, this Patrick practiced law in St. Catharines for more than fifty years, was the President of the Lincoln County Law Association, a Chairman of the St. Catharines Separate School Board and one-time President of the St. Catharines Club. Patrick and Mary Gertrude had five children, four boys and one girl.

By the mid-1940's, the Kerwin family were all very busy: Patrick was a Justice with the Supreme Court; Mrs. Kerwin had family and social obligations; Isobel was married; son Pat was married and practicing law; George was off fighting in WWII; Philip was continuing to astonish everyone with his academic achievements.

During the war, George wrote his parents as often as he could and mentioned how he made extra money sewing clothing for colleagues but said nothing of earning additional amounts running a poker game. George, who rarely spoke of his experiences during the war, did tell the story one evening about running a game of stakes on a ship on their way to Africa. Once docked, the Captain unceremoniously kicked them off the ship for running said game so George and his fellow soldiers moved inland to continue the game. That night, the ship they had been on was bombed.

The Kerwins' youngest son, Phil, entered the University of Toronto at the age of 16 and graduated four years later with a Bachelor of Arts Honours Degree. On October 21, 1944, tragedy struck the Kerwin family when this youngest member of the family died at age 21 in an automobile accident while working as a production assistant for the National Film Board unit engaged in Victory Loan work in New Brunswick. A newspaper clipping saved by Mrs. Kerwin told the story of Phil's death:

> Killed instantly Saturday night when a small truck left the road between Geary and Petersville (New Brunswick) and turned over in the ditch. The truck was proceeding from Fredericton toward Saint John when the accident occurred. An honour graduate of the University of Toronto last June, Phil John Kerwin joined the staff of the National Film Board about two months ago, where his ability was quickly recognized. He was born in Guelph 21 years ago and received his education there and in Toronto and Ottawa; attending St. Patrick's School and Lisgar Collegiate. He took an honour course in English at University of Toronto, graduating with the degree of Bachelor of Arts in June this year. Surviving, besides his parents, are: one sister, Mrs. John McKenna; and two brothers, Patrick Kerwin, a lawyer in St. Catharines and Lieut. George Kerwin, in Italy with the R.C.A.[151]

The few times I gently tried to ask about my Uncle Phil in later years, my grandmother, Georgina, did not wish to discuss it. The

---

151 Unnamed newspaper article, Georgina Kerwin's collection.

subject was still too painful for her and to my knowledge the topic was never addressed again during her lifetime.

At the end of the war, George Kerwin, now at home, announced that he was to wed a lovely young Belgian woman by the name of Claire Elisabeth Roland, of Châtelet, Belgium. In 1947, Claire flew from post-war Europe to New York where George met her, staying briefly with friends of Patrick and Georgina. George would later tell his family that the friend's wife relished the fact that she met the bride-to-be before his mother did. From there, George and Claire took the train to Ottawa where they were married in early February of that same year. George started working with International Business Machines (IBM) in Burlington, and they lived in an apartment in Hamilton until they bought a house in Burlington, once the first of their two children was on the way.

Now all the Kerwin children were married and starting families of their own, but with Philip sorely missed from the Kerwin fold. A good friend of the family once related she felt that the 'joie de vivre' in Georgina's eyes dimmed at the loss of her youngest child.

By 1948, the Kerwins were on their own in the big house at 490 Wilbrod Street and it was starting to feeling empty as well as a bit too much to keep up. They decided to look for a smaller place, maybe even an apartment. Patrick's superior, The Rt. Hon. Thibaudeau Rinfret, Chief Justice of the Supreme Court, suggested his own apartment building, a three-storey walk-up, located down the street at 177 Wilbrod Street, the second building from the corner of Cumberland Street. Patrick and Georgina happily moved to quite a spacious first floor apartment just across from their parish church, St. Joseph's Catholic Church. The apartment took up the entire floor, had large rooms for entertaining, a private study for Patrick and a dumb-waiter that we grandchildren later played in when they were not looking. Chief Justice and Mrs. Rinfret were their upstairs neighbours on the third floor. Many decades later, while attending the University of Ottawa, I was invited to a classmate's apartment for a study group in that very apartment. It was nice to re-visit this place I had been to so many times as a youngster — not something we often get to do in life.

~

In September of 1949 Mr. Justice Kerwin and Mrs. Kerwin took the train out west to attend the Canadian Bar Association Annual Meeting in Banff, Alberta. Then, on their return trip to Ottawa, they stopped in Saskatoon, Saskatchewan, for a few days where Justice Kerwin, and fellow traveller, Justice Estey (originally from Saskatoon), were honoured at a dinner by the Saskatoon Bar Association. Once back in Ottawa, Justice Kerwin, the senior Puisne Justice in the Supreme Court, again acted as Administrator of Canada in place of the absent Governor General and Chief Justice.

The Library of Parliament at one time had a large reading-room carrying a myriad of titles but, in recent years, this room was closed to the Library, and is now used as a meeting room in the Parliament Buildings. The Library has a record of books Patrick signed out from the collection, not tomes on law or procedure, but mysteries and biographies. During a visit to the Library of Parliament, I was shown a list of books signed out by Patrick in 1947 that included such titles as: *Something About Midnight* by Olsen; *King of the Beggars* by O'Faolaize; *Patrick Hastings Autobiography*; *White South* by Innes; *The Two Graphs* by Rhodes; *The Cardinal* by Robinson to name but a few. More titles would have been included had the penmanship of the person recording the transactions been legible.[152] This gives us an idea of what Patrick read for pleasure during some of his tenure with the Supreme Court of Canada.

By this time in their lives, Patrick and Georgina had begun to holiday in Prince Edward Island (PEI) during the summers. They would pack up the car and drive to PEI, taking a few days to get there. Of course, at that time, there were no four-lane highways; the trip was taken on two-lane roads through every town and village along the way, which, while interesting, made for a slow trip. Spending a month or more each summer near Cavendish, the Kerwins came to know a number of people in that locale including the Chief Justice of the PEI Courts, Justice Thane A. Campbell, who was later quoted as saying about his friend on the Supreme Court, "he has been prominent in forensic and judicial circles ever since his admission to the bar of Ontario in 1911".[153]

---

152 "Supreme Court Sign-Out Ledger", Rare Book Sctn., Library of Parliament (1947), 639.
153 *Guardian*, Feb. 4, 1963, 3, from research provided by Professor Bale, Queen's University.

On June 2, 1953, Queen Elizabeth was crowned Queen Elizabeth the Second with a grand ceremony in England. In Canada, there were many celebrations including the official government activities to which Justice and Georgina Kerwin were invited. An estimated 100,000 people celebrated on Parliament Hill. [154] As Governor General Vincent Massey watched from a stand in front of the Peace Tower, 145 planes flew overhead and spelled out "E II" in giant letters. Silver spoons marking the occasion were sent to Canadian children born on that day.

The Honourable Justice Kerwin and Mrs. Kerwin were invited to attend the ceremony held on Parliament Hill and afterwards a reception held in the Railway Committee Room (used by Opposition leaders for more than a century).

The Government of Canada

has the honour to invite

The Honourable Patrick Kerwin and Mrs Kerwin.

to be present at the National Ceremony in observance of

The Coronation

of

Her Majesty Queen Elizabeth The Second

on Tuesday the second of June
Nineteen Hundred and Fifty-three at three forty-five p.m.
Parliament Hill, Ottawa

A reception in the Railway
Committee Room will be held after
the ceremony

Uniform
Morning Dress or Business Suit
Decorations
R.S.V.P. to the
Under-Secretary of State, Ottawa

A ticket of Admission to the Platform will be mailed on receipt of acceptance

Patrick and Georgina's invitation to Parliament Hill for the celebration of the Queens's Coronation, 1953. That evening, the Kerwins attended the State Ball held at Rideau Hall, the Governor General's residence.

---

154 Mr. David Lee, one of my reviewers, was in front of the Parliament buildings that day and said it rained.

~

To Celebrate Her Majesty's Coronation

The Aide-de-Camp in waiting
is desired by

His Excellency The Governor-General
to invite

The Hon. Mr. Justice Patrick and Mrs. Kerwin

to a State Ball on Tuesday the 2nd of June 1953

at 9.30 o'clock p.m.

Decorations

An answer is requested to the A.D.C. in waiting
repeating date and time.

State Ball invitation for Patrick and Georgina, June 1953.

A 1953 description of Patrick's personal life in the magazine, *Manitoba Ensign*, said,

> When he can steal away from his work (even Supreme
> Court judges do plenty of night homework), Mr. Justice
> Kerwin takes a great deal of interest in his 10 grandchildren,
> finds what time he can for bridge and gets his exercise at golf
> (the score is a judicial secret).[155]

Professionally, Patrick was reputed to be a quiet, reserved man. However, a social friend, Cyril Malone, a well-known Regina lawyer, said of Justice Kerwin, "I got to know him during the Second World War quite by accident and found him to be a charming man, learned, interested in people and he loved to talk." (Family Archives).

---

155 Kuhn, "Personality Panel", 45.

Justice is never more just
than when it is prompt.

—Patrick Kerwin

Chapter 11

Chief Justice of the Supreme Court

On July 1, 1954, Canada's eighty-seventh birthday, Justice Patrick Kerwin was named the tenth Chief Justice of the Supreme Court of Canada. The appointment of Justice Kerwin to this position, at the age of sixty-three, moved him from being the senior justice to the top position in Canada's highest court. The announcement was made by Prime Minister Louis St. Laurent following a Dominion Day cabinet meeting. Governor General Vincent Massey swore in Justice Kerwin as Chief Justice at a Government House ceremony.

The declaration on the following page from Queen Elizabeth II includes the Seal of Canada and was signed by Stuart S. Garson, Attorney General of Canada and Minister of Justice.

The bible that was used for the ceremony has been kept in the family and is now in the possession of Paul R. McKenna, grandson of the Chief Justice. It is the Catholic Douay version of the Holy Bible.[156] The inscription in this bible reads:

> To the Honourable PATRICK KERWIN upon the occasion of his being sworn as Chief Justice of Canada and as a Member of the Queen's Privy Council of Canada.

The bible was signed by Vincent Massey, Governor General; Louis St. Laurent, Prime Minister; R. B. Bryce, Clerk of the Privy Council.

The new Chief Justice's first official act was to swear in his replacement Justice Douglas Abbott. The 55-year-old Puisne Judge of the Supreme Court of Canada had spent nine years as a member of the Liberal government, and had been Finance Minister. He was an English-speaking Protestant whose appointment changed the traditional balance between English- and French-speaking members and between Roman Catholics and Protestants. Before Chief Justice Rinfret's retirement, there were four Roman Catholic and five Protestant justices; as Patrick became Chief Justice, there were three Roman Catholics and six Protestants.

---

156 The Holy Bible, (New York: J. Kennedy and Sons, 1914), John Murphy Company.

Royal declaration appointing Patrick Kerwin as Chief Justice, 1954.

The role of the Chief Justice of Canada has four main aspects:

Judge, administrator of the Supreme Court, head of the Canadian judiciary, and a public representative for the Supreme Court of Canada.

The Chief Justice of Canada's major responsibilities are to:

- Preside at all sittings of the Supreme Court at which he or she is present. The Chief Justice also chooses the panels of Justices that hear Supreme Court of Canada cases.

- Be the head of the Court's staff who are members of the Federal Government public service.

- Chair the Canadian Judicial Council, made up of the chief and associate chief justices and judges of all courts whose members are appointed by the Federal Government. The Canadian Judicial Council is a federal body created under the *Judges Act* with the mandate to promote efficiency, uniformity, and accountability, and to improve the quality of judicial service in the superior courts of Canada.

  The Council is also mandated to review any complaint or allegation against a superior court judge.

Canada
Elizabeth the Second, by the Grace of God of the United Kingdom, Canada and Her other Realms and Territories Queen, Head of the Commonwealth, Defender of the Faith.
To the Honourable
Patrick Kerwin
A Puisne Judge of the Supreme Court of Canada,
Attourney General of Canada

Greeting: **Know You**, that reposing special trust and confidence in your loyalty, integrity and ability, We have constituted and appointed, and We do hereby constitute and appoint you the said Patrick Kerwin to be
Chief Justice of Canada

To have, hold, exercise and enjoy the said office of Chief Justice of Canada unto you the said Patrick Kerwin with all and every the powers, rights, authority, privileges, profits, emoluments and advantages, unto the said office of right and by Law appertaining during your good behaviour.
In Testimony Whereof, We have caused these Our letters to be made patent and the Great Seal of Canada to be hereunto
affixed Witness.
Our right Trusty and Well-beloved Counsellor, Vincent Massey, Member of Our Order of the Companions of Honours, Governor General and Commander in Chief of Canada.

At Our Government House, in Our City of Ottawa, this first day of July, in the year of Our Lord one thousand nine hundred and fifty-four and in the third year of Our Reign.

By Command.
Recorded 3rd August, 1954.
Film 12, Document 33.
Acting Deputy Registrar General of Canada   Secretary of State of Canada

Transcript of Royal declaration appointing Patrick Kerwin as Chief Justice. (facing page).

- Act as a deputy to the Governor General of Canada for giving Royal Assent to bills and signing other official documents. The senior Puisne Justice of the Supreme Court steps in if the Chief Justice is not available.

- Become Administrator of Canada and assume the duties of the Governor General if the Governor General of Canada dies, becomes incapacitated or is out of the country.

At the beginning of the fall term of the Supreme Court, Justice Taschereau spoke of the great satisfaction of the judges of the

Court that Justice Kerwin had been named Chief Justice. Justice Taschereau added, "We members of the court are convinced Chief Justice Kerwin will continue to discharge with dignity the high traditions of the post."[157]

Chitty's Law Journal congratulated him on becoming Chief Justice, writing:

> Congratulations to Chief Justice Kerwin, C.J.C.
>
> We extend our heartiest congratulations to Mr. Justice Kerwin on his promotion to the high honour of Chief Justice of Canada .... On October 25th next he will be sixty-five so we may confidently expect that the presidency of the Court of the last resort for Canada will be in his hands for the next ten years .... During his tenure of office in the Court he has contributed greatly to the work of the Court and without drawing any invidious distinction we think we can safely say that his judgments during that period have been as often quoted as those of any other member of the Court.[158]

In numerous newspaper articles at the time, Patrick was noted as a veteran jurist having been a member of the Supreme Court of Canada for just over nineteen years. Noted as a highlight of his long career was the judgment earlier in 1954 that broke the 4–4 tie in favour of granting a Jehovah's Witnesses' appeal against a Québec law forbidding them to distribute religious tracts on the streets in the province.

A July 1954 edition of the *Ottawa Citizen* newspaper reported that Justice Kerwin had been made a member of the Privy Council:

> Kerwin Made Member of Privy Council
>
> Coincident with the appointment of the Hon. Patrick Kerwin as Chief Justice of the Supreme Court of Canada, he was also made a member of the Privy Council. The swearing in took place within a few hours of his being made the Chief Justice.
>
> It was pointed out that the previous Chief Justice was not made a privy councillor for nine years after his elevation to this post. The latter took place upon the occasion of the Coronation.

---

157 Chief Justice Taschereau, Speech, Family Archives.
158 "Inter Alia", *Chitty's Law Journal*, Vol. 4, No. 7, July 1, 1954, 161.

Today, as Chief Justice Kerwin receives his congratulations, co-mingled with felicitations over the chief justiceship are those on his being made a privy councillor.[159]

Time magazine reported in their July 1954 issue:

... Ontario-born Lawyer Kerwin, a Tory and a Roman Catholic, is the senior member of the court, and has long been ranked by Canadian lawyers as one of its best justices.[160]

~

In years prior to Patrick's appointment, the Chief Justice of the Supreme Court of Canada was named to the Judicial Committee of the Imperial Privy Council in England, thus acquiring the title given to all members of the Imperial Privy Council, "Right Honourable". When appeals beyond the Supreme Court of Canada were terminated in 1949, chief justices no longer became members of Her Majesty's Privy Council in England, but now were made members of the Canadian Privy Council, and thus held the corresponding title, "Honourable", as did other members. After 1968, however, the title, "Right Honourable" was restored in recognition of the office.[161] This is why Patrick is one of the few Chief Justices listed with the title, *the Honourable* Patrick Kerwin, along with the first two Chief Justices of the Court early in its history, the Honourable Sir William Buell Richards and the Honourable Sir William Johnston Ritchie.

The new Chief Justice's salary would now be $25,000 a year while the other Justices received $20,000 per year. According to the Bank of Canada inflation calculator, Patrick's salary would be $232,857 per year in 2017 dollars.[162]

The other jurists of the Supreme Court of Canada at the start of Patrick's tenure as Chief Justice were Hon. Robert Taschereau, Hon. I.C. Rand, Hon. Roy L. Kellock, Hon. J.W. Estey, Hon. C.H. Locke, Hon. J.R. Cartwright, Hon. Gerald Fauteux, Hon. Douglas Abbott.

The appointment marked a change from the traditional succession of a Roman Catholic followed by a Protestant. Justice Kerwin, an English-speaking Roman Catholic, succeeded Justice Thibaudeau

---

159 "Kerwin Made Member of Privy Council", *Ottawa Citizen,* 1954, 33.
160 "Canada – The Realm", *Time Magazine,* July 1954, 32.
161 Snell and Vaughan, *The Supreme Court,* 68-71.
162 www.bankofcanada.ca/rates/related/inflation-calculator Accessed June 2017.

Rinfret, a French-speaking Roman Catholic who retired June 21 at the age of 75.

P.C. 1954-998

PRIVY COUNCIL

CANADA

Certified to be a true copy of a Minute of a Meeting of the Committee of the Privy Council, approved by His Excellency the Governor General on the   1st July, 1954.

The Committee of the Privy Council, on the recommendation of the Right Honourable Louis S. St-Laurent, the Prime Minister, advise that the Honourable Patrick Kerwin, one of the Puisne Judges of the Supreme Court of Canada, be appointed Chief Justice of Canada.

Asst Clerk of the Privy Council.

Appointment as Chief Justice. Copy of Privy Council Meeting Minute, 1954 (Library and Archives of Canada).

Before the appointment was made official, there was uncertainty as to who would be appointed, as Patrick had been initially appointed to the Court by the Bennett Conservative government. So, the question at hand was, would a Liberal Prime Minister (St. Laurent) appoint Patrick, a Catholic Tory, to the highest position in the Court? In this light, Chief Justice Rinfret's retirement presented a quandary for Prime Minister St. Laurent. The logical successor was Justice Kerwin as Patrick was the senior Justice on the Court, but he, like Rinfret, was a Roman Catholic. It is hard today to understand how troublesome these questions of religion and ethnic background were when governments considered high judicial appointments.

> St. Laurent called on retired Chief Justice Lyman Duff for advice, and to his credit, Duff told him to ignore the question of religion; Kerwin, who had come to the Supreme Court of Canada after trial court experience in Ontario and earned his spurs in Ottawa, merited the appointment.[163]

The story heard around the family dining room table over the years was that Sir Lyman Duff walked into Prime Minister St. Laurent's office and said that he would never vote Liberal again if they did not appoint Patrick as Chief Justice. I am not sure if this tipped the scales on this decision or not but St. Laurent followed Duff's counsel, however it was delivered.

Nonetheless, not all was calm in the court with this appointment. Justice Roy Kellock, aged sixty-four, who was second only to Patrick in writing decisions for the Court, soon resigned from the Supreme Court after over thirteen years of service. "Officially, Kellock used poor health as an explanation, though there were suggestions that he was unhappy in a Court led by Patrick Kerwin rather than by himself."[164]

Before Patrick was appointed as Chief Justice there were comments made that Justice Kellock (a Baptist) was being considered, as shown in the following newspaper article:

> If the promotion went to Mr. Justice Kerwin, Mr. St. Laurent would be following the traditional practice of giving the chief justiceship to the senior judge of the court. However, the appointment would break the other tradition whereby the post alternates between Catholic and Protestant appointees. Mr.

---

163 Williams, *Duff: A Life*, 269.
164 McCormick, *Supreme at Last*, 14.

Rinfret and Mr. Justice Kerwin are both Catholics. For this reason Mr. Justice Kellock has been suggested for the post.[165]

Before his appointment to the bench, Patrick's political affiliations since his days in Guelph had been with the Conservative Party, but when, in 1954, the position of Chief Justice of Canada fell vacant, the judicial competence of Patrick was so universally recognized that the Liberal government of the day accorded to him the highest appointment in the courts of this nation.

Another problem with his appointment, as reported in the media, was Patrick's poor health. Rumours circulated that he would soon be retiring, although he in fact served almost nine years before his death (slightly longer that the average tenure for a chief justice at the time), these rumours meant that the Court operated against a background of uncertainty.[166]

In recalling the appointment, Patrick's friend and Chief Justice of the Prince Edward Island courts, Thane A. Campbell recalled (Family Archives),

... the selection was amply justified. His judgments have been marked by a clarity of language, and by a keen appreciation of the jurisprudence and precedents which he was called upon to consider and apply. His devotion to the sometimes arduous duties of his office was constant, even to the extent of overtaxing his strength. His administrative ability was outstanding, both in directing the business of the court and in acting as deputy to His Excellency the Governor General ...I count it my good fortune to have known him as an extremely gracious host and congenial companion.

The *Saint John Telegraph-Journal* wrote about a distinguished visitor:

Chief Justice Patrick Kerwin, of the Supreme Court of Canada, is coming to St. John to-day, accompanied by Mrs. Kerwin, in the course of a vacation motor trip in the Maritime Provinces. This is the distinguished jurist's first visit to the city since his elevation to the foremost judicial office in the nation, and he will receive a warm welcome. His numerous friends here were delighted to learn of his appointment, and they have been looking forward to extending congratulations to the new Chief Justice personally.

---

165 *Globe & Mail*, July 1, 1954, 1-2, from Professor Bale, Queen's University.
166 McCormick, *Supreme at Last*, 37.

Following the retirement of Chief Justice Thibaudeau Rinfret in June, the federal cabinet at a Dominion Day meeting selected the then Justice Kerwin, the senior member of Canada's Supreme Court, to succeed him, and Chief Justice Kerwin was sworn in by Governor General Massey at a ceremony at Government House, Ottawa. The Announcement of the appointment by Prime Minister St. Laurent was received with approval throughout the country.

In his new position Chief Justice Kerwin presides over deliberations of a court which is now not only the highest in the land but also the highest appeal tribunal in which legal actions brought in this country can be taken. The Supreme Court of Canada has assumed new significance since 1949, when the Federal Government took the historic step of abolishing appeals to the Judicial Committee of Her Majesty's Privy Council.[167]

~

With Patrick's many years on the Supreme Court of Canada and the few on the High Court of Ontario, he knew how to accurately separate the essential from the irrelevant, the pertinent from the repetitious. And, as head of this court, he did much to expedite the court's handling of cases. It was his view that one of the court's main responsibilities was to ensure timely judgments, as "justice delayed was justice denied"[168].

Patrick was a tough, serious-minded jurist, and ran the court business with a firm hand tempered by a sense of fairness. He was recognized for his efforts to ensure that counsel before him had ample opportunity to present their cases. Nevertheless, he could become quietly impatient at repetition. With Patrick, the law was never a matter for slow and leisurely procedures so, if a lawyer appearing before him seemed to be belabouring a point, he would likely have said, "Yes, we know all about that. Now have you anything else to say?"

The *Montreal Gazette* provided some interesting insight into the man who headed the court, writing:

> Nor was he a judge who departed from the matter at hand
> to indulge in humorous remarks. His face was the very
> picture of judicial gravity and concentration, with his firm,
> solid expression and the turned down corners of the mouth.
> If some lawyer happened to introduce a joke in the course of

---

167 "A Distinguished Visitor", *Saint John Telegraph-Journal*, Aug. 11, 1954.
168 Attributed to British PM Gladstone.

his pleading, he would find in that stern countenance no flicker of response. He was not on the highest bench of the land to encourage humour.

In his own judgments there was a remarkable directness, a coming quickly to the real point. The language in which he wrote his judgments was free of the rotundities and flourishes that easily tempt judicial minds. They were terse and simple, and usually brief.[169]

In an undated *Globe & Mail* article titled "Absolutely Without Bias", newspaper reporter Harold Greer wrote of the new Chief Justice:

Mr. Kerwin is well equipped by training and temperament for his new office. He never gets ruffled in court, is always courteous to counsel. A quiet-spoken, quiet-living man by nature, his training in law has made him cautious to a fault; he refuses, for example, to reveal his views except through his judgments handed down from the bench.

Few jurists enjoy higher respect in the legal profession. Judges, of course, are supposed to be impartial, but no man can escape his own personality. Those who disagree with him will declare without hesitation that Mr. Kerwin is fair-minded, absolutely without bias or prejudice.[170]

In the opinion of the *Canadian Press*:

Chief Justice Kerwin seldom showed any emotion while hearing argument, sometimes in sharp contrast to other justices who often exchanged brief bantering or ideas with pleading lawyers...But a touch of red could sometimes darken his features if he had to caution a lawyer for irrelevancies a second time .... With a young lawyer making his first appearance or with a layman appearing to argue his own case, the Chief Justice always tried to be helpful, often making allowances for inexperience.[171]

~

R. v. Coffin

At the start of Patrick's tenure, a notable, well-documented and even controversial case started in the Québec Provincial court where arguments were heard concerning the case of Wilbert Coffin. This story began in June 1953 on Québec's Gaspé

---

169 *Montreal Gazette*, Feb. 5, 1953.
170 Harold Greer, "Absolutely Without Bias", *Globe & Mail,* Sep. 11, 1954, 11.
171 CP Biographical Service, Sketch 1142, Sep. 30, 1959, 2.

Peninsula where three men from Pennsylvania (Eugene Lindsey, his son Richard Lindsey, 17, and Frederick Claar, 20) were reported missing. Their bodies were found a month later deep in the woods, sixty kilometres from the nearest town. Coffin, who was found to have many items belonging to the men in his possession, was sent to trial in July of 1954 even though the evidence against him was seen by many as mostly circumstantial. In the court he was convicted of murder and, on August 5 of that year, he was sentenced to hang. Wilbert Coffin applied to the Supreme Court of Canada for leave to appeal. Justice Douglas Abbott, former Liberal Finance Minister and newly appointed to the court, heard the application and turned it down. "Justice Abbott who was a rookie just appointed to the high court admitted having ' little experience in criminal matters.' "[172]

At that time, motions for leave to appeal could be heard by a single member of the court. Later this was amended such that these motions must be heard by at least three members of the Supreme Court of Canada. As of August 1956, a murder case required five Members of the Court to hear the application. In all other motions the quorum is three, as in civil cases.

Chief Justice Kerwin took a great interest in this court matter that had not come before him and, speaking on behalf of himself and some members of the Court, he told Justice Minister Stuart Garson that if they had heard the application, they would have granted Coffin leave to appeal. Garson worked quickly to get cabinet approval for an order-in-council referring the case to the full court. The court (*R. v. Coffin* [1956] S.C.R. 191) ruled in a 5 to 2 judgment that it would have confirmed the conviction and death sentence.

Roncarelli v. Duplessis

As discussed in a previous chapter, one of the highlights of Patrick's career had been his judgment in the Saumur case granting a Jehovah's Witnesses' appeal against Québec officials forbidding them to distribute religious tracts (pamphlets) on the streets in the province.[173] This case gave rise to another in 1959 in the Supreme Court, *Roncarelli v. Duplessis*, (1959, S.C.R. 121), a case that dealt directly with the subjects of individual freedom and civil liberties in Canada. This case began in 1946 with

---

172 *Kingston Whig Standard*, Jan. 22, 1986, 38., from Professor Bale, Queen's University.
173 *Saumur v. The City of Quebec*, [1953] 2 S.C.R. 299.

Maurice Duplessis, Premier of Québec and Attorney-General, systematically ordering the arrest of a group of Jehovah's Witnesses who had distributed leaflets boldly criticizing established religions including the Roman Catholic, a powerful institution in that province in those days. Duplessis argued the religious sect's rhetoric was a clear threat to public order. Frank Roncarelli, owner of a very select restaurant, Quaff, in the heart of Montreal, supplied tens of thousands of dollars in bail for his fellow Jehovah's Witnesses. The Liquor Commission of the Province of Québec, on explicit instructions from the premier, cancelled Roncarelli's liquor license and barred him forever from holding such a license. The fact that the restaurant's liquor license was invalidated threw the restaurant into ruin, as later heard in an interview with Roncarelli on the CBC television programme, 'Front Page Challenge'.

Roncarelli decided to fight back and sued Duplessis. The case explored the intricacies of civil liberties and was heard before the trial and appellate courts over a period of twelve and a half years.

The plaintiff, Roncarelli, the proprietor of the restaurant and the holder of a license to sell intoxicating liquor, sued the defendant personally for damages arising out of the cancellation of his license by the Québec Liquor Commission. He alleged that the license had been arbitrarily cancelled at the instigation of the defendant who, without legal powers in the matter, had given orders to the Commission to cancel it before its expiration. This was done, it was alleged, to punish the plaintiff, a member of the Witnesses of Jehovah, because he had acted as bailsman for a large number of members of his sect charged with the violation of a municipal by-law relating to the distribution of literature.

In the end, in January 1959, the Supreme Court of Canada ruled in favour of Roncarelli. Premier Duplessis was ordered to personally pay damages to Roncarelli. In the Supreme Court Case history, Patrick's decision read:

> THE CHIEF JUSTICE : — No satisfactory reason has been advanced for the Court of Queen's Bench (Appeal Side) setting aside the finding of fact by the trial judge that the respondent ordered the Québec Liquor Commission to cancel the appellant's licence. A reading of the testimony of the respondent and of the person constituting the commission at the relevant time satisfies me that the trial judge correctly decided the point. As to the other questions, I agree with Mr. Justice Martland. [Cancellation of the permit was the result of an order given by the defendant to the manager of the Commission. There was, therefore, a relationship of cause

and effect between the defendant's acts and the cancellation of the permit].

The appeals should be allowed with costs here and below and judgment directed to be entered for the appellant against the respondent in the sum of $33,123.53 with interest from the date of the judgment of the Superior Court, together with the costs of the action.[174]

"Would your case be the only one where a person had sued the premier of a province?" a Front Page Challenge panellist asked Roncarelli in a television interview. "That's right — dictator I prefer," Roncarelli corrected then added, "and I won".

Justice Rand wrote in his oft-quoted reasons that the unwritten constitutional principle of the 'rule of law' meant that no public official was above the law, that is, they could neither suspend it nor dispense with it.

The fallout from this case has affected Canadian law in many ways. As the Ottawa attorney, James Harbic, said, "This affects the personal freedom of everyone in Canada and beyond."[175]

The opinion of David Lee, a member of the Bar of the Province of Québec, on this case was that, "It is a case considered important in administrative law in other Commonwealth countries."[176]

An obituary for Patrick Kerwin published in Kingston, Ontario, stated that,

> A devoted Catholic, he [Patrick] showed his dedication to the law and the principle of religious liberty in the rulings against decisions of Québec courts curbing the religious freedom of members of Jehovah's Witnesses.[177]

It is reassuring to know that the press of the day believed the Chief Justice of the Supreme Court of Canada was able to show impartiality even though he was of a different religious persuasion. The newspaper indicated that the lack of influence of Patrick's religious background in his weighing of the question of liberty was a hallmark and an example for other members of the judiciary at whatever level. On this subject, he took a broad liberal attitude that left its mark on the fabric of Canadian society.

O'Grady v. Sparling

---

174 Supreme Court Judgments, *Roncarelli v. Duplessis,* 1959 S.C.R. 121, 125.
175 James Harbic, B.A., B.L., J.D., Barrister and Solicitor/Notary, Interview Dec. 27, 2012.
176 David Lee, Member of the Bar in the Province of Quebec, Quote Jan. 2013.
177 *Canadian Register* of Kingston, Ontario, Feb. 9, 1963.

Another case that is deemed a major decision of the Kerwin court is that of *O'Grady v. Sparling*. This dealt with the constitutional problems created when the federal and provincial legislatures generated overlapping rules. In a simplified explanation, the Federal Government has jurisdiction over the criminal law and provincial governments have jurisdiction over local matters, such as the streets and highways; but some criminal offences involve automobiles and highways — and sometimes both the federal and provincial governments will identify and use their jurisdiction to regulate a problem such as dangerous or drunk driving.

> A person charged under the Manitoba *Highway Traffic Act* with driving without due care and attention argued the invalidity of provincial legislation because Parliament had "occupied the field" when it created the criminal offence of criminal negligence in the operation of a motor vehicle.[178]

The appeal was dismissed for the reason that "there is no conflict between the provisions in the sense that they are repugnant" and "the two pieces of legislation differed both in legislative purpose and legal and practical effect". The reasons for judgment were written by Justices Judson, with Kerwin, Taschereau, Fauteux, Abbott, Martland, and Ritchie concurring. Justices Cartwright and Locke were in dissent.

Switzman v. Elbling

A case noted as a landmark decision by the Kerwin Court was that of *Switzman v. Elbling* and the A.G. of Québec (1957 SRC 285), where Québec's 'Padlock Law' was struck down. The Supreme Court of Canada struck down a Québec statute that allowed the province to padlock any premises suspected of promoting communism, both without warrant or the need for any evidence. In the 1940's, this law had been considered one of the most offensive violations of civil liberties in a generation. It was so vague that it was used against unionists, Jews, Jehovah's Witnesses, Communists and people on the political left in general. Victims could only appeal to the Attorney General and, in this case, it was Duplessis who was both Attorney General and Premier. His government enacted the 'Padlock' Law in 1937.

The case concerned Max Bailey and John Switzman, a resident of a Park Avenue apartment in Montreal. In February 1948, Bailey, a former Montreal City Councillor and a Communist,

---

178 McCormick, *Supreme at Last*, 51.

wanted to sublet his apartment to John Switzman, a prominent Marxist, who turned the apartment into a local Communist hub. The landlady, Freda Elbling, tried to prevent Switzman from keeping the apartment for fear of having the building appropriated by the province under the Padlock Law. Failing that, the landlord applied to the court to have the lease cancelled. In his defence, Switzman challenged the Padlock Law as a violation of freedom of speech and as *ultra vires* (beyond the powers). At trial and on Provincial appeal, the courts found in favour of the landlady. The Supreme Court found in favour of Switzman on both issues in an 8 to 1 decision.

In writing his reasons for judgment, Justice Ivan Rand rejected the argument that the restrictions on expression were similar to the "ordinary civil restriction of libel or slander," which would have been valid topics of provincial legislation as affecting the right "between subject and subject". He expressed the view that:

> The ban is directed against the freedom or civil liberty of the actor; no civil right of anyone is affected nor is any civil remedy created. The aim of the statute is, by means of penalties, to prevent what is considered a poisoning of men's minds, to shield the individual from exposure to dangerous ideas, to protect him, in short, from his own thinking propensities. There is nothing of civil rights in this; it is to curtail or proscribe those freedoms which the majority so far consider to be the condition of social cohesion and its ultimate stabilizing force.[179]

These arguments made clear that our fundamental freedoms are guaranteed by *The British North America (BNA) Act, 1867*, whereby freedom of speech, of association, of the press, and freedom of religion are some of the fundamentals accepted as the norm and guaranteed by that statute. This was so because, as stated in the preamble of *BNA Act, 1867*, that *Act* expressed the desire for the Provinces to be federally united "with Constitution similar in principle to that of the United Kingdom", where those guarantees existed already. This was the basis for fundamental liberties in our law before any were set out expressly in the *Constitution Act, 1982*. Ivan Rand was a clear proponent of this doctrine.

Switzman v. Elbling was the occasion of Kerwin's signature comment: "In cases where constitutional issues are involved, it is important that nothing be said that is unnecessary".[180] What he

---

179 scc-csc.lexum.com/scc-csc/scc-csc/en/item/2748/index.do Accessed July 2016.
180 Supreme Court of Canada, *Switzman v. Elbing and A.G. of Quebec*, 1957, S.C.R. 285: 289.

deemed necessary and sufficient in that case was to declare the Québec Padlock Law, which prohibited the use of premises for the purposes of disseminating communism or bolshevism, and made it unlawful to print or distribute material propagating these views, beyond the powers of provincial authority.

In writing their reasons for judgment, four justices joined Patrick in holding that law "attaching penal sanction to the propagation of a particular ideology" was an invasion of the federal Parliament's criminal law jurisdiction, as conferred upon it by section 91 (27) of *BNA Act* (as it then was). This was a pragmatic instance of liberty. It was also characteristic of Patrick's approach in such cases.[181]

However, the bottom line was an overwhelming eight-to-one (Justice Taschereau dissenting) decision to declare the Padlock Law unconstitutional.

Mr. Berger's day in court

In 1958, a young lawyer, Thomas R. Berger, appeared before the Supreme Court of Canada and described the events as follows:

> Very early on I went to the Supreme Court of Canada. It was in 1958, my second year at the bar, on an application for leave to appeal in an arson case. Three of the nine judges of the court would sit to hear applications for leave. I appeared before Chief Justice Patrick Kerwin and two of his colleagues. I had arrived in Ottawa two days before to review the law. In those days before photocopying, you had to get the volumes of the law reports containing the cases you intended to rely on out of the library, bring them to the courtroom on a trolley, and line them up on the counsel table. I must have had twenty or thirty volumes lined up, stretching from the lectern into the middle distance. W. R. (Bill) Burke-Robertson, a prominent Ottawa lawyer, who appeared for the Attorney General of B.C. in opposition to my motion, brought only one volume, the *Criminal Code*. An austere rebuke.
>
> Chief Justice Patrick Kerwin said, "Mr. Berger, you're not going to read all those cases to us, are you?" I don't remember my reply. But it was not a good start. Nor a good finish. I did not get leave to appeal.[182]

Divorce in Canada

---

181 Randall P. H. Balcome, Edward J. McBride, and Dawn A. Russell, *Supreme Court of Canada Decision-Making: The Benchmarks of Rand, Kerwin and Martland* (Carswell,1990), 181.
182 Thomas R. Berger, *One Man's Justice – A Life in the Law* (Douglas & McIntyre, 2002), 11.

Divorce in the 1950's was not an easy thing to accomplish in Canada, especially for those living in Québec, Newfoundland and Labrador. They could not get divorced in any way if they were Catholic unless there was special legal dispensation, given by Parliament. Divorce Petitions went to the Committee on Private Bills and there were often up to 400 petitions a year.

In 1959 Prime Minister Diefenbaker was approached by a man on this issue after Parliament and the Senate were already in recess. This was in part due to Diefenbaker inviting the audience members in election campaigns to write him. His mail often provided a court of last resort to individuals. Many Canadians, when official government avenues were closed to them, discovered that a letter to Diefenbaker frequently brought remedial action, occasionally overruling a decision already given by a civil servant, or cabinet minister, and once even involving the prerogative of the Governor General.

On May 6, 1959, Eric Reisinger of Montreal came to Ottawa to pick up the papers for his divorce which he assumed had undergone all of the parliamentary procedure involved in such actions. He was horrified to discover that his divorce bill had not yet been granted royal assent, and that no royal assent ceremonies were planned for the immediate future. Since Reisinger had already planned his second wedding for the Saturday afternoon of the week he was in Ottawa and had invited many guests, he felt in such a desperate predicament that he went to call on the Prime Minister. After he had explained the situation, and Diefenbaker had checked whether the bill really only lacked the one final step, a royal assent ceremony was arranged. "That evening Chief Justice Patrick Kerwin, the Deputy Governor General, gave royal assent to the Reisinger bill, in a ceremony which set a precedent, since it included no public bills."[183]

Trade Agreement

Another Royal Assent was announced in a Press Release from the Office of the Prime Minister in 1960. It read:

Date June 8, 1960   For Release: Immediate
Pour Publication:

The Prime Minister, the Right Honourable John G. Diefenbaker, announced today that the Deputy Governor General, the Chief Justice of Canada, the Honourable

---

183 Peter C. Newman, *Renegade in Power: The Diefenbaker Years* (McClelland and Stewart, 1963), 86-87.

Patrick J. [*sic*] Kerwin, will give Royal Assent to the Canada - Australia Trade Agreement which has been passed by both Houses of Parliament, together with other Legislation, in the Senate Chamber at 2.45 p.m., on Thursday, June 9.

The Prime Minister of Australia, the Right Honourable R. G. Menzies, will be present and seated on the floor of the Senate.[184]

Obscene Literature

In another case, a controversial book, *Lady Chatterley's Lover*, was ruled by the Supreme Court of Canada in 1962 as not obscene in a 5–4 decision.[185] The court's decision meant that the D. H. Lawrence novel could be sold in Canada because it did not violate a section of the *Criminal Code* prohibiting obscene literature. This was the first time the Supreme Court had been given the task of determining whether a novel was obscene. The five justices of the majority were Justices Cartwright, Abbott, Martland, Judson and Ritchie. Chief Justice Kerwin was one of the dissenting judges, along with Justices Taschereau, Fauteux and Locke.

In his dissenting opinion, Patrick stated:

It was unnecessary to deal with the argument that the Crown having cross-examined the witnesses, could not now say that their evidence was inadmissible, because Parliament has prescribed that under s. 150(8) an objective test be applied. The rule in *R. v. Hicklin* is not the one to be followed in applying s. 150(8) of the Code. Under that subsection, a publication is deemed to be obscene if (a) a dominant characteristic of the publication is (b) the undue exploitation (c) of sex. The claim of the witnesses and of the judgments in the Courts of England and the United States that the dominant characteristic of the book is to show the evils of industrialism in England and the damage it does to the human soul is not substantiated by a careful reading of the book. The use of "four-letter words" by itself might or might not make a book one in which sex was exploited unduly so as to make that feature a dominant characteristic, but they could not be treated in isolation from the scenes depicted in which they were used. The witnesses called on behalf of the accused have not succeeded in showing that this is a work of art in which there is no undue exploitation of sex and that that is not the dominant characteristic of the book. Although the evidence was competent to show the merits of the book as a work of art, the tribunals would still

---

184 Office of the Prime Minister, Press Release, June 8, 1960, Library of Parliament, courtesy of Barbara Pilek, Chief Librarian.
185 Supreme Court of Canada, *Brody, Dansky, Rubin v. The Queen*, [1962] S.C.R. 681.

have to determine whether a dominant characteristic of the book was the undue exploitation of sex. In the present case, the answer must be in the affirmative.[186]

~

In the Kerwin court, the overall reversal rates from the lower courts were fully 10 percent lower than those of the Rinfret Court. In general, despite its high personnel turnover during Patrick's tenure, the performance of the Kerwin Court represents business as usual. Although with a slightly larger caseload, the Court managed to have significantly shorter decisions, fewer reversals of provincial appeal court decisions, and less-fragmented decisions.

The Kerwin Court was somewhat less divided than its predecessor; over its nine years, there were on average about two opinions delivered for each decision, down from almost three for the Rinfret Court. Unanimous opinions accounted for roughly one-half of all the cases, almost exactly double the proportion for the Rinfret Court.[187]

In order to cope with the increased business, the members of the Court in the 1950's recommended, and Parliament enacted, that the First Term of the Court should commence earlier than before, causing it to open (as today) on the fourth Tuesday in January; the Second on the fourth Tuesday in April and the Third on the first Tuesday in October. Sittings were now almost continuous, save for short adjournments for Christmas and Easter plus a longer one for the summer. As it is today, it was impossible for the Court to decide each appeal immediately upon the conclusion of the argument, or even in the few hours available after the actual time spent on the bench. A period was required to consider the arguments presented and, in many instances, to conduct further research, particularly when constitutional questions were involved, and lastly, for the Justices to confer before coming to their settled view of each case. The greater part of this necessary time can only be found during these recesses.

A person within the legal community who was closely associated with the Chief Justice in his early years was R. B. Hungerford. Back during his time in Guelph, Patrick hired Hungerford in 1918 to help with the workload once Patrick's partner in law, Hugh Guthrie, was made a Federal Cabinet Minister. They worked hard in those early years dealing with a

---

186 Ibid., 682-3.
187 McCormick, *Supreme at Last*, 41.

full workload on a variety of subjects and, during this time, the two became quite close. Hungerford had taken over the practice in Guelph as the lead partner when Patrick was appointed as a Justice on the Ontario Court. Many years later, these old friends met in Ottawa for the last time (two years prior to Patrick's death), going over old times in recollection. Hungerford later described the Chief Justice as a pleasant and unassuming person, whom nobody would ever think was the third ranking official in Canada, superseded only by the Governor General and the Prime Minister. "He also described Patrick as 'erudite and meticulous who was a person who would at no time take advantage of his rank' ".[188]

---

188 *Guelph Mercury,* Feb. 4, 1963, 9.

Dissents, Concurrences, and Decisions, by Judge
Reported Supreme Court Decisions, 1954-1963 [189]

Judge	Panels	Divided panels	Wrote Decision	Contributed to Decision	With majority	Concurrences	Dissents
					%		
Chief Justice **Kerwin**	392	233	26.0	47.4	60.1	26.6	13.3
Taschereau	445	226	16.6	26.5	71.7	19.9	14.2
Rand	237	180	19.8	65.4	35.0	48.3	16.7
Kellock	110	83	25.5	61.8	45.8	47.0	7.2
Estey	53	39	18.9	41.5	59.0	30.8	10.3
Locke	439	268	14.6	46.5	39.2	42.2	18.7
Cartwright	520	289	15.4	46.3	34.6	33.9	31.5
Fauteux	446	214	15.9	24.7	72.0	17.3	10.7
Abbott	456	227	12.3	20.2	71.8	17.2	11.0
Nolan	49	36	14.3	22.4	59.0	33.3	5.6
Martland	317	115	18.3	24.9	64.3	23.5	12.2
Judson	310	129	26.1	31.9	72.1	12.4	15.5
Ritchie	230	84	18.7	27.8	65.5	22.6	11.9
Hall	12	7	8.3	33.3	42.9	14.3	42.9

189 McCormick, *Supreme at Last*, 43.

...a barrister who knows his case,
who presents it in a clear manner,
embellished perhaps, but with discretion,
need have no fear of not having a fair hearing.

—Justice Patrick Kerwin in an address to the Lawyers' Club,
entitled "Law and Literature",
Toronto, 1952

Chapter 12

Life as the Chief Justice
1954 - 1963

It has been said that Canada's tenth Chief Justice of the Supreme Court of Canada went about his work with a smile of kindness in his light blue eyes. He was known to take a moment to pause and talk with friends, enjoy a rubber of bridge, a rare game of golf or relax reading a clever "whodunit". This was in contrast to when he was in the Court or acting as Administrator of Canada for the Governor General, and he set himself a little apart from the people. But there may have been times where many a person, perhaps sharing space at a drugstore counter for lunch, would have been unaware that the pleasant man next to them who just passed the ketchup, was, in order of precedence in the Canadian hierarchy, third only to the Governor General and the Prime Minister.

Researching the life of my grandfather was made more difficult by not locating much correspondence he authored. Luckily, one such item was located. In July of 1954, Patrick wrote a letter to his son, George. Written on Supreme Court letterhead that read, 'Chief Justice's Chambers, Supreme Court, Ottawa', Patrick described a portion of the events surrounding his appointment as Chief Justice that occurred just prior to him and his wife leaving Ottawa for their holiday in Prince Edward Island.

Green Gables Bungalow Court, Cavendish, P.E.I.

Saturday, July 17/54

Dear George,
...On Saturday June 26th I prorogued Parliament about 6 pm. The P.M. and Senator Macdonald [the Gov't leader in the Senate] met me and the G.G. sec'y & my aide-de-camp at the Senate entrance & we proceeded to the quarters of the Speaker of the Senate. For once there was no waiting & we then, after leaving our hats, marched in the usual procession to the Senate chamber (being televised on Thursday) where I sat on the Throne; the P.M. & Senate leader bowed & took their place on my right &

left respectively. I bade all "Pray be seated" in English and French & the Speaker then commanded the Gentleman Usher of the Black Rod to summon the Commons. The Usher bowed three times at intervals to me which I acknowledged & departed. It was then while we were waiting for the Commons, that the P.M. rising from his seat & leaning over a table told me I would be appointed for which I thanked him. This of course was whispered. He asked when I was leaving for holidays. I told him I had intended to leave Monday July 5th but of course would delay my departure. He explained (what I already knew) that the G. G. would return to Ottawa only on the morning of July 1st for the Trooping of the Colours & was leaving that evening; that several changes in the Cabinet were being made & he would like to have me sworn in first & then the ministers; he said he would let me know as soon as arrangements were made.

On Wed. June 30th one of his secretaries telephoned me in the morning that the Cabinet would meet at three pm the next day & that Mr. Abbott would like to be sworn in as the new Judge by me after I was sworn in (the CJ, by statute has to be sworn in by the G.G.). Later the current under-secretary of the Privy Council Hill telephoned me that he would come for me and have me at Gov't House at 4 (as a matter of fact there was an earlier Cabinet meeting on Wednesday afternoon and that evening Hill brought me the papers to complete the business transacted on that occasion).

Thursday AM mother and I attended the Trooping of the Colours on Parliament Hill & about 3:40 pm Hill came for me. I had already obtained from Leduc (the Court Registrar) the roll to his coming cabinet. The cabinet ministers who were exchanging portfolios & the two new ones & I & Hill etc., met in the Drawing Room. The P.M. went direct to the G.G.'s study where he advised the G.G. of the appointments which, of course, the G.G. approved. Then Abbott & I & Hill went in, shook hands, and the oath of CJ was administered to me. I was about to hand the Bible to Hill when the P.M. said that the G.G. had seen fit to approve the Cabinet's recommendation that I be made a Canadian Privy Councillor. This was quite unexpected as it is a great honour. I so expressed myself to the G.G. & P.M. whereupon the latter said he thought he should have one surprise. I was then sworn in as a P.C. & took the oath of secrecy and signed the P.C. Roll which has been in use since Confederation. Sir John A. Macdonald's was the first signature in it. Then I swore in Abbott who signed the Judges' Roll. He & I returned to the Drawing Room while the ministerial changes were being effected. The G.G. & others came in & we all had a glass of champagne & sandwiches. Then home! It was over!

The first message of congratulations had already arrived; a cable from J.T. Hackett Q. C. of Montreal who was in England. He must have been prescient as, of course, it was sent before the appointment was made. Telephone messages, wires and letters have been coming ever since. I kept three stenographers busy in Ottawa all day Friday, Saturday morning and all day Monday & Tuesday. Mother & I left Wed. morning for Quebec with the mail that arrived that morning .... Other mail was sent on & on Friday morning I kept a stenographer in Quebec busy for two hours taking dictation. She typed at her home that afternoon & I signed the letters Saturday morning. We left Monday AM & arrived here Wednesday afternoon. Some letters I feel I must answer by hand (6 or 7) & about thirty more have been sent me by Campbell. There will be more & in about two weeks we will go to Charlotte-town (25 miles away) & I will dictate answers.

This is long but I thought you would be interested. We expect to leave Aug 12th & leave Ottawa for Lake Erie about Aug 19th. We will see you & Claire & family after that or perhaps you will come to the Rathbone Inn for a day & see us there.

Of course Isobel's baby was born the day I prorogued Parliament. That morning I presided in Court; we [illegible] judgments & arguments in the Fall. The previous Monday C.J. Rinfret presided for the last time. I had arranged for represent-atives of the Provincial Bar Associations to be present. Sir Lyman Duff came at Rinfret's invitation & sat with us. After Rinfret announced judgments, I spoke first, on behalf of the Court bidding farewell to the C.J., then Duff, then the representatives of seven provinces, then an old friend of Rinfret, who then {illegible} replied. The Rinfrets asked the Judges & their wives & those who had spoken & of course their own children & grandchildren and in-laws, to their apartment for champagne & sandwiches. I presided in court Tuesday, Wed, Thurs & Friday. All in all, what with the uncertainty of the previous months, and all the activities of the last weeks, it was a trying time. Mother and I were tired & needed the four days at Quebec before travelling here.

Vern & Rose took their holidays coming thru Ont. to Buffalo & then thru the States to Quebec & the four of us stayed at Kanes'. Vern & Rose left Sunday AM for Ottawa & we gave them the key to our apartment. We stopped at Ethel's on the way, & she came Friday & stayed in Quebec with a friend until Monday. The Kanes expect to go for Aug 2nd.

Now, to turn to yourselves, I hope Claire & Michael & Shawn & you are well. We are anxious to see all of you in August but write us here at the address above.

Our best love to each one and thank you again for your letters.

Affectionately,

Dad[190]

---

190 Letter from Patrick to his son George, July 1954 (Family Archives).

The Prime Minister mentioned in this correspondence was the Right Honourable Louis St. Laurent. The Governor General was Vincent Massey. The reference to 'Campbell' in the letter refers to W. Ken Campbell, a long-time friend and personal aide to the Chief Justice. The comment about his daughter, Isobel, having a baby on the day he prorogued Parliament refers to the birth of the author of this book. Mentioning Vern & Rose, Patrick was speaking of his brother and sister-in-law. The Kanes in Québec refers to Mrs. Kerwin's older sister, Queenie (Alice), and husband Mattie Kane. Lastly, Ethel is thought to be a cousin of Mattie Kane.

~

Acting Deputy Governor General of Canada

Patrick acted for the Governor General on numerous occasions, including in 1959 for Governor General Vanier. In a document titled, "Commission appointing the Honourable Patrick Kerwin Deputy Governor General", dated September 23, 1959, the Acting Under Secretary of State wrote on behalf of the Governor General:

> Know you that being well assured of your loyalty, fidelity and capacity, I, Major-General Georges Philias Vanier, Governor General of Canada, under and by virtue of and in pursuance of the power and authority vested in me by the Commission of Her Majesty Queen Elizabeth II, under the Great Seal of Canada, dated August 1, 1959, constituting and appointing me to the Governor General of Canada do hereby nominate, constitute and appoint you the said PATRICK KERWIN, to be my Deputy within Canada and in that capacity to exercise, subject to any limitations or directions from time to time expressed or given by Her Majesty, all the powers, authorities and function vested in and of right exercisable by me as Governor General, saving and except the power of dissolving the Parliament of Canada.[191]

The document went on to further confirm and outline the powers involved.

---

191 Library and Archives Canada, File MG26-K.

The newly appointed Governor General, General Georges Vanier, takes the Oath of Office, 1959. The three principals in this photo are: G.G. Vanier, Mrs. Vanier and Patrick.

In his memoirs Governor General Vanier observed,

The public in Canada is often unaware of the extent of the Governor General's activities. There have been times in our recent history when it has been said by some that the governor-generalship was redundant and that the Chief Justice might perform whatever duties were worth retaining. I am not aware that any Chief Justice was ever asked for his views. The answer would probably have been, one job is enough![192]

Governor General Vanier and Patrick became good friends during this time and, when state business required it for official trips within Canada, the G.G. would loan Patrick and his wife the private train car used by the Governor General. Family tales tell of one such time where Patrick was acting for the Governor General with respect to state obligations in Québec City one summer. The Chief Justice and his wife enjoyed the use of the private train car but neither made a fuss about it. When queried about it a number of years later, my grandmother replied simply, "It was nice", but never added any more to the subject. She was not one to be pushed for information; if she had decided that she had said enough on a subject, the topic was then closed.

Governor General Vanier cited Lord Dufferin (Governor General 1872-1878) as responsible for the Governor General's residences, like the Citadel, in the following manner:

> Lord Dufferin, when he held the post, showed great imagination when he turned a part of the old fortress we call the citadel at Québec into a second vice-regal residence. Most of his successors used it, until it fell into disrepair and had to be restored under the stimulating guidance of Lady Willingdon. The Citadel is often referred to as a summer residence, which conjures up a picture of an indolent form lying in a hammock, a drink at hand, lazily turning the pages of a current novel. That is not my experience of the Citadel. As busy a social and official programme was carried on there each September as took place at other times at Government House in Ottawa. One month each year was, indeed, far too short for what had to be done.[193]

One interesting bit of history in regard to his time in Québec City was pointed out by Governor General Vanier dealing with the cloistered communities in that region.

---

192 Vincent Massey, *What's past is prologue - the Memoirs of Vincent Massey* (Macmillan of Canada, 1963), 466.
193 Massey, *What's past is prologue*, 470-471.

The Governor General has certain privileges in French Canada unknown to the general public — indeed unknown to me until I assumed the vice-regal post. They cannot but interest people with a sense of history. During the French regime, the Governor had the right to visit cloistered communities. After the conquest, the heads of these houses asked the British governors to continue the exercise of this historic privilege and, ever since, the Governor General of the day has done so. By custom, he is permitted to take members of his staff and family but no one else.[194]

It is not known if Patrick visited this community while acting for the Governor General.

Patrick acted on behalf of the Governor General, both as a Justice and as Chief Justice of the Court, many times. Some of these instances included:

1945 - October, acted on behalf of the Governor General;
1946 - November, acted on behalf of the Governor General;
1947 - July, prorogued Parliament;
1947 - July, read message from the King to Privy Council concerning the marriage of Princess Elizabeth to Lieutenant Mountbatten;
1949 - September, Opening of Parliament;
1950 - June, prorogued 2nd session of 21st Parliament;
1950 - August, gave Royal Assent to bill ending Rail Strike;
1951 - May, gave Royal Assent to 100 bills;
1952 - June, gave Royal Assent to 110 bills, including 84 divorce bills;
1953 - May, prorogued Parliament;
1954 - June, prorogued Parliament;
1955 - July, prorogued Parliament;
1955 - May, received the Letter of Credence from the Ambassador of Portugal, His Excellency Dr. Luis Esteves Fernandes;
1955 - September, received the Letter of Credence from the Ambassador of Norway, His Excellency Arne Christian Gunneng accompanied by Lester Pearson;
1955 - September, received the Letter of Credence from the Ambassador of Cuba, His Excellency Dr. Juan Antonio accompanied by L. Pearson;
1956 - March, received the Letter of Credence from the Ambassador of Mexico, His Excellency Manuel Maples Arce;
1956 - March, gave Royal Assent to two emergency grain bills;
1956 - April, received the Letter of Credence from the Ambassador of Sweden, His Excellency Oscar Thorsing;
1957 - March, gave Royal Assent to 204 bills;

---

194 Ibid., 472.

1957 - September, received the Letter of Credence from the Ambassador of Israel, His Excellency Arthur Lourie;

1957 - September, received the Letter of Credence from the Ambassador of Tunisia, His Excellency Mongi Slim;

1958 - January, acted on behalf of the Governor General;

1958 - March, received the Letter of Credence from the Ambassador of Dominican Republic, His Excellency Milton Merrence;

1959 - May, gave Royal Assent to bills;

1959 - July, received the Letter of Credence from the Ambassador of Italy, His Excellency Ferrarios Salgano;

1959 - July, prorogued 2nd session of 24th Parliament;

1960 - January, gave Royal Assent to bills providing emergency financial assistance to Prairie farmers;

1961 - June, gave Royal Assent to a number of bills;

1961 - July, acted on behalf of the Governor General;

1962 - December, gave Royal Assent to 13 bills and adjourned Parliament until January 21st, 1963.

Picture given to Patrick and Georgina by Governor General and Mrs. Vanier.

Acting as Administrator of Canada, Patrick was requested to prorogue the second sitting of Canada's 22nd Parliament (January 7 - July 28, 1955). Things did not go the way predicted for this usually sombre event, as described in the local newspaper:

Chief Justice Patrick Kerwin, administrator of Canada, today turned the table on the Commons. He informed the House that he couldn't make it in time to prorogue parliament at 12:45 p.m. as scheduled but would be on hand at 1.15 p.m. No reason was given.
Yesterday, the Chief Justice acting in the absence of

Governor General Massey, was ready to prorogue parliament at 5 p.m. but the Commons didn't finish its business and prorogation was set over until today.[195]

~

For quite a number of years the Kerwins spent part of their summers up at the Bakers' cottage at Cedarhurst Beach on Lake Simcoe. As previously noted, these two couples had been friends since their early days in Guelph. The Kerwins were invited to come and stay as long as they liked and often did so anywhere from three to six weeks at a time. One summer while there, Patrick was sworn in as the Administrator of Canada at the cottage. The Governor General had left on a vacation trip to England on the weekend and, on Monday, the Great Seal of Canada was flown from Ottawa to Muskoka Airport then driven to Beaverton where Chief Justice Kerwin was vacationing. In a ceremony attended by Acting Under Secretary of State, Cattanach, two aides, Louis McCann and Charles Doyle along with Arthur Hill, Deputy-Clerk of the Privy Council and W. K. Campbell, Private Secretary of the Chief Justice, the Chief Justice was sworn in as Administrator of Canada.

On this notable occasion, Patrick was quoted as saying,

> Having taken the necessary oath I have thought fit to issue this proclamation:
>
> I do hereby require and command that all and singular Her Majesty's officers and ministers in Canada do continue in the execution of their several and respective offices, places and employment, and that Her Majesty's living subjects and all others whom these presets may concern do take notice thereof and govern themselves accordingly.[196]

Sibling grandchildren of the Bakers, Barb and Bill McCollum, recall that, once Patrick had been sworn in by the contingent from Ottawa, the Seal of Canada was left with the Chief Justice and also a handsome (in Barb's opinion) young plain clothes officer from the Royal Canadian Mounted Police to protect the substitute Governor General. He was initially introduced as a 'friend' of the Kerwins. It must have been an interesting assignment for the officer as it turned out he was as good at water skiing as

---

195 "Just One Last Delay", *Ottawa Citizen*, July 28, 1955, 1.
196 "Takes Over Reins of Canada", *Windsor Star,* July 20, 1961, 21.

he was at providing protection for the Administrator of Canada and his family.

According to Bill McCollum, on the occasion of Patrick acting on behalf of the Governor General, the Kerwins arrived on the train. He recalled,

> ...the Ont. Northland stopped at the Cedarhurst station (such as it was) and let the C. J. off ... he was travelling in the G.G.'s railway car, with all sorts of regal emblems on it. This gave rise, I'm sure, to a great deal of tongue-wagging. Don't forget that the first scheduled stop for the Northland after leaving Toronto, was Washago, north of Orillia, and the train stopped for no one, except, of course, the Queen's representative in Canada.[197]

Both Barb and Bill recall one fine summer's day at the lake when a call was received at the cottage from one of the Prime Minister's Aides for the Chief Justice. Georgina took the call and told a very surprised young man to wait for a minute as the Chief Justice was busy taking out the garbage and would be a few minutes. This caused uproarious laughter for all at the cottage that day.

They both recall that Patrick loved to play cards and would play bridge or cribbage with the adults and canasta or cribbage with the children. Even though Professor Baker and friends were avid fishermen, Patrick was not. Patrick would rarely accompany the men on the boat but, if he did go, he would bring a good book and read while the others waited for a bite. Barb McCollum remembers one time Patrick did accompany the fishermen on the boat on one condition: when he ran out of cigarettes, they would return to shore. She also recalls that when her grandparents and the Kerwins were together, there was a lot of laughter — mostly from the ladies. She said that Mrs. Kerwin had "such a sense of humour at times and I remember both grandmothers often sitting together on the couch just laughing up a storm. Oh, what wonderful memories."[198]

Barb McCollum was very happy to discuss her time with the Kerwins at the summer cottage. She told of going to get the daily mail in Beaverton with Patrick, saying,

> I think they had a blue car, but I may be mistaken on that one. And we sometimes stopped at the Frosty Treat for an ice

---

197 Email to the author from William (Bill) McCollum, Oct. 16, 2013.
198 Email to the author from Barbara McCollum, Oct. 21, 2013.

cream on the way home. He always told me not to tell mom because we usually went in the late afternoon and mom thought it would spoil my appetite.[199]

Patrick's preferred make of automobile was a Studebaker (model: Lark; colour: light blue).

Barb was very fond of the Kerwins. In 2014 she wrote to tell me more about their times at the cottage, saying, "Your grand-dad and I always seemed to connect. He would laugh and carry on especially when he beat me at crib. He really sharpened my skills but always seemed to win. I had won some chess tournaments and they both wanted to see my trophies".

Her lasting impression of Patrick was summed up when she wrote, "I think he liked being around the people just as much as the card games. He was such a sweet man."

A newspaper article kept by Georgina describes how the Administrator of Canada visited the Stephen Leacock Home in Orillia ON:

> The man who is presently the chief representative of Her Majesty the Queen in Canada paid an informal visit to Orillia last night. His Excellency Chief Justice Patrick Kerwin was made administrator for Canada in the holiday absence of His Excellency Governor General Vanier in a ceremony at Beaverton Monday. In company with friend Prof. and Mrs. A. W. Baker of Beaverton, Chief Justice Kerwin and Mrs. Kerwin visited the Stephen Leacock Home and was introduced to the entire town council meeting in the council chamber.
>
> On his visit here Chief Justice Kerwin, Mrs. Kerwin and Prof. and Mrs. Baker were accompanied by Ald. J. A. McGarvey, chairman of reception and publicity for the town. They were entertained at a dinner by the town and visited the Leacock Memorial Home.
>
> The party paid an informal and unexpected visit to last night's council meeting where Mayor A. J. Truman introduced his Excellency to the councillors.
>
> Mrs. Kerwin remarked that when he came to this area he was ill, "This air up here does wonders for you", she said.[200]

An avid bridge player, voracious reader and sometime golfer, Patrick was known to have led a quiet life away from the social swirl in Canada's capitol. Once he was named Chief Justice, he was not able to find much time for golf anymore. It was not all

---

199 Email to the author from Barbara McCollum, Oct. 16, 2013.
200 *Packet and Times*, July 29, 1960, 3.

bad though as he rarely had to tee off at that first hole at the Royal Ottawa Golf Club — it was said that the first hole unnerved him greatly as all the members and guests in the clubhouse would be watching one's first shot, which was, in his opinion, most often not one's best shot of the day.

Always the kind, calm and busy grandfather, when he and our grandmother came to our home for Sunday dinner, Patrick would sometimes drop his wife off in the afternoon, say hello to all assembled, and then excuse himself to do some work at the office. He was always back in time for dinner. Coming to dinner and spending time with some of his grandchildren became a weekly ritual for Patrick and Georgina and they only missed it due to prior obligations, ill health or absence from the city. We missed having our grandfather and grandmother come to dinner when they could not make it but, being children, we sometimes missed the homemade cookies that our grandmother made as well.

One such Sunday in the late 1950's, after our grandparents had arrived at our home and Patrick was about to leave again to do some work at the office, he impulsively invited my older brother, Pat, to come along to see the office. This was not the first time my much older brother was invited along to his office but it was the first time that our long-time neighbour (and brother by proxy), Terry McManus, was invited to tag along. Patrick probably was helping our mother by removing one of the more prolific "instigators" out of the mix at home for a short while.

To keep themselves busy, both boys brought their bags of marbles to find out who was the best at mibs and taws. In those days, a large bag of alleys was a prized possession for any ten-year-old boy but it was also a sign of one-upmanship to have the bag that held one's collection be a purple Seagram's liquor bag (without the bottle, of course). On the way down to the courthouse, my brother Pat and Grandfather Patrick were talking in the front seat of the Studebaker when Patrick asked his grandson how he liked the new courthouse. My brother asked how old it was and Patrick informed young Pat that it was around 10 or 11 years old. In reply Pat exclaimed, "Whoa, that's OLD!" Pat's grandfather was not impressed with the response in any way and very little was said after that as they travelled to the courthouse.

They entered through the underground parking lot at the back of the building and the Chief Justice put the young lads in the care of elderly Commissionaires at the front desk in the large foyer of the Grand Entrance Hall. Patrick suggested the boys play with their alleys in the large marble hall, resplendent with the double staircases that lead up to the main courtroom. With its seven tall windows, this elegant setting provided a well-lit playroom on this bright Sunday afternoon for these active boys.

The two started playing a few feet apart at first but, slowly, as the game progressed, they began moving further apart from each other. After a while the game degraded to the sport of trying to hit each other with the projectiles across the breadth of the thirty-two-metre hall. But the best was yet to come (and to this day each of them believes it was the other's idea): at one point hurling marble alleys across a marble floor became tiresome so to mix things up, my brother, Pat, took Terry's still almost full bag and ran to the top of the first flight of stairs shouting, "Watch this!" as he turned the bag upside down. Did you know that alleys really do take off at a great rate when bouncing on marble steps down to a marble floor? Almost like throwing a multitude of India Rubber balls as hard as you can. The commissionaires, older fellows who had probably seen action in WWII, stood still, as if frozen — no need for anyone to break a hip over these impulsive young tykes.

Finally, one brave commissionaire shuffled along the floor up and towards my brother who was still at the top of the stairs and sporting a wide grin of true accomplishment. The bag was unceremoniously ripped from Pat's hand with orders barked sharply at the boys, "It's time to pick these all up! NOW!"

Not very long after this stroke of creative mischief had taken place, the Chief Justice of Canada, having completed the afternoon's tasks in his office, was proceeding down the grand staircase. As he approached, Patrick noted five bodies (two boys plus three commissionaires) down on their hands and knees, all of whom seemed to be searching for something in the grand hall in a strained silence.

As he observed this scene, the Chief Justice asked the commissionaires, "So, gentlemen, how did it go?"

Responses from the guards of the Supreme Court of Canada were positive in nature and the Chief Justice was advised that they were helping the boys find all their alleys as some of them had somehow spread through the spacious room. Shortly thereafter, the scene then included a sixth person, the Chief Justice of Canada, on hands and knees looking for all the alleys that had been spread far and wide. After all, it was his grandson and not a word was said about the boys' full behaviour.

~

At convocation in October of 1954, the University of New Brunswick conferred an honourary Doctor of Laws degree on the newest Chief Justice of the Supreme Court of Canada. Robert Cattley, first official orator at the University, gave the introduction in the following terms:

> Patrick Kerwin, member of Her Majesty's Canadian Privy Council, Chief Justice and Deputy Governor General of Canada, is a man of great wisdom, greater modesty and an infinitely courteous and diplomatic spirit. One of our most respected jurists and an acknowledged authority on Constitutional Law, he is rightly and deservedly supreme over what is now the final and Supreme Court of the land. To this august post he brings a fair mind, an even temper and a faultless reputation for justice without bias or prejudice. Formidable though his titles and weighty his authority, no appellant has ever wanted for an impartial ruling at his hands; and many a young practitioner has cause to bless his Lordship's tolerance and human sympathy.[201]

On the same occasion, the *Saint John Telegraph-Journal* wrote:

> The head of Canada's highest court paid tribute Friday at Saint John, to accomplishments of the University of New Brunswick's Law School faculty in Saint John. Chief Justice Patrick Kerwin of Ottawa told a UNB Convocation gathering that the teaching of law was of paramount importance and responsibilities resting on any faculty of law were onerous.[202]

On Saturday November 20, 1954, a dinner was held at Convocation Hall, Osgoode Hall to honour the "recently appointed Chief Justice of Canada, the Honourable Patrick Kerwin". Always pleased to speak at Osgoode Hall events, Patrick was happy to have a moment to share his thoughts at the dinner. Among those present were old friends and former colleagues of the Chief Justice, Judge R. Stewart Clark of Guelph, J. Kenneth Blair, president of the South Wellington Bar Association, E. G. Thompson, Q.C., representing the Perth County Law Association, W. P. Gregory, Bencher (Governing Body) of the Law Society of Upper Canada. There is a copy of this speech in the Appendix.

The Chief Justice and Georgina Kerwin were the guests of honour at the annual St. Mary's Ball in Montreal in December

---

201 Robert E.D. Cattley, "Honoris causa: the effervescences of a university orator."
    (Fredericton: UNB Associated Alumnae, 1968).
202 *Saint John Telegraph-Journal*, Oct. 16, 1954.

1954. The event was held at the Windsor Hotel in aid of the Ladies Auxiliary and the St. Mary's Hospital Maternity Committee. This meant taking the train to Montreal, attending the event, staying overnight and then returning by train the next day.

On May 11, 1955, in a luncheon speech to the Canadian Club held in Ottawa the recently appointed Chief Justice was quoted as saying, "It is not enough that the Court should be right; it must also seem to be right".[203] It was also a belief of his that the people deserved to know and understand the laws under which they live. It was his aim to make his Court not be a refuge for lawyers laden with books and fat fees, but a place of reason and light based on man's experience.

In June 1955, Patrick was given an honourary Doctor of Civil Law at convocation for Bishop's University, in Lennoxville, Québec. Patrick was one of six accorded this honour.[204] At this event, the introduction of the Chief Justice of the Supreme Court of Canada stated:

> The Rt. [sic] Hon. Chief Justice Patrick Kerwin was named to the Supreme Court of Canada in 1935, and became Chief Justice on July 1st, 1954. As such he is deputy to the Governor General and administrator of the nation in his absence, and he presides over the highest court of justice in the Dominion, the court that plays a major role in shaping the lives and destinies of Canadian citizens. Chief Justice Kerwin has devoted his life to the study and application of law as the expression of fundamental principles of ethics and equity by which men and nations can and must live together in peace and harmony.[205]

Whereas most newspaper articles on the subject of the honourary degree gave a standard listing of Patrick's life, family and accomplishments to date, one article went further than most in noting,

> Patrick Kerwin is a man whose whole life has been devoted to the law, not merely as a profession but as the very force that guarantees the order and the dignity of life. In his long service on the bench he has shown how deep is his recognition of the truth that the law is not only the regulator of human affairs, but the expression of those fundamental principles of equity by which all men must live, whether as nations or

203 Chief Justice Kerwin, Address to the Canadian Club, May 11, 1955.
204 Bishop's University Archives Convocation Pamphlet, June 11, 1955.
205 Ibid.

persons.[206]

His direct style of speaking, with simple sentences and short comments might have led casual visitors to Patrick's court into thinking that this man might not be of the best judicial tradition of learning and ability. But a lawyer who was the recipient of his penetrating questioning or thought on subjects knew differently. The *Globe & Mail* wrote, "Chief Justice Kerwin is recognized as an extremely able, hardworking and shrewd jurist and a good executive."[207]

~

Patrick's activities outside the court at that time included membership on the board of regents with Ottawa University from 1948 until 1960 and Chairmanship of the lay advisory board of St. Patrick's College, a Catholic school. In December of 1949, Patrick received a Christmas card from the Archbishop of Ottawa, Monseigneur Alexandre Vachon, thanking him for his "help to the University of Ottawa and St. Patrick's College". (Family Archives).

Among the Chief Justice's duties was fulfilling the many requests to deliver speeches at events in addition to his regular duties and filling in for the Governor General. For example, in the years 1956 and 1957 alone, some of the speeches Patrick gave were:

- Loyola College convocation in Montreal;
- Lincoln County Bar Association in Niagara Falls;
- Convocation at St. Patrick's College in Ottawa;
- Assumption University of Windsor on the occasion of receiving an Honourary Degree of Doctor of Civil Law;
- University of Toronto on the occasion of receiving an Honourary Degree of Doctor of Laws;
- Boston University Law School;
- Opening of the Superior Court in Montreal;
- Newman Club in Kingston, Ontario; and
- Sarnia Chamber of Commerce.

In a 1956 *Detroit News* article, the author wrote of Patrick and brother Vern's annual reunion:

---

206 Unnamed newspaper article, Georgina Kerwin's collection.
207 *Globe & Mail*, Saturday, July 9, 1955.

MOTARBOARDS AND GOWNS — A SYMBOL OF RENOWN

Five distinguished Canadians and a British Government representative who received honorary degrees of Doctor of Laws at the University of Toronto convocation chat informally prior to yesterday's campus ceremonies. From left are: Charles Harold Hale, Chester Samuel Walters, Edith Kathleen Russell, Canada's Chief Justice Patrick Kerwin, Dr. Clifford D. Graham, provincial deputy minister of agriculture (he received his degree at a previous convocation), and Lt.-Gol. Sir Archibald Nye, British High Commissioner for Canada.

Patrick at the University of Toronto where he received an honourary degree of Doctor of Laws, May, 1956.

... the Kerwin boys, Pat now 66, and Vern now 62, have got together for a real reunion at least once a year..."There is never a date set for our annual meeting", said Vern, "One of us gets lonesome for the other and we get together".

This year the reunion was spurred when official business called the justice to neighbouring Windsor. He was luncheon guest at the Essex County Bar at Elmwood, and delivered the address at the annual convocation and presentation of diplomas to students of Assumption College.

At this convocation, Justice Kerwin received the college's Honorary Doctor of Civil Law degree.

But the justice came down a day early for the affair, and morning found him dressing carefully before a mirror in Vern's spare bedroom at 1499 Campbell rather than in a Windsor hotel.

Yesterday saw the justice, in his great ermine-trimmed robes, back at the highest court of all Canada, and

184

probationers in Circuit Court wondered what Vernon Kerwin was grinning about.

Maybe he will be grinning at what he remarked about, when the austere Chief Justice was dressing in his home: "You know, he has to come over here to let his hair down." The justice is very bald.[208]

In June of 1957, the *Saskatoon Star-Phoenix* summarized Patrick's speech at the Boston University School of Law for the second annual Law Day celebration:

Chief Justice Patrick Kerwin of the Supreme Court of Canada said today the law is part of the warp and woof of our civilization and that without rules our society could not exist.

But the individual was of prime importance in our communities and he must "be free in body and spirit".

In his address Kerwin said:

Barring such matters as sedition, libel, slander and indecency, the individual in a free community may not only hold to his ideas but he may set them forth in words or writing without fear of untoward consequences.

Unless these rights are preserved, of what avail are the activities buying and selling, of manufacturing, of the arts and sciences? Without that freedom, all else will have been in vain. And that, I suggest, is the law's chief contribution to the peace and prosperity of a nation.[209]

In October of 1957, Patrick and Georgina travelled by train to his hometown where he was slated to give a speech at the fall meeting of the Sarnia Chamber of Commerce. He also wanted to visit his sister, Mrs. George Beatty, and was able to celebrate his sixty-eighth birthday on October 25 in the place of his birth with friends and family.

In his speech to the 300 attendees at the dinner held at Kenwick Terrace, the Chief Justice said, "If the way of the transgressor in modern times was hard, the work of the judiciary was far from easy too".[210] He also recalled playing in Quinn's Band there more than 50 years ago when the building was a skating rink.

Then Patrick spoke about the long and interesting history of Chambers of Commerce, citing the first as being created in

---

208 "Chief Justice of Canada Visits Detroit Brother", *Detroit News,* Oct. 30, 1956.
209 "Law Guarantees Freedom Kerwin Tells Bostonians", *Saskatoon Star-Phoenix,* June 1, 1957, 1.
210 Chief Justice Kerwin, Address to Sarnia Chamber of Commerce, Oct. 25, 1957.

France as long ago as the year 1400. "Their purpose", he told the audience, "was to stimulate national unity, encourage freedom of enterprise and the preservation of individual liberty. Without organizations similar to the Sarnia chamber, where each member did his utmost to respect the law, the businesses and many traders would suffer."[211]

On the subject of his work, Patrick believed that the first task of the judiciary in modern times was to ascertain the intention of the lawmakers. He added that it was absolutely necessary that there should be rules to regulate the manifold activities of a myriad of peoples. Otherwise, he warned, chaos would result and only the strongest would survive in a perpetual state of strife. In concluding, he said:

> ...the individual may live his life and earn the daily bread for
> the support of himself and his dependents in his own way, —
> so long as he does not invade the similar rights of others.[212]

At the end of the guest of honour's speech, a vote of thanks was offered by the host and was followed by the presentation of a multi-tiered birthday cake bearing 68 candles for their guest. Patrick was touched and proceeded to work his way around the cake to blow out the multitude of candles. Entertainment that evening was provided by the singer, Joyce Sullivan, a popular vocalist and CBC radio host.

The Mayor and the city then presented the guest of honour with the civic scroll, only given to distinguished visitors, that read:

October 25, 1957

To the Honourable Patrick Kerwin
Privy Councillor,
Doctor of Laws,
Chief Justice of Canada

We, the Mayor and Aldermen of the City of Sarnia on behalf of the Citizens of the City of Sarnia, pay honour to your distinguished person on the occasion of your visit to our City, the City of your birth on the 25th day of October this Year of Our Lord, One Thousand Nine Hundred and Fifty Seven.

It is with great pride that we welcome back to our City a son who has so distinguished himself in his chosen profession,

---

211 Chief Justice Kerwin, Address to Sarnia Chamber of Commerce, Oct. 25, 1957.
212 Ibid.

whose character, talents and qualities have been so noted, that the highest government in Canada has seen fit to elevate him to the position of highest honour, whose wide learning has been fitly recognized by Universities throughout the land and whose very life and success reflect some considerable glory on the City that gave him birth.

Welcome Patrick Kerwin
And
Godspeed

It is the hope, the prayer, of our people that you will continue to grow in stature and in wisdom, that you may continue to serve our country with ever greater ability and sureness, and that your future assured success will be matched with like happiness.

M. M, Gowland, M.D.,
MAYOR

A 1963 Sarnia newspaper article recalls Patrick's visit in 1957, stating that Patrick expressed concern at the growing incidence of costly lawsuits from automobile accidents and said there was an urgent need for education in driving. But he also had a "twinkle in his eye" as he recalled falling from his bicycle at Lochiel and Christine in 1905 and breaking his arm (the newspaper article describing this fall reprinted in this book did not include the 'broken arm' part of the story). This same newspaper interview continued:

Chief Justice Kerwin took his post seriously and he discharged his judicial duties in a manner most befitting such high office. He was master of the courts over which he presided and to say he was learned in the law of the land would be a gross under-statement. But, he also had an Irish sense of humour.[213]

As Chief Justice, Patrick's reputation was that of a firm, serious-minded and fair jurist. He rarely granted interviews or saw anyone in his chambers except on legal or administrative business.

Colleagues knew Patrick as a tireless worker, but in 1958 exhaustion forced him to take a six-month leave of absence for a rest from overwork. It was Georgina's firmly held belief that it was also due to the effects of having worked in the stench of the old court building on a special project for Prime Minister Mackenzie King on hot summer days years earlier.

---

213 Unnamed newspaper article, Georgina Kerwin's collection.

In an article in the *Globe & Mail* , Ralph Hyman wrote,

> Noted for his terse, straight-to-the-point reasons for judgment, Chief Justice Kerwin on several occasions helped upset judgments of the lower courts in Quebec in the matter of religious freedom for Jehovah's Witnesses. Conscientious and painstaking, he took six month's leave of absence in 1958 to regain his health which had become undermined through overwork.[214]

An article in the *Ottawa Citizen* headlined "Kerwin Retiring 'Soon'" gave their take on the Chief Justice's health,

> Retirement of the Chief Justice Patrick Kerwin of the Supreme Court of Canada may be expected in the near future. Chief Justice Kerwin has been in ill-health in recent months and it is understood that he plans retirement at an early date. His successor will likely be Mr. Justice Charles H. Locke.[215]

~

In 1959, Patrick and Mrs. Kerwin came to the aid of their daughter, Isobel, when her husband, their son-in-law John McKenna (lawyer), suddenly died of a heart attack. With seven children to take care of, a house to pay for and no life insurance to rely on, Isobel never forgot the kindness and support her parents (and brothers) showed during this unimaginably difficult time. Isobel's honours degree in English served her well as she soon started writing shows for the CBC television network. For a time she wrote book reviews as well as questions for the popular "Reach for the Top" quiz show for high school students, testing the questions out on her younger children to see if they were difficult enough for the show. Isobel later managed to carve out a career teaching English at Carleton University, and later as a professor on staff at the University of Ottawa.

Early in the 1950's, the Kerwins had moved from their large home at the east end of Wilbrod Street to a large apartment directly across from St. Joseph's Church near the western end of the same street. In the early 1960's, there was a fire one night in the detached garage behind their building. As his daughter Isobel recalled,

> Even though your grandfather was a wise and sensible man, this wasn't always the way in all things. When the

---

214 R. Hyman, "Gallery of Canadians, Painstaking Chief Justice", *Globe & Mail,* Jan. 20, 1962.
215 "Kerwin Retiring 'Soon' " *Ottawa Citizen,* Nov. 7, 1958, 32, from Professor Bale, Queen's University.

garage fire occurred, it, of course, happened in the middle of the night. By the time your grandparents woke up, the garage was fully engulfed in flames. Your grandfather immediately put some shoes on and threw a coat over his pajamas and housecoat so he could "rescue" the car [a late-model Studebaker, his favourite type of automobile]. Your grandmother had quite a time convincing him not to run into a burning garage to save a car. "After all," she explained, "We can replace the car, but not you!" Fortunately, this did get his attention and stopped him from running out to the burning garage. As your grandmother later explained, "I'd seen the garage from the window, and it was on fire every-where. The firemen were there working at the flames and I'm sure the car was already gone." A couple of weeks later they arrived at our home for their regular Sunday dinner with your grandfather driving a shiny new blue Studebaker Lark.

As there were numerous grandchildren in Ottawa, we would visit our grandparents in smaller numbers so as not to overwhelm them. I recall being taken out to dinner at a restaurant (Murray's in the Lord Elgin) by my grandparents and told I could have anything I wanted. A bit overwhelming for this eight-year old but it was nice to spend time with them. My sister, Sheila, recalled that on one of her overnight visits to see them, our grandfather taught her how to shuffle a deck of cards and she was just thrilled. Later, I found out that our grandfather had taken up smoking a pipe to replace his cigarette habit.

My cousin, Michael Kerwin, related a story about our grand-parents: "My father [George Kerwin] said that Grandad had suggested a family vacation in P.E.I. with all the children, spouses, and grandchildren. Dad politely suggested that this, perhaps, would not be much of a quiet holiday for them both and nothing ever came of it."

In late 1962, our mother took us to visit the place where our grandfather worked. We were permitted to enter Court's parking garage and, from there, took the elevator up to the floor where the Justices' offices are located.

We were met by Helen McKenna, a cousin of my father's, who worked at the Court and volunteered on her day off to guide us through the building. I recall touring the library, a very large, well-lit room that had little cubby hole rooms very high up. Some of these were accessible and were arrived at via a large, wide-stepped ladder. In the attic room we toured there was a book nearly as big as I was on a lectern.

In touring Patrick's office, as an eight-year-old, it impressed me very much that he not only had a private washroom but also had a shower. Later, we children were asked to wait in a large meeting room and, while there, we found great pleasure in sliding along the long table in our sock feet. This was immediately ended once discovered by the adults.

Even at that young age I was impressed at what a stunning building it was, and that impression continues to this day.

At another time, my brother Patrick decided he would like to show his good friend, Jimmy (Jim Harbic), the building where the Chief Justice worked so, being bold and creative, he opted to do it himself and not bother others by asking permission. The two took the bus downtown and got into the Supreme Court building via the garage at the back. It seems no one noticed two twelve-year-olds traipsing through the building (not today's security standards, to be sure). Brother Patrick showed Jimmy the courtroom, meeting rooms, the judges' chambers and his grandfather's office. Once the private tour was completed, the boys went off to have a cola and fries at Woolworth's with nobody the wiser to their exploits.

Harbic recalled another, authorized, visit to the Court with members of our family where they got a bit of a tour and sat in the courtroom while in session; he was very impressed with it all. After the session broke at noon, the Chief Justice took them to lunch which Jim also remembers liking very much as well.

~

In July of 1962, the man Patrick replaced as Chief Justice, Thibaudeau Rinfret, died at the age of eighty-three. This was a person that he knew well and socialized with, as their apartments were in the same building on Wilbrod Street. Patrick, his colleagues and Georgina all attended the funeral for his former superior. Chief Justice Rinfret was interred at Notre-Dame-des-Neiges Cemetery in Montreal.

The last Justice of the Supreme Court to be sworn in by Chief Justice Kerwin was Emmett Hall on January 10, 1963. Justice Hall, along with his wife, son and daughter-in-law, attended the swearing-in ceremony held in a chamber just off the courtroom. Hall was only the third justice ever named from Saskatchewan.[216]

According to Peter McCormick, the Kerwin Court continued the work begun by the Rinfret Court in the gradual and cautious

---

216 Dennis Gruending, *Emmett Hall - Establishment Radical* (Fitzhenry & Whiteside, 2005).

evolution of a Canadian jurisprudence that was not simply an echo of previous or current English decisions, and this is demonstrated by the "footprints" the court left in the form of its frequently cited decisions.

> The Kerwin Court's citation practices remained strongly focused on the Judicial Committee and the other English Courts, but it was beginning to shift toward the use of Canadian authorities, especially the Supreme Court itself and the most prominent of those Canadian authorities was still former Chief Justice Duff. [217]

The early Kerwin Court, like the Rinfret Court before it, was almost entirely staffed by judges appointed in the 1940s, established in their ways and approaching the end of their careers. The later Kerwin Court represented the first renewal of the Supreme Court, dominated (in numbers if not always in performance) by newly appointed judges.

Official Visit to Venezuela, 1955

The Chief Justice and Georgina Kerwin travelled for business quite frequently, attending dinners or meetings where the Chief Justice was being honoured and, often, delivering a speech. Georgina, who entertained widely, travelled out of a sense of duty and enjoyment; Patrick, who preferred to stay home, travelled for duty. However, they both quite enjoyed their trip to Caracas, Venezuela in late 1955.

On October 18, 1955, E.D. McGreer, Chief of Protocol, Department of External Affairs, sent a confidential message to the Canadian Embassy in Caracas, Venezuela. He wrote to the Ambassador that the President of the Federal Court of Venezuela, Dr. G. Manrique Pacanins, had extended an invitation to the Chief Justice of the Supreme Court of Canada to attend the celebrations in Caracas to commemorate the centenary of the establishment of the Civil Code of that country put forth by the Venezuelan, Andrés Bello. McGreer then asked for an indication of the number of Chief Justices (or Presidents) of various Supreme Courts who were expected to attend, the duration of the ceremonies and to provide their own view as to whether "we should be in attendance".[218]

---

217 McCormick, *Supreme at Last*, 57.
218 Library and Archives Canada, 1955/10/18-1955/11/16, File RG25-A-3-b.

In its telegram reply, dated October 25, 1955, the Canadian Embassy in Caracas advised that all of the Latin American Supreme Court representatives had been asked as well as Canadian and American Supreme Court representatives. A copy of this telegram was immediately forwarded to the Chief Justice of the Supreme Court of Canada. Shortly thereafter, the Chief Justice of Canada accepted the invitation.

This visit engendered much administrative action. One letter provided biographical information on Andrés Bello, a brochure on Venezuela in Spanish, a book on Venezuela from the Pan American Union (now the Organization of American States, which Canada officially joined in 1990), information on the clothing and habits of Venezuelans and on inoculations required for the trip. Also in this correspondence was the notation of the Ambassador of Venezuela that he was delighted the Chief Justice had accepted the invitation and he was taking the necessary "steps to secure air passage for you leaving on Sunday and leaving Caracas on the following Friday". Further, the Ambassador wanted the Chief Justice to know that "November climatically was the best month of the year in Caracas so that a light summer suit would be appropriate".[219] Lastly, McGreer advised that Anderson of the Department of External Affairs would be preparing a few remarks in Spanish for him. The biographical information on Andrés Bello provided to the Chief Justice read as follows:

> Andrés Bello born in Caracas, Venezuela. After having been associated with the revolutionary movement against Spain, he was sent in 1810 on a political mission to London. He resided there for 19 years, acting as Secretary to the Legation of Chile, Columbia and Venezuela, and spending his free time in study, teaching and journalism.
>
> In 1829 he was given a post in the Chilean Treasury and settled in Santiago. He took a prominent part in the intellectual life of the city, particularly in founding the National University (1843) of which he became Rector. He was nominated Senator and died at Santiago in 1865. He was mainly responsible for the Civil Code promulgated in 1855. He wrote a number of prose works on law, philosophy, literary criticism and philology, as well as poetry.[220]

On November 2, 1955, a handwritten letter was sent to the Embassy of Venezuela, in Ottawa, stating,

---

219 Ibid.
220 Ibid.

The Department of External Affairs presents its compliments to the Embassy of Venezuela and has the honour to request that an appropriate visa be affixed to the enclosed passport No. D-2703 of the Honourable Patrick Kerwin, Chief Justice of the Supreme Court of Canada who is proceeding at an early date to Venezuela to attend the ceremonies marking the 100th anniversary of the Establishment of the Code of Andres Bello.[221]

A further memo dealt with the subject of "Notes re Speech for the Chief Justice" and included a copy of the speech (in English) and observed, "All Latins are more flowery than we are; they regard us as cold. The draft is, deliberately, more flowery than it would be in English. Reference to "Bolivar" is a must; in Caracas they almost worship his memory" then warns, "My English text is probably far from elegant; I wrote in Spanish and dictated a free-translation in English."[222] Arrangements were also made for Patrick to rehearse the speech in Spanish which he was to deliver. The speech enclosed with the November 2 memo was:

Mr. President (Note: greeting to be checked) — In rising to address this distinguished assembly, I find myself in some doubt as to whether I should begin by expressing my thanks to Dr. Pacanins for his kindness in inviting me or whether I should rather first of all express my regret for my slight knowledge of the beautiful Spanish language, which restricts me to these few poor words.

As this deficiency does not need to be underlined, I hasten to offer my very sincere appreciation for having been given the opportunity to attend this outstanding meeting.

For me, a Canadian, it is double happiness to be here in Caracas. The jurists of my country very seldom have the opportunity to meet their colleagues in other countries of the Americas and to exchange ideas with them and it is an honour to be here in the company of the most learned and illustrious jurists of the Hemisphere.

At the same time, I have the privilege of visiting for the first time the capital of this great country, Venezuela, which can be called the cradle not only of the great liberator, Simon Bolivar, but of liberty itself in this part of America.

...

[Kerwin's speech continued]

---

221 Library and Archives Canada, 1955/10/18-1955/11/16, File RG25-A-3-b.
222 Ibid.

How can one adequately praise the magnificent city which is Caracas today! Worthy of all admiration indeed is the imaginative labour which His Excellency the President, Don Marco Perez Jiminez, as well as so many eminent architects and engineers have dedicated to the great task of expansion and embellishment of Caracas. They have achieved an impressive success.

In celebrating today, the centenary of the Civil Code, Venezuela honours the memory of a native son of her own soil and an adopted of the sister republic of Chile, Andres Bello, whose fame as a jurist and man of letters is almost legendary. On this very special occasion   I am honoured in bringing to this distinguished group the felicitations and the friendly thoughts of the Government and people of Canada to which, with all my heart, I add my own.[223]

An update from the Canadian Embassy in Caracas, Venezuela, indicated "... six countries have so far accepted the invitation to send representatives to the ceremonies beginning November 22. Supreme Court judges (magistrates) will come from Brazil, Chile, Columbia, Mexico, Peru and the United States."[224]

Chief Justice Returns From South America

Hon. Patrick Kerwin, chief justice of Canada, has returned from attending a ceremony at Caracas, Venezuela, celebrating the 100th anniversary of the promulgation by Andres Bello of the civil code of that country.

Chief Justice Kerwin flew to Caracas and return as the guest of the Venezuelan government. Mr. Justice Hugo Black represented United States Chief Justice Earl Warren. The chief justices of several Central and South American countries likewise attended.

Hon. Mr. Justice Robert Taschereau was acting chief justice of the Supreme Court of Canada during Chief Justice Kerwin's absence.

18 Cases

The Supreme Court this morning began hearing of 18 Ontario cases on its docket. At the current fall session, the court has already heard 29 cases, seven held over from a previous term, 13 from Western Canada, three from the Maritimes and six from Quebec.

December 5 is the date of a special hearing by the Supreme Court of the cabinet "reference" on the Wilbert Coffin murder case.

The court will continue to sit right up until the eve of Christmas, but it is probable that as many as eight cases listed on the docket will have to go over until the court's winter term in the New Year.

Patrick and Georgina Kerwin's return to Canada announced, and the Court's spring session outlined. 1955.

---

223 Patrick's Venezuela Speech. Library and Archives Canada, 1955/10/18-1955/11/16, File RG25-A-3-b, Translated by Lorraine and Bill Rooney.
224 Ibid.

194

The Chief Justice and Mrs. Kerwin would take the train to New York from Ottawa on Sunday, November 20 and, the next day, would fly to Caracas and a "Mr. McKay would be meeting the Chief Justice and his wife when they arrive on the Washingtonian" and would speak with the Chief Justice on that day or on the way to the airport Monday morning to play the part of the "cautious advisor".

The Programme for the Kerwins' 1955 Venezuelan trip:

November 22

11 am   Reception by the Federal Court and the Court of Cassation. Champagne toast
4 pm   Reception in Miraflores hosted by the President of the Republic
8:30 pm Commemorative academic ceremony

November 23

11 am   Ceremony at the National Cemetery
         Afternoon Reception by the Municipal Council
9 pm   Banquet for the Delegates offered (hosted) by the Venezuelan Ministers of Internal Relations, Education and Justice

November 24

9 am   Visits to the house where the Liberator and Andres Bello were born; the university district; the Elliptical Room; the Military School and the Andres Bello High School
6 pm   Joint reception with the Academy of Political and Social Sciences and the College of Lawyers of the Federal District

November 25

Free day

November 26

7 am   Visit to the General Penitentiary of Venezuela
6:30 pm Cocktail reception sponsored by the Federal Court and the Court of Cassation representing the Judiciary. The ceremony will be held in the Armed Forces Circle.

November 27

Return

Official Visit by Queen Elizabeth, 1957

One aspect of the Chief Justice's duties included attending functions, dinners and parties, something he was often not very fond of, but some of which he quite enjoyed. One of these was the visit of Queen Elizabeth and Prince Philip in October of 1957. Georgina saved the programme outlining the events that began with the Royals' arrival at RCAF Station Uplands in Ottawa.

On her first official visit to Canada as the monarch, Queen Elizabeth II spent four days in Canada's capital, and officially opened the first session of the 23rd Parliament of Canada on October 23, 1957.

The programme detailed events from beginning to end, almost minute by minute, starting with item #1, "15:15 hours, the RCAF Training Command Band commences to play". At 16:25 hours, the Royal Aircraft lands and the Royal Standard is broken out followed by a 21-gun salute. The item listed at 16:41 hours was:

Prince Phillip, Queen Elizabeth and Patrick (bottom left) at the opening of Parliament, October 1957.(City of Ottawa Archives, MG: 393, Code: AN-P-003727-026,1957-10-23).

Following the inspection of the guard, the Prime Minister presents the following people to Her Majesty:

Chief Justice and Mrs. Kerwin
Dean of the Diplomatic Corps and Mrs. Ustun
Mayor of Ottawa and Mrs. Nelms
Chief of the Air Staff and Mrs. Campbell
Commanding Officer, RCAF Station Uplands and Mrs. Mussells.

Chief Justice Kerwin meets Queen Elizabeth II and Prince Philip, 1957.

The opening of Parliament was followed by a state dinner in honour of Her Majesty at Government House, known as Rideau Hall (the official home of the Canadian Governor General, located on Sussex Drive in Ottawa). While in Ottawa the Queen also laid a wreath at the National War Memorial, spoke to the country on CBC radio and television, presided at a meeting of the Queen's Privy Council for Canada, attended numerous events and state receptions, inaugurated work on the 'Queensway' superhighway that was to be built through the city of Ottawa, and was the guest of honour at a dinner at the Prime Minister's home at 24 Sussex Drive. A busy schedule for anyone, to be sure.

Queen Elizabeth, Prince Philip and many dignitaries at state dinner; Patrick 2nd from right October 1957.

~

Official Visit of President Kennedy, 1961

In May of 1961, President Kennedy of the U.S.A. and his wife made their first official visit to Canada. The whole affair was carefully planned down to the minute and included having President and Mrs. Kennedy meet Chief Justice Kerwin and Mrs. Kerwin a few times during the trip.

The Kerwins meet the US President and Mrs. Kennedy, as well as the Governor General and Mrs. Vanier, 1961.

Georgina Kerwin at home in their apartment on Wilbrod Street, Ottawa. 1961.

Georgina kept the original minute-by-minute programme detailing the arrival of the Kennedys at 4:30 p.m. at RCAF Station Uplands on Tuesday, May 16, 1961.

P.M.   PROGRAMME

4:37   The President is escorted to the dais.
         The Royal Guard of Honour, the Colour Party and the Central Band accord a Royal Salute. Twenty-one gun salute commences.
4:38   The President inspects the Guard of Honour accompanied by the Guard Commander, the President's military Aide and the Commanding Officer.

4:43   Following the inspection of the guard, the Governor General
        introduces to the President and Mrs. Kennedy:

>   Chief Justice of Canada and Mrs. Kerwin
>   Dean of the Diplomatic Corps and Madame Lacoste
>   Chairman Chief of Staff and Mrs. Miller
>   Mayor of Ottawa
>   Commanding Officer and Mrs. Mussells.

President presents the members of his suite.

The events continue until all the welcomes, speeches and replies were made by those designated to do so. Within the Programme, it is noted that the Royal Guard of Honour and the Colour Party are composed of personnel from RCAF Training Command and are described as (Family Archives):

> The Royal Guard of Honour comprises one hundred men, including three officers, one warrant officer, six non-commissioned officers, and ninety airmen, commanded by Flight Lieutenant R. J. Henderson.
> The Colour Party comprises eight men commanded by Flight Lieutenant A. A. Jagoes.

The event had started at exactly at 3:15 p.m. that afternoon just prior to the arrival of the honoured guests and ended exactly at 5:10 p.m. with the guests departing the viewing stands.

At 8:00 PM that same day, a State Dinner was held in honour of the President and Mrs. Kennedy at Government House in Ottawa. Georgina kept the pamphlet announcing the dinner, which included the seating plan. President Kennedy and Governor General Vanier were seated in the middle of the head table, Chief Justice Kerwin was seated two seats to the right of the President, between Mrs. Vanier and Mrs. Diefenbaker, the Prime Minister's wife. Georgina Kerwin, sitting three seats to the left of the Governor General, sat between Prime Minister Diefenbaker and the Ambassador of France.

"President Kennedy greatly admired the Canadian genius for ordered ceremony, and the Vaniers were struck by his humility and by Jacqueline Kennedy's lack of sophistication." [225] Many years later, when asked about meeting the President and Mrs. Kennedy, our grandmother, Georgina, said that Mrs. Kennedy was quite a pleasant person to speak with.

---

225 Robert Speaight, *Vanier - Soldier, Diplomat & Governor General* (Collins, 1970), 383.

ARRIVAL OF

THE PRESIDENT OF THE UNITED STATES OF AMERICA

AND MRS. KENNEDY

R.C.A.F. STATION UPLANDS, OTTAWA
TUESDAY, MAY 16, 1961 AT 4.30 P.M.

ADMIT TO STAND IN HANGAR NO. 11

Hon. Patrick Kerwin, P.C.

HOLDERS OF TICKETS ARE REQUESTED TO BE IN
THEIR PLACES NOT LATER THAN THIRTY (30) MINUTES
BEFORE THE ANNOUNCED TIME OF ARRIVAL.

C

16

ARRIVAL OF

THE PRESIDENT OF THE UNITED STATES OF AMERICA

AND MRS. KENNEDY

R.C.A.F. STATION UPLANDS, OTTAWA
TUESDAY, MAY 16, 1961 AT 4.30 P.M.

ADMIT TO STAND IN HANGAR NO. 11

Mrs. Kerwin

HOLDERS OF TICKETS ARE REQUESTED TO BE IN
THEIR PLACES NOT LATER THAN THIRTY (30) MINUTES
BEFORE THE ANNOUNCED TIME OF ARRIVAL.

C

15

Tickets for admission to the airport.

On the subject of the Kennedy visit, Barb McCollum could not wait to get to the Bakers' cottage on Lake Simcoe that summer so she could speak with Georgina about meeting Mrs. Kennedy. Barb recalled that Georgina spoke well of Mrs. Kennedy.

In a June 12, 2014 email Barb wrote:

After our greeting, I remember sitting down with your grandmother and asking her all about the Kennedys. They had been to Ottawa just the month before and she told me some great little stories. She just loved Mrs. Kennedy and said that she (Jackie) had told her she was a little nervous because it was their first trip abroad and that she had had a nice discussion with the First Lady. She said that Mrs. Kennedy told her that all she wanted to do was make a good, happy, comfortable home for her husband in the White House, but again mentioned that she was a tad nervous because it was their first foray. I think your grandfather was totally taken by her as well as by the President. I will never forget that discussion.

~

Canadian Council of Christians and Jews

202

One of Patrick's outside interests included working with the Canadian Council of Christians and Jews. This organization sought to promote justice, understanding and amity among the many racial, religious and ethnic groups in Canada. It sought the establishment of a social order in which the ideals of brotherhood and justice would become the standards for human relationships. In order to achieve these ends, the organization began to promote what it called "Brotherhood Week".

In 1963, Patrick was acting as co-chairman of Brotherhood Week, which was set for the week starting February 16, 1963, just over two weeks after his death as it turned out. It was Patrick's viewpoint that, in a country such as Canada, it was necessary for each person to accommodate himself to the views of others. The press release issued by this group was published across Canada — the following is the article as it appeared in the *Ottawa Citizen* newspaper:

Brotherhood Week Feb. 16 1963 opens on Sunday

Brotherhood Week, which opens this Sunday, has been proclaimed by federal, provincial and municipal leaders across the nation.
Programs on the theme of the week have been arranged by schools, churches, service clubs, and many other organizations.
In a country like Canada, each person must accommodate himself to the views of others, the late Chief Justice Patrick Kerwin of the Supreme Court of Canada said in a statement prepared as co-chairman of the week.
Co-chairman Dr. Marcel Faribault has called on all Canadians to rededicate themselves to tolerance, truth, and friendship as the basis of civic and political order.
Celebrated in one or two communities 16 years ago, Brotherhood Week has been developed by the Canadian Council of Christians and Jews into a national observance.[226]

In Patrick's own statement, issued only a few days before his death, he explained his stance on the organization,

The name of the organization [Canadian Council of Christians and Jews] should be self-explanatory, but I have often wondered if such were the case. It should remind us all that Canadians are descendants of various forebearers and that the two named sections of the population should serve

---

226 "Brotherhood Week Feb. 16 1963 opens on Sunday", *Ottawa Citizen*, Feb. 16, 1963, 9.

to emphasize not only the advisability but the necessity of each person accommodating himself to the views of others. By doing this we will ensure a happy and prosperous Canada and give evidence of that love of freedom which should animate the hearts and minds of all mankind.

A newspaper article kept by Georgina was written by Patrick. This undated item read:

Present Campaign to Determine Catholic History of Future

By The Hon. Patrick Kerwin, P. C.
Honorary Patron

To a great extent, the history of our Archdiocese in the years immediately ahead will be determined by the success of this campaign.

Canada is in one of its greatest periods of transition and growth. Out of this boom period, a new and even greater era will emerge. Catholics of the Archdiocese are faced with a unique obligation. They must match the dynamic material expansion of their country by helping to provide an intellectual and spiritual leadership which will rightly direct all the new growth.

Our most pressing need is trained spiritual leadership. We can produce this responsible leadership, in the clergy and laity, only by providing for the training of our young men.

By building adequate educational facilities, we will be conferring untold benefits upon both the Church and our community for generations to come.[227]

---

227 "Present Campaign to Determine Catholic History of Future", uncredited newspaper article, Georgina Kerwin's collection.

THE STATE AND THE LAW

Among the prominent figures at the official opening of the Second Commonwealth and Empire Law Conference in the Supreme Court Building this morning were, left to right, Chief Justice Kerwin of the Supreme Court of Canada; Justice Minister Fulton, Attorney General of Canada, and Viscount Kilmuir, Lord Chancellor of England.

(Journal Photo by Dominion Wide)

Patrick (left), at opening of the Second Commonwealth and Empire Law Conference, The *Ottawa Journal*, 1960.

It is not enough that the Court should be right;
it must also seem to be right.

—Chief Justice Patrick Kerwin in a speech
given to the Canadian Club
Ottawa, May 1955

Chapter 13

February 1963 and Beyond

On Saturday, February 2, 1963 Patrick died of a heart attack in their Wilbrod Street apartment. At the time of his death his wife and his son, George, who was visiting, were with him. Flags on Parliament Hill flew at half-mast that day marking the death of a valued and vital Canadian.

The *Guelph Mercury* wrote:

> Chief Justice Kerwin, who also held the title of administrator
> of the Government in the absence of the Governor General,
> was active until the time of death. An associate who talked to
> him a few hours before he died said he appeared to be in
> good health. [228]

This was the death of a kind and beloved husband, father, grandfather, and loyal and respected friend to many. This man was third in order of precedence in the Canadian Government, and Chief Justice of the Supreme Court of Canada; the man who brought his considerable expertise and experience to the Court; the man whose administration had brought order and efficiency to the Court; the man who had acted as the Administrator of Canada many times when the Governor General of the day was away from Canada. His contribution to the law in Canada was, to say the least, and in the opinion of many, substantial.

Patrick Grandcourt Kerwin had served on the Supreme Court of Canada for a total of twenty-seven years, six months and twelve days. This almost matched the time served by Justices H. E. Taschereau and R. Taschereau but not quite as long as Chief Justice Rinfret (twenty-nine years, eight months and twenty days) or the longest serving, Chief Justice Duff (thirty-seven years, three months and ten days).[229]

In his time as a Justice of the Supreme Court and then as the Chief Justice of the Court, Patrick worked alongside a number of Prime Ministers, each bringing their own influence to appointments

---

228 *Guelph Daily Mercury*, Feb. 4, 1963, 8.
229 Courtesy of Professor Gordon Bale, Queen's University, 2012.

to the Court and to matters of the day. Chronologically listed, they were:

The Right Honourable Richard Bedford Bennett
(appointed P. Kerwin to the Supreme Court)
The Right Honourable William Lyon Mackenzie King
The Right Honourable Louis Stephen St. Laurent
(appointed P. Kerwin as Chief Justice of the Supreme Court)
The Right Honourable John George Diefenbaker

A state funeral was held at St. Joseph's Roman Catholic Church, located just across the street from the Kerwin home. A pontifical high mass was solemnized with Archbishop M. J. Lemieux officiating. The church was filled with family, friends and many dignitaries. I watched from the apartment window across the street with my younger sister and brother. Our mother had decided that our older siblings could attend but that we younger children (Kathleen (6), Matthew (4) and I (8)) were to watch from across the street in our grandparents' apartment while under the watchful eye of a very nice lady. It was a strange and unsettling experience since I did understand that he was gone. I also recall reading the notes attached to the many, and seemingly over-flowing, number of flower arrangements that had been received from around the world — the three of us were very impressed at this and were not entirely certain where all the countries were. The number of arrangements threatened to overtake the entry and large living room of the apartment. But the one I remember most vividly is the multi-coloured floral wreath from Queen Elizabeth II and her husband — it seemed huge to us children at the time and was taller than any one of us. We watched the procession as everyone filed into the church, watching for Prime Minister Diefenbaker and others whom we youngsters recognized by ourselves or with the help of our sitter. We were sorry that our very kind and sweet grandfather was no longer with us.

I remember him sitting in his leather rocking chair in his study. I recall the smells, textures and arrangement of his study and my grandfather, always the gentle, patient and kind man we had not known long enough.

Prime Minister Diefenbaker said the death of the Chief Justice was a "great and tragic loss for Canada". The PM added that Patrick was —

...a distinguished lawyer, a great jurist and ... a kindly man. His devotion was to justice and freedom. I feel a distinct personal sense of loss in his passing and extend not only on behalf of the Government of Canada but personally heartfelt sympathy to his widow and members of his family ... as Chief Justice he earned the admiration and respect that has come to few.[230]

Patrick relaxing with his pipe and book, circa 1955.

Governor General Vanier said he was "shocked beyond words" to hear of the death, then added, "He was a dear devoted friend who was always happy to deputize for me, sometimes at great inconvenience to himself. For many years he has filled with grace and wisdom his exalted office. I shall miss his friendship and help."[231]

The Leader of the Opposition, Lester B. Pearson, said to be shaken by the news, stated he and his wife were "deeply shocked" at the unexpected death of the Chief Justice, "whom we have known for many years as a personal friend. Canada has lost a very great and devoted public servant."[232]

Others who attended the funeral included Chief Justice Dana Porter of Ontario, Chief Justice Lucien Tremblay of Québec and Chief Justice J. D. McRuer of the High Court of Justice of Ontario. Honourary pallbearers were: Diefenbaker, Justice Minister Fleming, the eight members of the Supreme Court, Justice J. K. Kearney of the Exchequer Court of Canada, Ross McKinnie, president of the Canadian Bar Association, and W. Kenneth Campbell, administrative officer of the Supreme Court and a devoted friend. Over four hundred members of the Federal and Ontario Governments, the City of Ottawa, the bar and bench, representatives of the diplomatic corps, friends and family attended the funeral. Patrick Grandcourt Kerwin (1889-1963) was buried at Notre Dame

230 *Ottawa Citizen*, Feb. 4, 1963.
231 *Ottawa Journal*, Feb. 4, 1963.
232 Ibid.

Cemetery in Ottawa, Ontario, next to his son, John Philip Kerwin (1923-1944).

Besides his wife, Patrick was survived by his daughter, Isobel (Mrs. John McKenna) and sons, Patrick Kilroy and George as well as his sister, Mrs. George Beatty, of Sarnia, his brother, Vernon L. Kerwin, of Detroit and fourteen grandchildren.

Georgina received messages of sympathy from all parts of Canada as well as from many other countries. The Queen sent a message of sympathy from the royal yacht Britannia after leaving Suva, Fiji, for New Zealand. The Queen's message read, "I am grieved to learn of the death of the Chief Justice of Canada. My husband and I send you our sincerest sympathy in your loss."

In a letter to Isobel offering sympathy, an old friend of hers, Mary McElroy, recalled, "...a twelve-hour bridge marathon with Patrick and Isobel during the war". Mrs. McElroy also said that, "I always had the feeling that, if I ever needed advice, I wouldn't hesitate to ask Mr. Kerwin. I respected and admired him so. He was a very remarkable and wonderful man."[233]

In a formal tribute at a Court meeting, held on the Wednesday after his death (February 6th), Mr. Justice Robert Taschereau, Acting Chief Justice, said the late Chief Justice made a "great contribution to the jurisprudence of the country and his judgments reveal his wisdom, his erudition and philosophic insight". Then, with his voice choked with emotion, Mr. Justice Taschereau said, "We bow before the grave of the late Chief Justice", then added, "I sat on the bench of the Supreme Court of Canada with the Chief Justice for twenty-two years and it was my privilege to fully appreciate his great qualities of heart and mind."[234]

On February 5, 1963 the *St. Catharines Standard* newspaper reported:

> The death of Chief Justice Patrick Kerwin in Ottawa on
> Saturday will be widely mourned, and in St. Catharines
> sincere sympathy will be extended to a son, Patrick Jr., well
> known city lawyer...The shock of his passing will be softened
> by the knowledge that in whatever he did, he served well.

During Patrick's time as Chief Justice, he was known for expediting the Court's handling of cases such that there were only a few cases on which judgments were still to be given at the time of his death.

---

233 Letter from Mrs. Mary McElroy, Ottawa, to Mrs. Isobel (Kerwin) McKenna, Feb. 1963.
234 The *Canadian Press*, Feb. 7, 1963.

In a book by Balcome, McBride, and Russell, a summary of Patrick's decisions and style were outlined as follows:

> A devotee of bridge, Kerwin preferred to play his judicial cards close to the vest. In such cases as *Saumur v. Québec (City)* [1953] 2 S.C.R. 299 and *Switzman v. Elbling* [1957] S.C.R. 285) he opted for a narrower ground of decision than some of his colleagues, particularly the more celebrated Rand. In the second *Boucher v. R.* [1951] S.C.R. 265) decision, and in *Roncarelli v. Duplessis* [1959] S.C.R. 121), our subject wrote much less than his more forthcoming brethren. Adherence to precedent, brevity of expression, and caution in experimentation with the law were the ABCs of Kerwin's judicial primer.[235]

Similarly, in the major cases of his judicial prime, Kerwin voted in a manner which respected individual rights while still balancing the well-being of the community. Moreover, his reasoning consistently won the support of his judicial peers. His record drew praise in his time and deserves credit in ours.

Patrick was described as:

> Not without his paradoxes, although, owing to an underplayed persona, they seemed relatively mild. He was an Irishman evidently unenchanted by language. He was a Roman Catholic who upheld the then vituperatively anti-Catholic Jehovah's Witnesses in their struggle with the Catholic authorities of Quebec. He was a man who could both eschew politics himself as a young lawyer and, in a convocation address many years later, urge University of Toronto graduates to stand for elective office, deeming it "an ambition which cannot be too highly praised". He was an important public official, ranked third in the official table of precedence for Canada, after the Governor General and the Prime Minister, who was little known to the public because he shunned publicity, infrequently granted interviews, and rarely bothered with the social whirl of Ottawa. In him, professional correctness, even aloofness, and personal kindliness formed an equable blend.[236]

> Kerwin was a major, even leading, participant in some historic assertions of authority by the Supreme Court of Canada on behalf of civil liberties. But all the while he advocated restraint in stating the reasons for these judgments. Crisp decisions and narrow doctrines were hallmarks of Kerwin's jurisprudence.[237]

---

235 Balcome, McBride and Russell, *Supreme Court,* 151.
236 Ibid., 184-185.
237 Ibid., 186.

Kerwin was low-keyed and understated, laconic and reserved. Here personal temperament and, as he perceived it, institutional requirement, appeared to conjoin. If law is a tyranny of words, then Kerwin would have been a constitutional monarch, unobtrusive and circumspect to a fault and, above all, sparing and guarded in utterance from the bench. Finally, Kerwin was a quiet man on "a quiet court in an unquiet country". The dual impact of a judge so situated and so disposed was both to restrict the risks and to limit the legacy of the institution that he strove to serve.[238]

When he was a member of the Supreme Court, and even when he was Chief Justice, Patrick remained little known to the Canadian public. This was certainly par for the course in his time. The attention centered on his colleague Justice Rand's more speculative opinions. As it happened, Patrick, although comparatively ignored by the scholars and critics, did not lack the esteem of his peers.

Justice Martland, who sat on the Court with him, maintained that Patrick was "underrated" as a judge. He said that there was "no flamboyance" about Patrick, that he had "great common sense," that he was an advocate of "the less said, the better," and that, in sum, "he was a very good Commander-in-Chief".

According to Martland, Patrick was a pragmatist; there was no arm-twisting of any kind. Martland stated that he was the type of Chief Justice who was always there and always anxious to help. Martland commented that "Kerwin had always been overshadowed by Rand and that, in his view, Kerwin had been overlooked for too long".[239]

Justice Abbott said of Patrick, "I think Kerwin was a very much underrated judge. Personally, I found him a very good judge. He was a well-trained common lawyer and a well-trained judge with great experience. I found him a good Chief Justice."[240]

Shortly after the death of Chief Justice Kerwin, the Minister of Justice and Attorney General of Canada, the Hon. Donald Fleming, told Prime Minister Diefenbaker that he was not going to be a candidate for re-election and would leave public life. The Prime Minister made no attempt to argue or alter his decision, but said, "I've been thinking about the death of Chief Justice Kerwin and thought you would be a good person to be Chief Justice." The

---

238 Balcome, McBride and Russell, *Supreme Court,* 187.
239 Ibid., Interview with Justice Martland by Dawn Russell, as conveyed to Russell in a letter Oct. 17, 1985.
240 Balcome, McBride and Russell, *Supreme Court,* 225.

proposal to be the possible successor to Kerwin was a surprise to Fleming in a time of turmoil in the Conservative government.

When the Prime Minister took this idea to the cabinet, not all were in favour. Some opposition was expressed to appointing one who was not already a member of the Court. A few weeks later, the PM showed Fleming a personal letter he had received from Governor General Vanier in which the Governor General recommended against the appointment on the same grounds and Vanier recalled that Sir Charles Fitzpatrick, then Minister of Justice, had been appointed Chief Justice in 1906, but had never been accepted by his colleagues on the Court.

Fleming felt the Prime Minister could not make up his mind on the subject of who to appoint to the post and said,

> All he accomplished by continuing to dangle it was to promote uncertainty and delay my plans to return to private life and resume my professional practice.[241]

Chief Justice Kerwin died in the midst of a cabinet crisis and a parliamentary conflict that would ultimately bring down Prime Minister Diefenbaker's government. During frantic attempts to save his government through restructuring the cabinet, some cabinet rebels viewed the sudden Supreme Court vacancy as an opportunity to remove the Prime Minister by offering him the post.

Diefenbaker wrote of this time:

> Later that Sunday afternoon, Senator McCutcheon had made the startling proposal that I become Chief Justice of the Supreme Court; he had checked it out with the other Judges, he told me, and they were agreeable. Indeed, he said to Olive [Diefenbaker], "Well, day after tomorrow your husband will be the first man who has occupied both positions in this country, and only one other person in a democracy will have done the same. Taft was President of the Unites States and also Chief Justice of the United States."[242]

---

241 Donald Fleming, *So Very Near - The Political Memoir of the Hon. Donald Fleming*, (McLelland and Stewart, 1985), thanks to Professor Bale, Queen's University.
242 John G. Diefenbaker, *One Canada, Memoirs: The tumultuous years, 1962-1967* (Macmillan of Canada/NAL, 1975), 163.

Diefenbaker added that they presented —

> ... in the face of this mass of resignations [of his Cabinet],
> I would agree to their appointment of me as Chief Justice of
> the Supreme Court of Canada ... the position that was to be
> my 'reward', is a prerogative power of the Prime Minister; they
> were in fact offering me what only I could give.[243]

In Peter C. Newman's book, *Renegade in Power*, he describes
George Hees, Minister of Trade and Commerce, appearing at 24
Sussex Drive to confront the Prime Minister with a desperate
proposal — be appointed Chief Justice of the Supreme Court of
Canada. Newman goes on to write, "Diefenbaker recoiled at the
suggestion, but asked Hees to wait. He went to another room and
telephoned Gordon Churchill (Tory House Leader), to tell him of
the offer. Churchill suggested Diefenbaker tell Hees to go to hell.
Diefenbaker did."[244]

The same day that Diefenbaker rejected the suggestion of the
chief justiceship, his government was defeated in the House. The
vacancy at the Court was not filled until after a general election
had taken place and a new government had taken office. On the
same day that Lester Person was sworn into office as Prime
Minister, April 22, 1963, Robert Taschereau, the Senior Puisne
Justice, was elevated to preside over the Court.

~

A few years after Patrick's death, Mrs. Kerwin had moved from
her apartment on Wilbrod Street in downtown Ottawa to the
home of her daughter, Isobel (Kerwin) McKenna and family, located
in the suburb of Alta Vista.

Patrick's granddaughter, Kathleen (McKenna) Thomas, daughter
of Isobel, and my younger sister, recalled our grandmother, Georgina,
speaking one day of the trip to Venezuela.

It was on January 13, 1976 when Kathleen was having a quiet
dinner with her grandmother that Georgina reminisced about the
trip she and her husband had taken to South America. Georgina
said they got to meet a great many interesting people including
the President of Venezuela, Marcos Pérez Jiménez. They had happily
toured around the capital city of Caracas, which they had both
found particularly beautiful and interesting. Then she and her

---

243 Diefenbaker, *One Canada*, 158-9.
244 Newman, *Renegade in Power*, 370-1.

husband had attended a dinner held in their honour where the meal was served on gold-plated dinner service with matching goblets for the wine. Georgina also recalled that her husband had purchased some exquisite jewelry for her on that trip as well as a picture that "reminded him of what she looked like on their wedding day". Kathleen still has this picture of an unknown young woman in a wedding dress that does, uncannily, very much resemble our grandmother on her wedding day.

Kathleen was the last person to have spoken with our grandmother. Later that evening Georgina died of a brain hemorrhage. Georgina (Mace) Kerwin is remembered for her strong support and dedication to her husband and family.

*It may appear when I have finished
that the title is too ambitious
but I can only hope that, unlike charity,
it will not be found to cover a multitude of sins.*

—Justice Patrick Kerwin in a speech to The Lawyers' Club
entitled "Law and Literature",
Toronto, 1952

Epilogue

From the start of his career, Patrick seemed uncomplicated, pleasant, and ambitious. Success, advancement, distinction and, finally, the highest laurel of the law all came to him. However, there was more to him than that.

In his many years in the courts, no one witnessed Patrick act rudely to counsel appearing before him nor was it ever known for him to lose his temper in court. It is wonderful to know that a man who acted with such decorum over the many years is still having his words heard through the judgments provided during his career.

Patrick Grandcourt Kerwin's innate sense of fair play and justice permeated his work from the time he practised law in Guelph, to sitting on the bench of the Ontario High Court, and Supreme Court of Canada. In his own life, he kept it simple and straightforward. As his daughter noted, "If you presented him with a good argument, he would weigh the issue on its own merits."

During a speech he gave upon receiving an Honourary Doctorate of Laws at the University of Toronto in 1956, Patrick spoke of the past, the future and the notion of 'goodness'. On that day in May, he stated,

> Having been born and practised law in Ontario, it is particularly gratifying that such an academic distinction should come to me from this University, situate in the capital of the Province and exercising a profound influence not only in Ontario but throughout Canada...

> It is a far cry from the early days of this institution and its predecessor, from the days of Upper Canada and muddy York, and from the times of comparatively slow motion in the way of travel. Since then great strides have been taken in all fields of human endeavour and the sons and daughters of this, and other universities have taken a prominent part in the march of progress, — not only in practical and mundane things but also in research and in the sphere of ideas and ideals. This in truth is an exemplification of the principle set forth by Newman in his *Idea of a University* that "the good is always useful".

Goodness for the individual and, therefore, for all mankind. As Canadians we are concerned with the meaning and effect of that quality, in Ontario, in the other Provinces and in the Territories. Its full force may be felt only if the rights of the individual as a human being be held in high regard and nothing be done, or suffered, to cast him from his pedestal. To put the matter no higher, each one who graduates from this University has a duty to himself, to his parents and relatives and to his professors to see to it that these rights are protected.[245]

The extent of Patrick's experience in the field of law brought to the fore for him this notion of goodness, that the individual was the most important aspect, as well as justice was best served when not delayed. His reputation was that of a fair and hard-working man. He had worked long and was not far from retirement age. But Patrick Grandcourt Kerwin was never able to retire and enjoy a time of ease and reflection. He was never able to enjoy the 'evening of life'; a time spent in relaxation, deliberation and relishing his grandchildren's achievements. As well, he was unable to have time to ponder a life well lived and a life of service to the public good.

Interesting bits of life intrude on one's self every now and then to help us recall times past and those things that have made an impression, no matter how small. I learned that Patrick had taken up smoking a pipe in order to stop smoking cigarettes. On that note, for me, the smell of his particular pipe tobacco is one reminder of time spent with my grandfather.

Even today, so many years later, when a gentle waft of that certain type of pipe smoke comes my way, I am reminded of him sitting in his squeaky leather rocking chair at home in the study. In my mind, there he is, having a few puffs then, and later, relighting the pipe for a few more minutes of enjoyment for him as he watched over us. It is a warm and poignant feeling that reminds me again how much I miss him.

---

245 Chief Justice Kerwin, Address at the University of Toronto, May 25, 1956, 1-2.

... a dear devoted friend who was always happy to deputize for me, sometimes at great inconvenience to himself. For many years he has filled with grace and wisdom his exalted office. I shall miss his friendship and help.

—Governor General
Georges Vanier
1963

Obituaries

Chief Justice Patrick G. Kerwin died at home on February 2, 1963.

Following is a selection of obituaries and tributes, collected by his wife as well as Ken Campbell (Patrick's personal secretary) and others.

The Honourable Patrick Kerwin, PC, 1889-1963.

Selections from *Chitty's Law Journal*, March-April 1963.[246]

He was sensible and sensitive. He understood the common people. With him, every lawyer had his day in Court. He was an example of dignity and courtesy. He had a profound respect for the Rule of Law which stemmed from his integrity and competence in our various systems of law.

He has made a great contribution to the jurisprudence of this country, and his judgments reveal his wisdom, his erudition and philosophic insights.

... sagesse et l'intégrité ne pouvaient qu'inspirer la confiance la plus entière.

—The Hon. Mr. Justice Taschereau

On the Bench he was dignified without being austere, courteous without being remote, gentle without yielding firmness, supremely modest, companionable, even-tempered, and good-humoured. In the noblest sense he was a Christian gentleman. There was a sublime simplicity about his life that demonstrated the true beauty of simplicity and the greatness of simplicity. He was indeed a very gentle soul.

—The Hon. Donald Fleming, Q.C., Minister of Justice

... le Canada perd un juge éclairé, imbu de justice, un juriste éminent, une personnalité frappante, un parfait citoyen et gentilhomme.

—Rodrigue Farley, Q.C.

---

246 *Chitty's Law Journal*, March-April 1963, 241-242. The full text of the article is reproduced at the end of this section.

The *Telegram* in Toronto wrote of Patrick upon his death:

History is often called whimsical, but when it chose Patrick Kerwin to be Chief Justice of Canada, it put the right man in the right place with a fine sense of timing. For by training and temperament he was able to enhance the sense of order that comes from the interpretation of the law.

His quiet speech, quiet living and impeccable courtesy richly contributed to the sense of order that emanated from the marble and mahogany building which serves as the highest court in the land.

His unruffled temperament was backed by profound scholarship in constitutional law. The authority of this combination was felt in Canada's transition during his tenure from a country dependent on Privy Council decisions to a more self-reliant status.

With quiet courage he broke a four-four tie in the court in quashing a conviction against a member of Jehovah Witnesses who distributed a tract call "Quebec's Burning Hatred for God and Christ". His words on that occasion are a milestone in the annals of religious liberty in Canada: "An intention to bring the administration of justice into hatred or contempt or exert dissatisfaction against it is not seditious unless there is also the intention to incite people to violence against it."

His death brings to a close a career distinguished by unwavering persistence, hard work and natural gifts, a career that will live in memory to the service performed to a grateful country and the inspiration it proves for others eager to serve.[247]

The *Globe & Mail* wrote:

Chief Justice Kerwin, who died in Ottawa on Saturday, was what a good jurist should be — an outstanding champion of the rights of men. His career demonstrated his belief in a principle he expressed in 1955 to an international conference at Harvard University: That the individual is the most important fact in the world.

Chief Justice Kerwin, before and after his appointment to the post in 1954, was, as well, a believer in the obligations of individuals in democracy. He felt, as he said in a 1956 University of Toronto convocation address, that "unless men and women of character are prepared to undergo sacrifices to occupy elective offices, the public and private lives of Canadians will suffer as a consequence."[248]

---

247 "The Order Maker", *Telegram*, Toronto ON, Feb. 5, 1963, 5.
248 "Chief Justice Kerwin," *Globe and Mail*, Feb. 5, 1963.

The *Globe & Mail* (continued).

He was a tough-minded realist who maintained a no-nonsense attitude in court and devoted his time to hard work, shunning the social whirl. But he was also a courtly figure of great personal charm.

Because appeals to the Privy Council had been abolished during the term of his predecessor, Chief Justice Kerwin was the first Canadian jurist to take over a Supreme Court that had the final legal voice in Canada. It was a laurel that he deserved, and wore well.

Many newspapers used the same *Canadian Press* (CP) story that came over the wires and some of following items were included in these stories:

His passing will be deeply felt in many places. An equally qualified successor will be hard to find.
(*Sarnia Observer* ON; from Professor Bale, Queen's University)

A tough, serious-minded jurist, he ran court business with a firm hand tempered by a sense of fairness.
(*Barrie Examiner*, ON)

He took great pains to ensure that counsel appearing before him were given ample opportunity to present their cases but became impatient at repetitious argument.
(*Brantford Expositor*, ON)

The court's acknowledged expert on constitutional law, Chief Justice Kerwin played a leading role in some of the most famous constitutional cases ever to come before the court for decision.
(*Barry's Bay Review*, ON)

During the nine years he served as Chief Justice, he did much to expedite the court's handling of cases. His view was that the court should do everything in its power to ensure that judgments were not unduly delayed.
(*Owen Sound Sun Times*, ON)

He leaves the nation's highest court as strong a defender of the law of the land and the rights of individual citizens as it has ever been; and no greater tribute can be paid any jurist.
(*Calgary Albertan*, AB)

His interests were wide and his vision national.
(*Globe & Mail*, ON)

A quiet, studious man, he was in the best traditions of the legal profession. By his character and his devotion to duty, he added lustre to his high office. May he rest in peace.
(*Antigonish Casket*, NS)

He brought a dignity and an inquiring mind to the post that helped it maintain the lustre given it by those giants of Canadian jurisprudence, Lyman Duff and Thibaudeau Rinfret.
(*Hamilton Spectator*, ON)

Patrick Kerwin, humanitarian and wise judge, takes his place among the great men Canada has produced.
(*Ottawa Citizen*, ON)

Chief Justice Kerwin deserved far better recognition by his countrymen. So does any man who qualifies for that high office.
(*Lethbridge Herald*, AB)

To head Canada's court of last resort was a great responsibility. No man could have felt that responsibility more deeply, or have sought to carry it out more rigorously.
(*Montreal Gazette*, QC)

Chief Justice W. B. Scott, of the Québec Superior Court: "His judgments were marked by a clarity and common sense and always commanded respect. Present and future generations of Canadians will be indebted to him for the heritage of his reported decisions."
(*Montreal Star*, QC)

Justice Minister Fleming said that as long as Canadians value the rule of law and devotion of men to public service they will have reason to remember their debt to Hon. Patrick Kerwin.
(*Hamilton Spectator*, ON)

His services to the administration of justice in Canada were very great and deserve remembrance.
(*Toronto Star*, ON)

Scores of dignitaries attended the last rites of the brilliant jurist who died Saturday at the age of 73.
(*Peterborough Examiner*, ON)

His visits to the old home town, although fewer these past years, took him not to the halls of the mighty but into the kitchens and old-fashioned parlours of the people among whom he was raised in Our Lady of Mercy Parish and school.
(*Sarnia Gazette*, ON)

Funeral service was held today for Hon. Patrick Kerwin, Chief Justice of Canada, a wise, humanitarian judge whose career left a permanent mark on Canadian society.
(*Saskatoon Star-Phoenix*, SK)

Never lacking in dignity, he yet insisted on what has been described as "a methodical, let's-keep-things-moving administration".
(*Montreal Gazette* QC)

Ross A. MacKimmie, Q.C. of Calgary, president of the Canadian Bar Association, said: "Canada has lost one of its ablest judges. He will be very much missed. He was a great administrator and completely and entirely impartial in his judicial work."
(*Windsor Star*, ON)

The full text of the article in *Chitty's Law Journal* (March-April 1963, 241-242) is presented on the following pages.

NOTES AND MEMORANDA FROM THE SUPREME COURT OF CANADA

A MEMORIAL TO
THE HONOURABLE PATRICK KERWIN
PRIVY COUNCILLOR AND SOMETIME CHIEF JUSTICE OF CANADA

PATRICK KERWIN

Born October 25, 1889

Called to the Bar of Ontario, Trinity Term, 1911.
Appointed King's Counsel, 1928.
Appointed puisne judge of the Supreme Court of Ontario September 28, 1932.
Appointed puisne judge of the Supreme Court of Canada July 20, 1935.
Appointed Chief Justice of Canada and sworn of the Privy Council July 1, 1954.

Died February 2, 1963

The memoranda hereunder are the addresses heard in the Supreme Court of Canada on Wednesday, the 6th day of February, 1963, and respectively made by The Honourable Mr. Justice Taschereau, The Honourable Donald Fleming, Q.C., Minister of Justice, Mr. J. J. Robinette, Q.C., and Mr. Rodrigue Farley, Q.C.

THE HON. MR. JUSTICE TASCHEREAU

It was with very deep sorrow that we learned of the death of the Chief Justice of Canada, the Honourable Patrick Kerwin.

Today, the Court wishes to express, after two days of mourning, its profound regret of the passing of this great and kind gentleman who presided over its destiny for the last nine years.

The late Chief Justice was born in Sarnia 73 years ago, and practised law at Guelph, Ontario, as a partner of the late Hugh Guthrie. He was appointed to the High Court of Justice of Ontario in 1932, and became a justice of this Court in 1935 and Chief Justice of Canada in 1954. On the same day he was appointed a member of the Privy Council.

I sat on the Bench of the Supreme Court of Canada with him for the past 22 years, and it was my privilege to fully appreciate his great qualities of heart and mind. These qualities, I know, endeared him to all his colleagues on the Bench. He was sensible and sensitive. He understood the common people. With him every lawyer had his day in Court. He was an example of dignity and courtesy. He had a profound respect for the Rule of Law which stemmed from his integrity and competence in our various systems of law.

He has made a great contribution to the jurisprudence of this country, and his judgments reveal his wisdom, his erudition and philosophic insight.

We bow before the grave of the late Chief Justice. His death is a great loss to the Bench and Bar which he has adorned for the last 50 years, and we wish to express to Mrs. Kerwin and to his family our deepest and most sincere sympathy.

C'est avec un profond sentiment de tristesse

que nous offrons notre plus sincère sympathie à Madame Kerwin et à la famille. La mort prématurée du Juge en chef du Canada a non seulement affecté ses nombreux amis, mais aussi tous les membres de la Magistrature et du Barreau. Le Juge en chef faisait non seulement partie du corps juridique, mais aussi de l'âme de la Magistrature et du Barreau, comme on fait partie de l'âme de son Église.

Il a été non seulement un grand juge, fier des libertés constitutionnelles et de celles de l'individu, mais il a été aussi un administrateur remarquable. Soucieux des droits des parties en cause, il ne permettait pas les retards qui pouvaient prolonger les litiges. Il était toujours anxieux que la justice fût dispensée rapidement.

Avec sa mort disparaît un magistrat de grande expérience, un juriste accompli, dont la sagesse et l'intégrité ne pouvaient qu'inspirer la confiance la plus entière.

Sur cette tombe qui vient de se fermer, la Cour Suprême du Canada dépose l'expression de ses regrets, et ses hommages et son admiration.

THE HON. DONALD FLEMING, Q.C., MINISTER OF JUSTICE

My Lords:—

In this moment of sorrow and separation it is meet that we should pay this last tribute in these halls of justice to the memory of a great Canadian. It is at once a privilege and a sorrowful duty to speak for the Government, for the Department of Justice, for the Canadian public and for the Canadian Bar Association.

I speak with restraint; the late Chief Justice would not have wished extended or fulsome praise. His service was monumental: the past twenty-eight years as a member of this the highest Court in and for Canada, the last nine years as its Chief Justice in these days of its ultimate jurisdiction in Canada, preceded by twenty-one years at the Bar of Ontario and three years on the trial Bench of the Supreme Court of Ontario. He was fitted then by experience, talents, study and devotion for his career on the Bench. His service has been of enormous proportions.

The integrity of the Courts, undergirded by the independence of the judiciary, supporting the rule of law, maintaining noble traditions, extending their benign protection to the rights of the individual—these are the glory of our free way of life. The integrity of the Court can be no greater than the integrity of the judges who compose it. The character of the judge is then of ultimate importance.

The Honourable Patrick Kerwin was a leading judge whose place in our history is secure. He has written many judgments which claim and will continue to claim an abiding place in Canadian jurisprudence. To his high and exacting duties he brought balanced judgment, industry, understanding, patience, conscientious devotion to duty and extraordinary administrative talents. On the Bench he was dignified without being austere, courteous without being remote, gentle without yielding firmness, supremely modest, companionable, even-tempered, good-humoured. In the noblest sense he was a Christian gentleman. There was a sublime simplicity about his life that demonstrated the true beauty of simplicity and the greatness of simplicity. He was indeed a very gentle soul.

It was my privilege to know him personally for more than thirty years and I shall always retain the memory of his friendship as one of the enriching experiences of my life.

For his public tasks he was nurtured and sustained by his home, his family, his faith.

I have been asked also to speak, my Lords, in my privileged capacity as the Honorary President of the Canadian Bar Association. I do so at the request of Mr. McKimmie, the President of the Association, who, as your Lordships will recall, came to Ottawa from the West yesterday in order to attend the funeral services for the late Chief Justice. In this regard may I very simply say that the late Honourable Patrick Kerwin lent so much to good relations between the Bench and the Bar in this country, so essential for the proper administration of justice. Always he exhibited courtesy to counsel, patience and fairness. One will not forget his assistance and the consideration he extended to junior counsel. These attributes have won him the affection and the regard and, I believe, the lasting gratitude of the Members of the Bar in all parts of Canada.

Cette Cour a subi une perte très lourde par la mort de son Juge-en-chef, l'honorable Patrick

Kerwin. Sa famille pleure le départ d'un cher mari, d'un père et d'un grand-père. Tout le Canada partage cette tristesse. Au nom du Gouvernement, au nom du Premier Ministre, au nom du ministère de la Justice, au nom de la population canadienne, au nom de l'Association du Barreau canadien, j'offre à la Cour Suprême du Canada ma sympathie chaleureuse, et ce tribut insuffisant au Juge-en-chef dont la mémoire sera à jamais retenue par les Canadiens.

My Lords, as long as Canadians value devoted service they will have reason to bear in grateful memory their debt to the late Honourable Patrick Kerwin.

JOHN J. ROBINETTE, Q.C.

My Lords:—

Speaking on behalf of the Law Society of Upper Canada, we join with your Lordships in expressing our deep and sincere sense of loss on the passing of Chief Justice Kerwin.

His Lordship had been a distinguished member of our Bar, and over the years we have watched with justifiable pride his work first as a Justice of the Supreme Court of Ontario, then as a member and finally Chief Justice of this Court.

He brought to the performance of his high judicial duties a wide knowledge of the law, an intuitive feeling for justice and a rare administrative capacity. We all know that as Chief Justice he was insistent in maintaining the high efficiency of the Court and the orderly progress of its work. Although he made it very clear to counsel when he thought they were wandering from the issues he invariably did it without harshness or any tone of rebuke.

He was very close to his family, and I think that probably one of the happiest occasions of his life was when his children so thoughtfully tendered a reception two years ago in his honour on the occasion of the 25th anniversary of his appointment to the Court.

We shall all miss him very much and we join in conveying to Mrs. Kerwin and his family our sincere and deepest sympathy.

RODRIGUE FARLEY, Q.C.

C'est avec consternation que tous ont appris, samedi dernier, le décès subit de l'Honorable Patrick Kerwin, C. P. Juge en Chef du Canada; cette nouvelle en a été d'autant plus inattendue et surprenante que l'Honorable Juge en Chef présidait activement cette Cour jusqu'à jeudi de la semaine dernière.

Dans la mort de son Honorable Juge en Chef, le Canada perd un juge éclairé, imbu de justice, un juriste éminent, une personalité frappante, un parfait citoyen et gentilhomme.

Je me permets de dire que nous, de la province de Québec, savons et nous souvenons que dès son arrivée à Ottawa en 1935 l'Honorable Juge en Chef commença à suivre des cours de français, le maîtrisa de telle sorte qu'il lui fut possible d'entendre plusieurs des causes les plus célèbres provenant de notre province et d'en prendre part aux jugements.

En terminant, à la famille de l'Honorable Juge en Chef et à tous ceux que cette perte touche de près, nous offrons nos plus sincères sympathies, ajoutant que s'il est lui-même disparu, la mémoire de ses oeuvres restera longtemps dans nos esprits.

Sound Advice

Kerwin tells members of the Lansing Bar: [249]

... these words serve to remind us that law and equity must be molded to meet conditions as they change; that law must be administered impartially and that while the quality of mercy must not be strained "Reason", as Coke put it many years ago, — "Reason is the life of the law".

To students at Osgoode Hall: [250]

However, its history does exemplify one matter that I wish to emphasize and that is, while you have now been admitted to the Bar and the practice of your chosen profession, your studies are by no means over. Just as, while Osgoode Hall is fenced in the manner considered appropriate many years ago, what transpires within its walls is not precisely the same as what occurred therein at that time, so, while the legal learning you have acquired is necessary, it must be remembered that the law is a jealous mistress and demands of you, and all her devotees, an assiduous devotion to her cause. The common law is not static but develops from era to era, and sometimes from year to year. ...

Human nature and the vagaries of its conduct are such that at first you will find it hard to separate the wheat from the chaff, the important points from the irrelevant, and it is only by application that you will be able to overcome the difficulties and obstacles. That process requires not merely busyness but also research.

Where will you find the sources from which to draw your inspiration and knowledge? In the decisions of the courts, in statutes and regulations, in recognized textbooks of authority, and in essays and articles by competent craftsmen. ...

Each one of you, however, will have office work to do or oversee, and it is in that connection that you should decide never to mingle your clients' funds with your own. ...

---

249 Kerwin, "Administration of Justice in the Canadian Federal System", Address to the
    Lansing Bar, Lansing, Michigan, U.S.A. September 4, 1940.
250 Kerwin, Address to students, Osgoode Hall, June 29, 1950.

A sound rule is that you will avoid the occasions of evil to a very great extent by rigorously keeping your clients' funds separate from those of your own. ...

Each one of you should be willing to help the oppressed and the needy, and that is generally recognized by the setting-up of various associations among the Bar organizations for that specific purpose. Lend your assistance and your talents to these and to all worthy causes in your community. Take your place among the leaders of an enlightened democracy. ...

As you progress in your practice, while cherishing the history of the past, do not forget that it has been a history of evolution. Never be satisfied that things are all for the best in the best of all possible worlds and do not permit any of the legal associations which you may join to deteriorate into a mutual admiration society. Ever be ready to take a stand for improvement!

To the Lawyers' Club of Toronto: [251]

However, a barrister who knows his case, who presents it in a clear manner, embellished perhaps, but with discretion, need have no fear of not having a fair hearing. Disraeli is reported to have described the legal mind as chiefly displaying itself in illustrating the obvious, explaining the evident, and expatiating on the commonplace. ...

Counsel must, therefore, be prepared to understand the basis of the legal rules upon which he relies and, if a judge asks, "Where does this power end?", it will not do for him to reply, "It is for the Court to say" because, undoubtedly, the judge will counter with "I am seeking guidance". If asked upon which of two conflicting propositions he relies in support of his case, counsel should not say that he will leave that to the Court. His duty is to put forward that which will assist in a determination of the litigation in his favour. Of course, he must be frank with the Court and acknowledge the existence of the other theory while, at the same time, contending for the opposite view."

---

251 Kerwin, "Law and Literature", Address to the Lawyers' Club, Toronto, Nov. 13, 1952.

At the University of New Brunswick: [252]

Freedom of thought and action does not come from the recitation of decided cases or the statement of principles enunciated in them, although each of these is necessary. The pupil must be taught not merely what the professor knows but he must be trained to think for himself so that he will appreciate the reason for a rule and apply it to circumstances as they arise. Then will he be able to distinguish those cases where the principle is inapplicable from those in which it will be proper to extend or amplify it. Nowhere is the general point put more clearly or expressively than by Cardinal Newman when, in his Sixth Discourse on University Teaching, he takes for granted, "That the true and adequate end of intellectual training and of a University is not Learning or Acquirement, but rather is Thought or Reason exercised upon Knowledge."

At a dinner at The Law Society of Upper Canada: [253]

There is no general complaint when physicians, surgeons, architects, scientists, operating in their particular spheres, use terms which have proved suitable to express their thoughts and carry on their investigations. Similarly it is necessary for the legal profession to employ a terminology which has developed through the ages, because, by trial and error, the right word or phrase has evolved to describe a situation or a problem. Surely it is not a matter for reproach that lawyers use those means to explain their client's cause in or out of court and thus enable his business to be brought to a conclusion in a shorter period of time. Legal terminology is a necessity, not merely for the practitioners but also in the best interests of the members of the public, whose servants they are. ...

There are bound to be disputations in some instances as to the applicable law, because no one pretends that law is an exact science. I am speaking now of the great mass of disputes in which a knowledge of human nature is requisite; and it is at this precise point that I venture to affirm that in a purely worldly

---

252 Kerwin, Address by the Chief Justice at the University of New Brunswick – Honourary Degree of Laws, Saint John, Oct. 15, 1954.
253 Kerwin, Address at Dinner given by The Law Society of Upper Canada, Osgoode Hall,\ To Honour our Chief Justice, Nov. 20, 1954.

sense the legal profession by its training, by its experience, and by the mingling of its members in other groups is the most appropriate that has been devised to permit the work of the world to proceed in peace. While this may appear self-evident to us, it is my suggestion that, if the practicing members be prepared on all occasions to take part in the activities of their fellow citizens, the groundwork of the complaints on behalf of some of these disappears. ...

The experience of the labourer who sought employment from a farmer may serve to exemplify the responsibilities resting upon the holder of judicial office. He was hired for one day to cut wood. The job was done satisfactorily and he was engaged to build a fence the next day. That task having been completed in good order, the man was told on the third day to separate potatoes into three piles — (1) First class; (2) Second class but still edible; (3) Fit only for the soil heap. About noon the farmer went to see how the work was progressing and discovered that his man had fainted. Upon being revived and asked what had happened he at first declined to say. The farmer pointed out that his work on the first two days had been well done and that there was nothing difficult about the current job. Finally, after much persuasion, the man replied that he could not face the responsibility of deciding which potatoes went where. It is, of course, of capital importance that justice be swift, but if, on occasion, the time appears to lengthen between argument and judgment, you might bear in mind the struggle involved in reaching a conclusion, — and particularly if the quorum consists of more than one.

At Harvard University: [254]

In truth the individual is the most important fact in the world in all enlightened systems and it must be the aim of the State to preserve his natural rights while at the same time ensuring that the rights of one do not interfere with those of another.

---

254 Kerwin, "Constitutionalism in Canada", Address at Harvard University in celebration of the two-hundredth anniversary of the birth of John Marshall, Sep. 25, 1955.

To the Lawyers' Club: [255]

Many years ago Cicero, although in rather oratorical style, put the matter thus: —

For the law is the bond which secures our privileges in the commonwealth, the foundation of justice. Within the law are reposed the mind, the heart, the judgment and the conviction of the state. The state without law would be like the human body without mind — unable to employ the parts which are to it as sinews, blood, and limbs. The magistrates who administer the law, the judges who interpret it — all of us in short — obey the law to the end that we may be free.

At the University of Toronto: [256]

Hartley Coleridge once asked, — and answered: — "But what is freedom? Rightly understood, a universal licence to be good".

That kind of licence which each graduate of this University takes with him should not be merely a certificate of fitness but it should also be a spur to his endeavours to maintain that freedom without which all else shall have been in vain. Therefore, a mere preoccupation with our own affairs is not sufficient and that is the reason for the suggestion that an interest in those of others is not only advisable but necessary. Realization of this problem will lead to a better understanding of that right which we expect to enjoy. The matter may be considered from the standpoint of race, creed, or occupation, and in each of these our forefathers have made their contribution. Where they have succeeded they have furnished a base upon which may be erected a super-structure which will embrace the manifold activities of our modern civilization. Where there was error, which indeed is bound to occur in all human endeavour, we must profit by their mistakes.

---

255 Kerwin, Address at dinner of the Lawyers' Club, Osgoode Hall, Toronto, Jan. 12, 1956.
256 Kerwin, Address at the University of Toronto on the occasion of receiving honourary degree, Doctor of Laws, May 25th, 1956.

At the opening of the Superior Court, Montreal: [257]

Despite all the slurs that have from time to time been cast upon the administration of law, its devotees, in the minds of all right-thinking people, serve a useful and indeed, necessary purpose in the affairs of mankind. Without law and order we would be relegated to the days of chaos and licence. In order to carry out the dictates of reason all civilized nations recognize that there must be rules of conduct and courts of justice to decide those questions that are bound to arise in connection with those rules. In order that they may work satisfactorily the courts must be kept pure and undefiled; and I think it may be fairly said that the people of Canada are satisfied that in this country these conditions exist.

Convocation Address, Montreal: [258]

It is by following the precepts and examples to which you have been exposed that the rule of law will continue to prevail through-out our land. The history of mankind shows that unless these values be kept constantly in mind our nation will suffer since the rule of law is concerned with the rights of the individual not merely in a material sense, but in an artistic, a moral and a spiritual sense. In the Grotius Society Transactions of 1945 Richard O'Sullivan points out:

> The validity of a system of natural law and of essential human rights was taught, and even taken for granted, by all the great common lawyers from Bracton, Fortescue and Littleton, through Thomas More and Christopher St. Germain, to Coke and on to Holt. For all these men, law is founded on ethics.

---

257 Kerwin, Address at the opening of the Superior Court, Montreal, Quebec, Sep. 12, 1957.
258 Kerwin, Convocation Address, Loyola College Montreal, Quebec, May 31, 1958.

Appendix

Hon. Patrick Kerwin, Chief Justice of Canada.
Chief Justice Kerwin was born in 1889.
He studied law at Osgoode Hall in Toronto,
was called to the bar of Ontario in 1911,
became King's Counsel in 1928,
and became a Justice of the Supreme Court
of Ontario in 1932. In 1935, he became a
Justice of the Supreme Court of Canada,
and in 1954 he became Chief Justice.

—Notes at a Celebration of the two-hundredth
anniversary of the birth of John Marshall
September 25, 1955

Career timeline for Patrick Grandcourt Kerwin (b.1889 - d.1963)

1903-1906 Clerk with Hanna, McCarthy & LeSueur, Sarnia
1906-1911 Student-at-Law Hanna, LeSueur & Price, Sarnia
1908-1911 Attended law school, Osgoode Hall, Toronto
1911-1932 Attorney at Law with Guthrie & Guthrie /
           Guthrie, Guthrie & Kerwin / Guthrie & Kerwin, Guelph
1928   King's Counsel
1932-1935 Justice of the High Court of Justice of Ontario, Toronto
1935-1954 Justice of the Supreme Court of Canada, Ottawa
1954-1963 Chief Justice of the Supreme Court of Canada, Ottawa

Education and degrees

1902   Sarnia Separate School
1906   Sarnia Collegiate Institute
1911   Osgoode Hall Law School, Barrister at Law

           Honourary degrees:

1937   Doctor of Laws, University of Ottawa
1954   Degree of Laws, University of New Brunswick
1955   Doctor of Civil Law, Bishop's University
1956   Degree of Civil Law, Assumption College, Windsor
1956   Degree of Laws, University of Toronto

Chief Justices of the Supreme Court of Canada[259]

Hon. Sir William Buell Richards	Sep. 30, 1875 - Jan. 10, 1879
Hon. Sir William Johnston Ritchie	Jan. 11, 1879 - Sep. 25 1892
Rt. Hon. Sir Samuel Henry Strong	Dec. 13, 1892 - Nov. 18, 1902
Rt. Hon. Sir Henri Elzéar Taschereau	Nov. 21, 1902 - May 2, 1906
Rt. Hon. Sir Charles Fitzpatrick	June 4, 1906 - Oct. 21, 1918
Rt. Hon. Sir Louis Henry Davies	Oct. 23, 1918 - May 1, 1924
Rt. Hon. Francis Alexander Anglin	Sep. 16, 1924 - Feb. 28, 1933
Rt. Hon. Sir Lyman Poore Duff	Mar. 17, 1933 - Jan. 7, 1944
Rt. Hon. Thibaudeau Rinfret	Jan. 8, 1944 - June 22, 1954
Hon. Patrick G. K. Kerwin	**July 1, 1954 - Feb. 2, 1963**
Rt. Hon. Robert Taschereau	Apr. 22, 1963 - Aug. 31, 1967
Rt. Hon. John Robert Cartwright	Sep. 1, 1967 - Mar. 23, 1970
Rt. Hon. Joseph Honoré Gérald Fauteux	Mar. 23, 1970 - Dec. 23, 1973
Rt. Hon. Bora Laskin	Dec. 27, 1973 - Mar. 26, 1984
Rt. Hon. Robert George Brian Dickson	Apr. 18, 1984 - June 30, 1990
Rt. Hon. Antonio Lamer	July 1, 1990 - Jan. 6, 2000
Rt. Hon. Beverley McLachlin	Jan. 7, 2000 - Dec 15, 2017

Justices of the Kerwin Court [260]

1954-1956: R. Taschereau, I. Rand, R. Kellock, J. Estey, C. Locke, J. Cartwright, G. Fauteux, D. Abbott

1956-1957: R. Taschereau, I Rand, R Kellock, C. Locke, J. Cartwright, G. Fauteux, D. Abbott, H. Nolan

1958-1959: R. Taschereau, I. Rand, C. Locke, J. Cartwright, G. Fauteux, D. Abbott, R. Martland, W. Judson

1959-1962: R. Taschereau, C. Locke, J. Cartwright, G. Fauteux, D. Abbott, R. Martland, W. Judson, R. Ritchie

1962-1963: R. Taschereau, J. Cartwright, G. Fauteux, D. Abbott, R. Martland, W. Judson, R. Ritchie, E. M. Hall

---

259 www.scc-csc.ca/court-cour/judges-juges/cfcju-jucp-eng.aspx Accessed Sep. 2014.
260 https://en.wikipedia.org/wiki/Template:Kerwin-court Accessed Apr. 2017.

Speeches

On Patrick's 70th birthday, he was presented with a bound copy of speeches assembled by his personal secretary, W. Kenneth Campbell. It is told that Patrick was not only quite surprised but also delighted at receiving a personal gift of this nature. These speeches encompass the time when Patrick was a Justice and, later, the Chief Justice, of the Supreme Court of Canada.

W. Kenneth Campbell wrote the following dedication to Chief Justice P. Kerwin:

TO
THE HONOURABLE PATRICK KERWIN, P.C.,
CHIEF JUSTICE OF CANADA
ON THE OCCASION OF HIS SEVENTIETH BIRTHDAY
OCTOBER 25TH, 1959
FROM ONE WHO HAS BEEN THE RECIPIENT OF SO MUCH
CONSIDERATION AND SO MANY KINDNESSES

Included with the bound book of speeches was a note written by Patrick's son, George Kerwin, in 1970, to those who received a copy of the speeches (his brother Patrick K. Kerwin and sister, Isobel Kerwin McKenna, Aunt Francis Beatty and Uncle Vernon Kerwin).

On his 70th birthday, dad was presented with a bound copy of some of his speeches by Ken Campbell, Administrator of the Supreme Court of Canada.

The manner in which the book was bound made it impossible to photo-copy without damaging the binding. If copies were to be made it would be necessary to type the book and make copies from the typed pages.

Mother, who had the book, loaned it to me so that a typed copy could be made. At the time, neither of us realized that it would take so long. Now, a year later, it is done and the original returned.

The reason for all of this was that I thought that the children, brother and sister of the late Chief Justice would like to have a copy of these speeches. In reading them, I think something of the man comes through. I'm sure that you, just as I, will find a mental picture of Kerwin, C.J.C., in front of you as you read. In some passages, this picture will

show him with a slight smile and twinkle in his eye — in
other passages with a serious and earnest expression —
but always radiating that gentle kindness, which was so
characteristic.

Christmas, 1970
George

While doing research on this subject at the National Library
and Archives in Ottawa, two years after my mother's death, I
found a note placed with a typed copy of the speeches donated by
my mother, Isobel Kerwin McKenna, to the Archives sometime in
the 1980's. The note reads as follows;

The original set of speeches was prepared and dedicated
by W. Kenneth Campbell, who was secretary to at least five
C.J.'s and who Father made Administrator of the Supreme
Court.
Campbell had the speeches printed and bound, and this is
a typed copy that my brother George Kerwin had made when
he was with IBM, which accounts for the marks at the sides
of the pages. A few minor spelling errors crept in at that time.

—Isobel Kerwin McKenna

A selection of speeches follow.[261] Other speeches can be found
in the National Library and Archives of Canada.

---

261 Every effort has been made to reproduce this collection of Kerwin's speeches as
actually written.

Index to Speeches

ADDRESS TO THE LANSING BAR, LANSING, MICHIGAN, U.S.A. SEPTEMBER 4, 1940

Administration of Justice in the Canadian Federal System

Without attempting a history, it is perhaps convenient to say at the outset that the charter of Canada is found in *The British North America Act, 1867* and amendments to it. This *Act* is considerably later than your Declaration of Independence and Constitution but was the culmination of struggles for responsible and representative government that commenced soon after the Treaty of Paris in 1763 and continued with The *Quebec Act* of 1774, The *Constitutional Act* of 1791, and the *Act of Union* of 1840.

In 1867 there were only four provinces, Ontario, Quebec, Nova Scotia and New Brunswick, but the provinces that have since been added or formed out of the territories acquired by the Dominion (five in number) occupy the same relative position. While the charter is found in a British statute, that *Act* was passed at the request of representatives of the four provinces and from time to time amendments have been made to it at the request of governments in the Dominion.

The executive power was by the *Act* vested in Queen Victoria and Her Successors, and for the due exercise of that power provision was made for the appointment of a Governor General as the representative of the Crown. Similarly, in each province, a lieutenant governor is appointed by the Dominion Government and in him the executive power in each province is vested. Under the system of responsible and representative government, that executive authority, in each case, must, of course, be exercised upon the advice of Government of the day, the members of which, under a Prime Minister of the Dominion or Premier of the Province, are responsible to Parliament or the Legislature. Canada is a self-governing Dominion in the British Commonwealth of Nations and as constitutional usage has progressed and been settled, either the Dominion or the Provinces exercise full sovereignty, free and untrammeled.

While those responsible for the conferences that led to the passing of the statute are known popularly as "The Fathers of Confederation", what was actually accomplished may be more accurately described as a federation. On the one hand, it was not a legislative union whereby all legislative power would be vested in one body acting for the whole of the country, nor, on the other hand, was it a joining together of the provinces to confer restricted powers upon a central government while they themselves retained the residuum. Certain subjects were allotted to the Parliament of the new Dominion and certain others were allotted to the legislatures of the provinces. Speaking generally, the provinces were to retain jurisdiction over purely local affairs while those in a larger sphere, consisting of such enumerated subjects as it was thought would tend to make a strong central government, were allotted to the latter, — with a proviso that Parliament (the Senate and House of Commons of the Dominion) should have jurisdiction to make laws for the peace, order and good government of Canada in relation to all matters not coming within the classes of subjects assigned exclusively to the legislatures of the provinces. That, of course, is directly the opposite of the arrangement that was made in your country as between the States and the Federal Government.

As has been mentioned, there is a list of enumerated subjects so that we find allotted to the Dominion such items as the public debt and property, the regulation of trade and commerce, postal service, militia, military and naval services and defence, navigation and shipping, sea coast and inland fisheries, currency and coinage, banking, bills of exchange and promissory notes, interest, bankruptcy and insolvency, patents and copyrights, Indians, naturalization of aliens, unemployment insurance (since 1940) and "the criminal law except the constitution of courts of criminal jurisdiction but including the procedure in criminal matters". Among the subjects allotted to the provincial legislatures are municipal institutions, local works and undertakings, property and civil rights and "the administration of justice in the province, including the constitution, maintenance and organization of provincial courts both of civil and of criminal jurisdiction and including procedure in civil matters in those courts". In conjunction with the comparison of the last mentioned enumerated heading in each division, must be taken subsequent provisions of the *Act* whereby the Dominion appoints the judges of the superior, district and county courts in each province, — and whereby the judges of the superior courts shall hold office during good behaviour, removable only by the Governor General on address of the Senate and House of Commons; and finally a provision whereby Parliament may provide for the constitution, maintenance and organization of a general Court of Appeal for Canada and for the establishment of any additional courts for the better administration of the laws of Canada.

The legislature of each province enacts the great body of laws that affect the everyday lives of the people but over and above any statutory enactments there remains the old common law of England ameliorated in many respects by the system of equity that arose many years ago to soften the rigors of the former. Owing to the accidents of history, reference must be made to different dates in the various provinces in order to ascertain the particular system of law and equity that prevails, — subject, of course, to amendment by statute. That statement must be further restricted to what are known as the common law provinces, including all but the Province of Quebec which stands in a different position and as to which I must say something later.

The duty of providing for the administration of these laws and also of the criminal law (although both the substantive criminal law and the procedure in criminal matters is entrusted to the Dominion) devolves upon the provinces and, again speaking generally, we find justices of the peace, magistrates, division or small debt courts, county courts and supreme courts. The members of all these courts are appointed by the provinces, except the members of the supreme and county or district courts. From time to time, no matter how appointed, these courts may be administering the old common law and equity, and statutes of the Dominion and of the provinces. We find, therefore, that in many cases they are expounding the same common law or common law and equity that will be found in many of the States of your union. From time to time reference is made in our courts to decisions in yours and vice versa.

Two recent examples may be mentioned. In 1939 the Supreme Court of the United States decided that a federal employee was not immune from state taxation, and Mr. Justice Frankfurter referred to a judgment in the Supreme Court of Canada in 1907 deciding a similar problem in the same manner. On that point our Court (and in a subsequent case, the Privy Council) felt that Chief Justice Marshall's famous declaration, "the power to tax involves the power to destroy", could not be justified so far as our constitution was concerned; and your highest court ultimately came to the same conclusion with reference to the constitution of your country. In the present year, in a patent case, the Supreme

Court of Canada, in a unanimous judgment delivered on behalf of the Court by the Chief Justice, determined that it could not be said that in no circumstances could the existence of an illegal combine be an answer to an action for infringement of a patent, and referred to a decision earlier in the same year, of the United States Supreme Court, where it was held *inter alia* that the regulation of prices and the suppression of competition among purchasers of a patented article was not within the scope of the monopoly conferred upon a patentee by the patent laws.

The Province of Quebec, as I have indicated, is in a different position from any of the others. That is because it was mainly in the territory now comprising that province, first known as Canada and later as Lower Canada that people from Normandy and other parts of France first settled. Their descendants, by the Treaty of Paris in 1763, acquired certain rights which the British Government meticulously respected and guaranteed from time to time. They were not reared in common law but on the customs of Paris as varied from time to time by Royal French edicts applicable to the colony, and finally their law in several matters was codified, just before Confederation, by what is known as the Civil Code. This is similar to a great extent to the Code Napoleon but differs from it in many respects. That code, subject of course to amendment by the Quebec Legislature from time to time, contains the rules for the conduct of the ordinary everyday affairs of life in that province. As one who was nurtured under the other system but who has now the responsibility of deciding, upon many occasions, disputes that arise in the Province of Quebec, my admiration for that wonderful work, the Civil Code, is still increasing. Some of its provisions have been incorporated into the common law provinces with great advantages to the latter. In addition to this code, there is also, of course, the Code of Civil Procedure which takes the place, again speaking generally, of what are known as Judicature Acts and Rules of Practice in the common law provinces. *Stare decisis* applies in Quebec but the views of recognized writers are more freely used than in the common law system and the opinions of the Cour de Cassation in France are treated with the utmost respect where the Code Napoleon and the Quebec Civil Code do not differ.

The purely Dominion courts require a separate word. In order to deal with such subjects as patents, trademarks, copyright, admiralty law and claims against the Dominion Government, Parliament has set up the Exchequer Court. It and the Supreme Court of Canada are the only two Dominion courts and at first a

Judge of the Supreme Court of Canada exercised the power of an Exchequer Court Judge. For some years, however, there have been a President and a Puisne Judge of the Exchequer Court with an appeal from their decisions to the Supreme Court of Canada.

The latter is a general Court of Appeal for Canada and the Dominion statute which governs the Court also provides for its jurisdiction. Speaking generally, there is in civil cases an appeal from the highest provincial court to the Supreme Court of Canada in all cases involving two thousand dollars but there is also provision whereby special leave may be granted. Without attempting to cover the practice and procedure in that Court, it may be noted that factums, not briefs, are filed, and that counsel are permitted any reasonable length of time for the amplification of the points taken in the factums. Both written and oral argument may be in English or French but in the great majority of appeals, even from Quebec, the English language is used. The evidence, however, in disputes arising in that province may be in either language and the transcription is often entirely in French. There are seven judges in all, of whom two must be appointed from the bench or bar of Quebec. The quorum is five but in capital cases or where constitutional questions are involved, all who are available take part in the hearing and judgment.

There is another jurisdiction which I should mention because, as I understand, there is no similar authority in any court in the Union. The Governor General in Council (which means on the recommendation of the Government of the day) may refer to the Supreme Court of Canada for its opinion certain constitutional questions, such as the validity of legislation already passed or proposed to be enacted. That is, such questions may be referred without any dispute having arisen *inter partes*. It was in pursuance of such authority that legislation dealing with unemployment insurance and various other matters was referred about 1936. By the use of this power, as well as by decisions in concrete cases, there have been developed certain rules in connection with the construction of *The British North America Act* but this was accomplished mainly by decisions of the Judicial Committee of the Privy Council in England. The story of that body is a particularly interesting one but its importance and variety would require more time than is now available.

Suffice it to say that in criminal cases there is an appeal to the Supreme Court of Canada when there has been a dissent, on a question of law, in the provincial Court of Appeal or by leave where a decision of one such court is found to be in conflict with that of another provincial court of appeal, and to point out that now there is no appeal to the Judicial Committee of the Privy Council in criminal cases. That was accomplished by an enactment of the Dominion.

Again exercising the power to refer questions for the Court's opinion, the Governor General in Council obtained the opinion of the Court that the Dominion Parliament could abolish appeals in civil cases from the Supreme Court of Canada or any Court in Canada to the Privy Council if it so desires. That opinion, I should point out, was a majority opinion, four judges being of one mind, one holding directly the contrary view and another differing in part. At present, in civil matters and in constitutional questions, there is no appeal from the Supreme Court of Canada to the Judicial Committee save by leave of the latter except in admiralty cases. That leave has been granted in connection with the matter to which I have just referred and the question will be argued and determined when the exigencies of war permit.

Since the administration of justice is confided to the provinces, there is in each an attorney general whose duty it is to see to the enforcement of the criminal law. What immediately follows applies chiefly to the Province of Ontario but may be taken as fairly typical. There are Crown attorneys in each county or district, to whom that duty is in most instances delegated, — all, of course, appointed and paid by the provinces. An accused person may be summonsed or arrested and brought before a magistrate. The latter may dispose of the less serious infractions summarily; in other cases he may do so with the accused's consent, and in others he holds merely a preliminary inquiry when he decides if there is enough evidence to commit the accused for trial by a higher court. It should be noted that the magistrate also exercises jurisdiction under the provisions of many provincial statutes. After a person charged with a crime is committed for trial, he may, in some instances, elect to be tried speedily by a county or district court judge without a jury; if he does not so elect and in all the more serious cases, he is held in custody or on bail for the next Court of Sessions of the Peace or Assizes when he will be tried by a county or district court judge or a high court judge, as the case may be, with a jury. In all these instances last mentioned, the evidence of the Crown must first be submitted to the grand jury. In some of the provinces the number of petty jurors has been decreased from the usual panel of twelve. There are different views as to the retention of grand juries but as it is a contentious subject, I do not enter upon it.

On the civil side, proceedings in the Superior Courts are commenced by a writ of summons or a document corresponding to it, pleadings are delivered, examinations for discovery held, and the trial had — compulsorily with a jury in some cases and at the discretion of either party in what are still described as common law actions. County Courts follow much the same routine, while in Division or Small Debts Courts proceedings are simple and inexpensive. Throughout, the costs of litigation are comparatively light. Appeals add to the cost but they are fairly regulated. For instance, after judgment in a Supreme Court action in Ontario, an appeal may be brought in many cases, to the provincial Court of Appeal, consisting of three or five judges, and thence to the Supreme Court of Canada in case the amount involved in the appeal is two thousand dollars or over or if special leave is obtained.

A few moments ago I referred to the fact that the determination of the constitutional question as to the power of the Dominion Parliament to abolish appeals to the Privy Council depended upon the exigencies of war. Because Canada is at war the Canadian people are devoting their hearts and minds to that all important fact first and foremost. But it does not mean that the system of law, the system for the peaceable determination of disputes, for the trial of persons charged with crimes is at a standstill. It still functions and with the same ease and promptitude that has characterized it throughout the years. The courts are still hearing and determining cases and the Privy Council is still sitting in London hearing appeals from Canada, Australia, New Zealand, South Africa, India, and the Colonies, and the constitutional question will be disposed of when the Dominion and the Provinces choose to apply for a hearing.

War or no war, representative responsible government continues; and continue it must so long as a free people decides and wills to remain free. Because freedom can only exist under the law; and that despite the flings that have from time to time been taken at it. Dickens' statement, through the lips of Bumble, that "the law is as ass: an idiot"; and Tennyson's reference to "that wilderness of single instances" are taken with the proverbial grain of salt. That does not mean, however, that things are ever perfect in this imperfect world. "We must not", Shakespeare tells us in Measure for Measure:

We must not make a scarecrow of the law,
Setting it up to fear the birds prey,
And let it keep one shape, till custom make it
Their perch, and not their terror.

Whether applicable to those who disrupt the country's peace or infringe its penal laws, or to those who take an unconscionable advantage of their position, these words serve to remind us that law and equity must be molded to meet conditions as they change; that law must be administered impartially and that while the quality of mercy must not be strained "Reason", as Coke put it, many years ago, — "Reason is the life of the law".

ADDRESS TO STUDENTS, OSGOODE HALL, TORONTO JUNE 29, 1950

Mr. Carson's invitation was predicated upon two propositions. First, that I was a graduate of Osgoode Hall and, second, that as it was not likely that any of this year's graduating class would soon appear before the Supreme Court of Canada, this would afford an opportunity for all to see a member of that Court in the flesh. These two points being incontrovertible, there appeared to be no reason that judgment should not go in his favour. Whether any useful purpose will be served is an entirely different matter.

Addressing myself particularly to the ladies and gentlemen in their new gowns, I will not follow the example of Dick, the butcher, by saying: — "The first thing we do let's kill all the lawyers". If that injunction were carried out, it would mean my own death warrant because each of His Majesty's justices remains a lawyer. To what extent his pronouncements on legal and equitable matters meet the approval of the practicing members of the profession is a moot point, particularly in the view of disappointed litigants and their legal advisers. However, that may be, it is as a lawyer that I desire very sincerely to complement each one of you upon the successful conclusion of your efforts of the past few years. You have been called to the Bar of the Province of Ontario, a not insignificant accomplishment. By your attention to the lectures, by your studies, both in and out of the lecture hall, you have finally fitted yourselves to pass, and have succeeded in passing the test of examinations and now, today, your efforts have been rewarded and you are full-fledged members, and not merely students, of the Law Society of Upper Canada.

I have always thought that "The Law Society of Upper Canada" is a full-blooded, richly endowed phrase that cried out to be relished and rolled around the tongue; but beyond that, it brings to mind the hardships of the early pioneers of this province and the struggles and accomplishments of the Society's members. It has a noble history that deserves your attention but I do no more than recommend its study to you from the pamphlets and articles on the subject. However, its history does exemplify one matter that I wish to emphasize and that is, while you have now been admitted to the Bar and the practice of your chosen profession, your studies are by no means over. Just as, while Osgoode Hall is fenced in the manner considered appropriate many years ago, what transpires within its walls is not precisely the same as what occurred therein at that time, so, while the legal learning you have acquired is necessary, it must be remembered that the law is a jealous mistress and demands of you, and all her devotees, an assiduous devotion to her cause. The common law is not static but develops from era to era, and sometimes from year to year. That is not to say that you are at liberty to disregard the principles you have learned at such great cost of effort and money, but that changing circumstances require you to seek to apply those principles to altered conditions. That is not an easy task. It requires thought and application. I know of no more melancholy sight than a young lawyer deciding that upon being called to the Bar, the time for action has arrived and that for study has passed. Nothing is farther from the truth. It is true that with the benefit of your training you are now launched upon your career and that considerable of your time will, it is hoped, be taken up with interviewing clients and advising them and, if necessary, presenting their causes in the courts of the country. But, be not deceived! Human nature and the vagaries of its conduct are such that at first you will find it hard to separate the wheat from the chaff, the important points from the irrelevant, and it is only by application that you will be able to overcome the difficulties and obstacles. That process requires not merely busyness but also research.

Where will you find the sources from which to draw your inspiration and knowledge? In the decisions of the courts in statutes and regulations, in recognized textbooks of authority, and in essays and articles by competent craftsmen.

As to the latter, you will already have received some guidance as to their respective values, and experience, plus study, will enable you to round out your education in that regard. Provincial and Dominion statutes we have always with us. With the complexity of modern life, it has been found necessary to deal legislatively with many matters that never would have occurred to our forefathers, but you must take conditions as they are. That being so, you will not be able properly to advise your clients without at least knowing where to put your hands quickly upon the relevant enactments. Such aids as statute citators are, therefore, indispensable either in your own office or your local law association's library. I do not refer to the Great Library at Osgoode Hall because I dare say that not all of you will swell the ranks of the Toronto practitioners. As to the regulations, the various governments have made considerable progress in making them available and they now may in general be found in the Dominion and Provincial Gazettes. Not many lawyers will have these in their offices but, again, you will be enabled to take advantage of the facilities of your local associations. That marks the importance of your not only becoming members of those organizations but also of taking an active interest in them so that they may be made strong and useful to you and to the public.

As to Courts, it suffices to say that in every civilized country they form a hierarchy of trial tribunals and courts of appeal, the number of each depending upon the exigencies of the times and the wisdom of the Legislatures acting in conformity with an enlightened public opinion. Speaking from an experience as one of the Justices of the Trial Division of the Supreme Court of Ontario, while members of the former may refer to their judgments as those of a Superior Court, Appellate Courts designate them as judgments of a lower Court. But it has been found through experience that such a system is necessary, and I mention it only to suggest that in reading the reports you will find it advisable to differentiate between the weight to be attached to the pronouncement of a single judge and that of an appellate tribunal. Perhaps, in view of the Treasurer's propositions, it would not be amiss if a word were said about the Supreme Court of Canada. As you know, it exercises an appellate civil and criminal jurisdiction throughout Canada but its powers to intervene are limited in various ways. For some years it has been the final Court of Appeal in criminal matters and, now, by recent legislation, it has, in new litigation, become the final Court in civil matters. While in certain cases it was possible in the past to appeal from a Provincial Court of Appeal, and that power still exists, leave may now be sought from the Supreme Court of Canada to appeal from any judgment of the highest court of final resort in a province, or a judge thereof, in which judgment can be had in the particular case. The right to appeal in criminal matters is dealt with by the *Criminal Code*. When you arrive at the stage where you are concerned with appeals to that Court, you will have recourse to the *Criminal Code* as amended and to the *Supreme Court Act* particularly as amended at the last Session of Parliament. One effect of this legislation is that a good part of the learning in connection with granting leave to appeal will be found to be unnecessary and, for that, I am sure you will not be unthankful.

I realize that not all of you expect to display forensic powers and become counsel at trials and on appeals, and I therefore leave to those practitioners with whom you come in contact, the duty to teach and exemplify the manners and conduct that are helpful and expedient in those arenas. May I add only that nowhere in your practice will you find it more advantageous to be prepared. To a litigant, his case is one of the most important things in the world and he is entitled to demand that his lawyer know his case and be ready to submit to the Court the facts in their most attractive setting and all the points of law that require consideration.

Each one of you, however, will have office work to do or oversee, and it is in that connection that you should decide never to mingle your clients' funds with your own. By failure not only to make but to keep such a resolution more hardship is caused the public and more ignominy is heaped, not only upon the individual concerned, but also upon the entire profession, than by any other cause. At the last convention of the Canadian Bar Association, Mr. Justice Jackson of the Supreme Court of the United States, in a committee meeting, referred to the fact that he often thought, when seeing a former member of the profession who had been cast out from his high estate: "There but for the grace of God go I". He explained that what he meant was that temptations come to some oftener than others and in greater intensity. A sound rule is that you will avoid the occasions of evil to a very great extent by rigorously keeping your clients' funds separate from those of your own.

"Funds" suggests "costs" and I am not so far removed from the practice of law as to belittle their importance. After all, it is by means of your practice that you expect to earn your living by the sweat of your brow and, as the labourer is worthy of his hire, no one in any walk of life should object to the lawyer being paid properly for his work. But the law is more than a means of livelihood and entirely apart from the mechanics of your practice, whatever its nature, is a much wider concept of a lawyer's duties to his profession, to his community, and to the state at large. These are not easy to define but all of them may, I think, be said to be included in one of St. Paul's epistles: — "Here now it is required among the dispensers that a man be found faithful"; — faithful to your conscience and faithful to the highest ideals of your profession, a calling that despite the occasional jeers of those not of the fold, is, in my opinion at least, one of the noblest to which most men and women may aspire. While Shakespeare and other writers of lesser statute may poke fun at us, I think that in their hearts they realized the necessity of the profession and of the sterling service its members render to mankind. Each one of you should be willing to help the oppressed and the needy, and that is generally recognized by the setting-up of various associations among the Bar organizations for that specific purpose. Lend your assistance and your talents to these and to all worthy causes in your community. Take your place among the leaders of an enlightened democracy. You will enjoy the esteem of your fellow-citizens and merit their approval, and it is only by such a course of conduct that you will render a commensurate return to the country which through its Legislatures confers such large and important powers upon your profession. The public are entitled to expect that conduct as a quid pro quo for the grant of the power and it's only by making a return in full measure that you may hope for a continuance of the existing status. As you progress in your practice, while cherishing the history of the past, do not forget that it has been a history of evolution. Never be satisfied that things are all for the best in the best of all possible worlds and do not permit any of the legal associations which you may join to deteriorate into a mutual admiration society. Ever be ready to take a stand for improvement! If you do this, then will the words of Edmund Burke, in his speech on Conciliation with America, remain true:

> In no country perhaps in the world is the law so general a study ... This study renders men acute, inquisitive, dexterous, prompt in attack, ready in defence, full of resources .... They augur mis-government at a distance, and snuff the approach of tyranny in every tainted breeze.

ADDRESS TO THE LAWYERS' CLUB, TORONTO, NOVEMBER 13, 1952

Law and Literature

When I was sworn in as a Justice of the Supreme Court of Ontario about twenty years ago, the late Mr. Tilley, as Treasurer of the Law Society of Upper Canada, in welcoming the new member of the Bench, noted that I had just come of age in the practice of law. On this, my second appearance before the Lawyers' Club, I have nearly reached the legal age as a member of Her Majesty's Courts of Ontario or of Canada. I answered your President's invitation for this event in May and I thought there would be no difficulty in putting in order some ideas that had occurred to me during those two periods but, in September, when he wanted to know the subject of my talk, a difficulty arose as to what answer should be given. It may appear when I have finished that the title is too ambitious but I can only hope that, unlike charity, it will not be found to cover a multitude of sins.

One definition of "literature" in the Oxford Dictionary is "literary work or production". This sends us to "literary" which is said to mean "of or pertaining to, or of the nature of literature, polite learning, ...; pertaining to that kind of composition which has value on account of its qualities of form". To make a composite of these citations one might say that literature is using words or phrases in a form of polite learning. Certainly it is not a mere knowledge of words and an ability to string them together but rather a method of expressing ideas in a pleasant imaginative manner.

The presentation of legal or equitable disputes and the settlement of them require a precision that generally confines the speaker or writer to a set form. However, there are occasions when something has been inserted in a lighter vein without at all derogating from the main object. These occurrences are not numerous and, so far as judgments are concerned, the law reports contain but few examples. Many of them tend to lighten the labour of one reading the reports by affording an oasis in an oft-times arid field.

Of course, it is no more a part of the judicial process to be merely entertaining than it is for a draftsman to write, as it is said was once done,

> I, John of Gaunt
> Do give and do grant
> To Sir John Burgoyne
> And the heirs of his loin
> Both Sutton and Potton
> Till the world goes rotten

but an eminent peer in the House of Lords did not disdain to copy (with due acknowledgment) from "Through the Looking Glass". Thus, in *Liversidge v. Sir John Anderson* (1942) A.C. 206, Lord Atkin at page 245: —

> I know of only one authority which might justify the suggested method of construction: "When I use a word," Humpty Dumpty said in rather a scornful tone, "it means just what I choose it to mean, neither more nor less". "The question," said Alice, "is whether you can make words mean so many different things." "The question is", said Humpty Dumpty, "which is to be master — that's all."

Lord Atkin brought the matter to a head by continuing: —

> After all this long discussion the question is whether the words "If a man has" can mean "if a man thinks he has". I am of opinion that they cannot, and that the case should be decided accordingly.

The fact that Lord Atkin was dissenting on this point does not detract from the object I had in mind in quoting his words.

In Lord *Advocate v. Mirrielees' Trustees* (1945) S.C. (H.L.) 1, a company commander in the early local defence volunteers was killed in a grenade accident. At that time no Home Guard commissions were granted and Major Mirrielees though he held a command had not commissioned rank. The question was whether he was a "common soldier" so that his estate could escape estate duty. The Lord Chancellor (Viscount Simon) solved the question by a reference to Shakespeare; "The epithet 'common'" his lordship says, "is, I think, introduced merely to exclude higher ranks". Thus, in Shakespeare's Henry V, act IV, scene 1, when the king on the night before Agincourt, is touring the battlefield in disguise and comes upon Pistol, the following conversation ensues:

Pistol — Qui va là?
King Henry — A friend.
Pistol — Discuss unto me, art thou officer? Or art thou
base, common, and popular?

It was accordingly held that "common" meant "below a certain rank" and the estate therefore was free of duty.

In *Jackson v. Barry Railway* (1893) 1. Ch. 238, Lord Justice Bowen, at 248 considered that the "icy impartiality of Rhadamthus" could not be expected of an engineer arbitrator — an expression adopted by Viscount Simon in a recent appeal to the Judicial Committee from British Columbia, *White v. Kuzych* (1951) A.C. 585 at 595. In *Boucher v. The King* (1951) S.C.R. 265, Chief Justice Rinfret, at 277, remarks: "It might well be said in such a case (that the Chief Justice had put) in the words of Milton, "License they mean when they cry liberty" or, as expressed by Mr. Edouard Herriot, "La Liberté doit trouver sa limite dans l'autorité légale". In *Rowe v. The King* in the same volume of the Supreme Court Reports, the point was whether an accused could be found guilty of murder under a provision of the *Criminal Code* whereby culpable homicide is murder if the offender uses any weapon during his flight after the commission, or attempted commission, of certain other stated offences. In a concurring judgment, Mr. Justice Kellock stated it had often been pointed out that "The wicked flee when no man pursueth", which, of course, is a reference to Proverbs XXVIII(1). I might mention that the first time I recollect having heard that in a Court of law was at a trial for manslaughter at Barrie. Its use there by counsel for the accused did not accomplish its purpose but, of course, unlike judges, counsel did not have the last word.

These examples substantiate, I think what I have already said, that there are occasions when such references may be made in judgments, — not only without taking the lawyer's mind away from the subject under consideration but really furthering his appreciation of it. At the same time it must be borne in mind that to a litigant, his particular piece of litigation is an all important matter; that Courts are established to settle disputes, and that a party is anxious to know exactly why he fared so well or ill, and particularly the latter. I do no more than state the well known truth that a system of law and procedure is necessary to any civilized country but I emphasize the functions of the various cogs in the hierarchy of courts because of a criticism that appeared some time ago of the practice of the Judicial Committee and the Supreme Court of Canada as to concurrent findings of fact in the Courts below. Over the years it has been found that this is a good working rule. After all, the great majority of disputes never proceed beyond the trial Courts where they are disposed of by the same set of judges whose judgments in other cases proceed to appeal. And, if a Court of Appeal comes to the same conclusion of fact, can it be denied that the litigant has had his day in Court on that issue? It appears proper that in a further appeal he should be called upon to demonstrate that both Courts were wrong. In *Perusse v. Stafford* (1928) S.C.R. 416 at 418, Chief Justice Anglin, speaking for the Court says: — "error in the finding not being demonstrated, — not being made manifest — it is impossible for us to interfere". Sir Lyman Duff often expressed it "He must put his finger on an error". This is difficult but not impossible, and the late Lord Greene considered that one of his greatest achievements at the Bar had been to persuade the House of Lords that a trial judge and a unanimous Court of Appeal had been wrong on a question of fact. Litigation must come to an end some time and I recall to your minds the circumstance that not many years ago in the Province of Ontario we had Divisional Courts, which ultimately were considered unnecessary. There were misgivings as to the change at the time, even in the minds of some of the most distinguished and most beloved members of the Bench but who can now deny it was a wise move and reduced the cost of litigation?

All this brings us to the question of the operation of the judicial function. In Mr. Justice Cardoza's book, *The Nature of the Judicial Process*, he writes thus of the tendency, in some cases in the United States, to disregard precedent: —

> How to reconcile that tendency, which is a growing and in the main a wholesome one, with the need of uniformity and certainty, is one of the great problems confronting the lawyers and judges of our day. We shall have to feel our way here as elsewhere in the law. Somewhere between worship of the past and exaltation of the present, the path of safety will be found.

and further: — "Symmetrical development may be bought at too high a price".

On the other hand, another eminent United States jurist, Judge Learned Hand, had this to say of a fellow member of the Federal Court of Appeals: —

He will not overrule a precedent, unless he can be satisfied beyond peradventure that it was untenable when made; and not even then, if it has gathered around it the support of a substantial body of decisions based upon it. As a corollary, he is not given to wide commitments when he writes, for he distrusts the guidance which the present evidence and the present argument give, if the issues be amplified beyond what is necessary to dispose of the controversy. He believes that the industry of other suitors to whom they may become vital, if expanded, is likely further to explore and illuminate them. Consistently with this, he does not seek to support his conclusions by resort to broad or speculative general principles; but, like an English judge, looks to the precedents or to the text for his warrant.

This topic could, of course, be expanded into a full-length treatise but I refer to two matters only. The first is our old friend *obiter dicta*. It is idle to say there never should be any, because jurisprudence, whether based on the common law or the civil, is ever growing, ever expanding, and it is impossible in every case for a judge to avoid *dicta*. Not merely are they sometimes necessary in order that the judge may demonstrate the reason for the faith that is in him but also that he may show the litigants and their advisers the line of reasoning by which he reaches his ultimate conclusion. Not all *obiter dicta* are of equal value and this truth is well exemplified by Viscount Dunedin in *Nixon v. Attorney General* (1931) A.C. 184, where he was able to hold not only that the authority of the *dicta* in *Considine v. McInerney* (1916) 2 A.S. 162; *Wigg v. Att. Gen. for the Irish Free State* (1927) A.C. 674; and Re Transferred Civil Servants (Ireland) Compensation (1929) A.C. 242 was "overwhelming," but that no weight need be given *dictum* in Lupton's Case (1912) 1 K.B. 107 since there, the Master of the Rolls (Cozens Hardy L.J. and Fletcher Moulton L.J.) had, to use Lord Dunedin's words, "slipped into that expression without exactly knowing what the result of it would be".

Furthermore, if a judgment is based on two distinct grounds, neither of these may be treated as *obiter*. That was decided by the Supreme Court of Canada in *Gravestock v. Parkin* (1944) S.C.R. 150, where the Court of Appeal for Ontario had determined that A, who appeared to have no interest in certain lands but who had paid to a county treasurer the amount necessary to redeem those lands after a tax sale, was a person entitled to redeem within the meaning of the phrase "any other person" in a section of the *Ontario Assessment Act*. However, the Court also declared that under the circumstances, its discretion should be exercised against the applicant and a prerogative *mandamus* refused. A motion to quash an appeal to the Supreme Court of Canada for want of jurisdiction was allowed on the ground that the latter reason of the Court of Appeal was not *obiter* and therefore there was no authority to hear the appeal under the then section 38 of the *Supreme Court Act*. That section is now section 44 of the *Supreme Court Act* as amended in 1949 except that the last five words in the present enactment are new. Section 44 reads: —

> 44. No appeal lies to the Supreme Court of Canada from a judgment or order made in the exercise of judicial discretion except in proceedings in the nature of a suit or proceeding in equity originating elsewhere than in the province of Quebec and except in *mandamus* proceedings.

To the same effect as the decision in *Gravestock v. Parkin* is that of the House of Lords in *Jacobs v. London Privy Council* (1950) A.C. 361 where, at page 369, Lord Simonds says: —

> There is in my opinion no justification for regarding as *obiter dictum* a reason given by a judge for his decision, because he has given another reason also. If it were a proper test to ask whether the decision would have been the same apart from the proposition alleged to be *obiter,* then a case which *ex facie* decided two things would decide nothing.

The second matter to which I refer is the suggestion that Appellate Courts, and particularly a court of last resort should seize every opportunity to expound all the law upon a given subject. The supporters of this proposition argue that it would settle the law for the lower tribunals and permit lawyers to advise their clients with greater safety. Such a suggestion is intriguing and in theory cannot be denied. However, in practice, it has not been found workable, at least to the extent that its advocates contend. For a consideration of the subject I might refer you in addition to the opinions of Mr. Justice Cardozo and Judge Hand's fellow judge, already mentioned, the views of an experienced counsel and judge, the late Mr. Justice Riddell. A hope had been expressed that in a cause then pending he should elaborate the relevant law in all its ramifications but, in speaking of the matter to a brother judge, he expressed the undesirability of so doing, and in fact refrained.

In the Jacobs case Lord Simonds referred to "the importance, I would say the paramount importance, of certainty in the law" to which he added "...is to determine what the law is, not what it ought to have been, is our present task". Sir Frederick Pollock in his essay, "Judicial Caution and Valour" (1929) 45 L.G.R. 293 at 295 puts the matter very well: —

> Caution and valour are both needed for the fruitful constructive interpretation of legal principles. The court should be ever valiant to override the merely technical difficulties of professional thinking, and also current opinions having some show of authority, in the search for a solution which will be acceptable and in a general way intelligible to reasonable citizens, or the class of them whom the decision concerns. Judicial valour of this kind is in no way akin to headstrong ambition or love of innovation for its own sake.

And again later at page 296 where he says:

> From this point of view the problem of judicial interpretation is to hold a just middle way between excess of valour and excess of caution. A too daring expounder is in danger of laying down sweeping rules without attending to the probable variations in the circumstances to which they will be applied; and then the application of his rule may have to be confined within tolerable bounds by a series of qualifications which leave it, to use a classical expression, well nigh eaten up by exceptions. On the other hand, the pedestrian timidity that shrinks from hazarding any general conclusion will only land us in a still less desirable state, that of having no principle at all, but a heap of unrelated instances which those who come after may or may not find to be consistent with one another.

My own view is that while it is not true to say that principles of wide application should never be enunciated, the necessary coincidence of time and event will arise only in infrequent and impelling circumstances.

And now as to counsel whose duty it is to place their cases before the tribunals for adjudication. If it is true that a Chancery Counsel of the old school many years ago remarked, "It is a sad thing to see a fine estate frittered away among the beneficiaries". Undoubtedly, that is not a statement that would find favour today in any branch of the legal profession. The first requisite is, of course, that counsel know all about his case because as it has been aptly put "whenever any lawyer commences to believe that he no longer needs to know the record, hardening of the forensic arteries has set in". Such knowledge must also extend to the relevant statutes so that the Court will not be in the position of the Queen's Bench in 1842 which carefully considered a statute that had been repealed fourteen years previously. Counsel may have difficulty in construing legislation such as is stated to have been enacted in Virginia, "An Act to Amend an Act making it penal to alter the Mark of an Unmarked Hog". The art of draftsmanship has improved but a statement of Arthur Symonds in 1835 should now be even more applicable. Symonds had been educated as an attorney and had acted as a draftsman. Finally he became Secretary to Mr. Poullet Thomson, then President of the Board of Trade and afterwards, as Lord Sydenham, Governor General of Canada. It was while holding the position of the latter's secretary that he testified before a Select Committee to consider the more careful preparation and revision of public bills, and upon his recommending that a committee be appointed, consisting of lawyers and a draftsman, the Chairman asked for his definition of the latter, to which he replied: — "A person who can express himself so as to be understood". If that is required in the one calling, it is at least as necessary in the art of advocacy.

Both Macaulay and Bentham passed severe strictures on the lawyers of their day, some of which may have been merited but others, I imagine, were without any basis. Counsel Pleydell puts the substance of the complaints more fairly in Guy Mannering: — "Law's like laudanum: it's much more easy to use it as a quack does, than to learn to apply it like a physician". And even Beatrix Potter, the authoress of *The Tale of Peter Rabbit*, and who I am sure had no bias in the matter, wrote timidly to her first publisher with reference to her father and a proposed agreement:

> I have not spoken to Mr. Potter but I think, Sir, it would
> be well to explain the Agreement clearly because he is a little
> formal having been a barrister.

You might be interested in the following deliverance of Lord Esher, Master of the Rolls, in *City of London Contract Corporation v. Styles*, 2 Tax Cases 239, at 243: —

> Mr. Moulton, however young he may look is verging
> towards middle age as a barrister, and for that reason I
> should think he must feel extremely happy that other
> engagements kept him somewhere else, but he certainly did
> leave the case in the hands of a counsel who has all the
> refreshing boldness of being a youthful barrister. To us poor

faded creatures — no, I will speak for myself — to a faded creature like myself, old and worn out in the law, it is most refreshing to hear bad points, as I said in the course of the argument, put as well as they possibly can be put, and they can only be put well by somebody who has the boldness and freshness of youth. It makes one feel as if one had gone back 40 or 50 years when one used to try to do the same thing oneself in that way, and perhaps sometimes succeed. I mean what I say, I mean that these points were put as well as they could possibly be put; but they consist only in words, they consist in darkening a case which is as clear as any case ever was, in darkening it and confusing it, as some very great people have the fit of doing, darkening and confusing the plainest possible propositions by multitudes.

Whether these remarks were taken to heart by the counsel in question is not a matter of record.

However, a barrister who knows his case, who presents it in a clear manner, embellished perhaps, but with discretion, need have no fear of not having a fair hearing. Disraeli is reported to have described the legal mind as chiefly displaying itself in illustrating the obvious, explaining the evident, and expatiating on the commonplace. In Macaulay's review of a new edition of Boswell's life of Johnson, the critic, after expressing amazement that a man like Johnson who reasoned all his premises so ably should assume his premises so foolishly, continues:

> It is the same with some eminent lawyers. Their legal arguments are intellectual prodigies, abounding with the happiest analogies and the most refined distinctions. The principles of their arbitrary science being once admitted, the statute-book and the reports being once assumed as the foundations of jurisprudence, these men must be allowed to be perfect masters of logic. But if a question arises as to the postulates on which their whole system rests, if they are called upon to vindicate the fundamental maxims of that system which they have passed their lives in studying, these very men often talk the language of savages or of children.

Counsel must, therefore, be prepared to understand the basis of the legal rules upon which he relies and, if a judge asks, "Where does this power end?", it will not do for him to reply, "It is for the Court to say" because, undoubtedly, the judge will counter with "I am seeking guidance". If asked upon which of two conflicting propositions he relies in support of his case, counsel should not say that he will leave that to the Court. His duty is to put forward that which will assist in a determination of the litigation in his favour. Of course, he must be frank with the Court and acknowledge the existence of the other theory while, at the same time, contending for the opposite view. He must be prepared to cover the ground expeditiously and, if it should come to pass that a limit be set on the time allowed for oral argument, it might be remembered that counsel would not be entitled as of right to compensation for that taken by judicial eminent domain.

Even in these days of unlimited opportunity, I suggest that when you are reading evidence in an Appellate Court, it is lost effort and lost time to repeat the words "Question" and "Answer". Nor is it necessary in reading judgments of the Courts below to set out the full names of cases cited and the references; it is an entirely different matter if, in argument, you are referring to decisions, in which case the Court requires the names, the proper names and dates of the report, and the pages. I might also suggest that in preparing a factum for use in the Supreme Court of Canada, you take note of a recent amendment to the rules whereby,

> When a statute, regulation, rule, ordinance or by-law is cited, or relied on, so much thereof as may be necessary to the decision of the case shall be printed at length, as an appendix to the factum, or ten copies of such statute, regulation, rule, ordinance or by-law may be filed for the use of the Court.

I emphasize the words "printed at length as an appendix to the factum, or ten copies may be filed for the use of the Court".

And now I have wearied you sufficiently. I conclude by reminding you that as against the imprecations that have been heaped upon the legal profession, all fair minded men continue to hold the administration of justice in high esteem. In that work you play an important part and, if the Courts, with your assistance, continue to do their share, two admonitions from the Bible will be fulfilled now as in the past. The first is from St. Paul's first epistle to the Corinthians: "Let all things be done decently and according to order", and the other is from the Prophecy of Amos: "But let judgment run down as waters, and righteousness as a mighty stream".

ADDRESS BY THE CHIEF JUSTICE AT THE UNIVERSITY OF NEW BRUNSWICK — HONOURARY DOCTOR OF LAWS SAINT JOHN, OCTOBER 15, 1954

May I first Sir thank you and the University of New Brunswick, for the great honour conferred upon me. My friends, Mr. West, Mr. Jamieson, Mr. Nicholson, Mr. Irving, Dr. Cheatam, Dean Curtis and Dean Cronkite, have requested that I should on their behalf tender their appreciation. It is a dignity that we will greatly cherish and hold in grateful remembrance.

The occasion is memorable, not merely for this graceful gesture on the part of this University, which is a reason personal to ourselves, but because, due to the generosity of your honourary Chancellor, Lord Beaverbrook, and by him, there has been this day dedicated to the service of the legal profession, and therefore to the service of the public, a new building fully equipped for the teaching of law. While primarily intended for the use of residents of New Brunswick, advantage will be taken of its facilities by others from various parts of Canada and from foreign shores. Those facilities include, it is needless to emphasize, not merely the physical structure, its embellishment and the fixtures and the books but also the members of the Faculty of Law of the University.

The teaching of law had its genesis in remote antiquity but throughout the centuries has developed in different countries in numberless ways. Here, as in the other common law provinces, you operate under a system different from one which has as its foundation, a code. The two great systems of law in Canada have different origins but, as has been many times pointed out by Chief Justice Rinfret, the aim of each is to do justice between man and man and between the individual on the one hand, and the community, whether it be a municipality, a province, or Canada, on the other. To those who have been nurtured in the former, the Common Law of England, as varied by applicable statutory enactments, is the rule to which they are accustomed and it is that law which, save for an excursion into comparative law, it will be the privilege and the function of the members of the

Faculty of Law of this University to instil into the minds of its students.

I assume that not everyone in this gathering is trained in the profession or expects to follow that branch of learning but every individual must be affected by the law at one time or another. One may not be concerned in a cause célèbre, but, being a gregarious animal, man is bound to feel its impact in his daily life, or perhaps his heir or beneficiary after he has departed this planet. It is, therefore, of the greatest importance that the law should be known to those who, by virtue of the training offered them, will be expected to be able to advise competently all who may consult them.

Contrary to the opinion of Mr. Bumble, the law is not "an ass, an idiot" and however imperfect it may appear to a disappointed litigant, its object is to regulate the transactions of, and the relationships among, various members of the human race. It is now a truism in all democracies that the rule of law is necessary for the well-being of their civilizations, but it is not necessary on the present occasion to enlarge upon the reason for this. It suffices to note that its bulwark is a free and independent judiciary which in England commenced in the reign of William the Third, with the Act of 1700, whereby it was enacted that Judges' commissions should run *quam diu se bene fesserint* (instead of *durante bene placito*) and their salaries ascertained and established, but that upon the address of both Houses of Parliament it might be lawful to remove them. So far as the Judges of the Superior Courts of the provinces in this country are concerned, a similar enactment is to be found in Section 99 of *The British North America Act* and as to the judges of courts set up by the Parliament of Canada, by provisions in the relevant statutes. Without presumption but with humility, one holder of judicial office, on behalf of all, ventures to affirm that the people of Canada have confidence in the ability, integrity and impartiality of the members of their judiciary.

However, the courts must rely upon the assistance and co-operation of the Bar, not merely in carrying out their obligation to apply the rule of law without fear or favour and under all circumstances, but also in ensuring the preservation of that function. The task allotted to each is not for the glory of the members of either but as a means of furthering the cause of democracy and keeping alive what Bliss Carman described as:

That master cry, If freedom die,

Ye will have lived in vain.

Freedom of thought and action does not come from the recitation of decided cases or the statement of principles enunciated in them, although each of these is necessary. The pupil must be taught not merely what the professor knows but he must be trained to think for himself so that he will appreciate the reason for a rule and apply it to circumstances as they arise. Then will he be able to distinguish those cases where the principle is inapplicable from those in which it will be proper to extend or amplify it. Nowhere is the general point put more clearly or expressively than by Cardinal Newman when, in his Sixth Discourse on University Teaching, he takes for granted, "that the true and adequate end of intellectual training and of a University is not Learning or Acquirement, but rather is Thought or Reason exercised upon Knowledge". At the same time there must not be overlooked the practical object of sending forth into a world men and women who will be able to advise others, draw pleadings, and argue in court. Into the current discussion as to the mode of attaining this desideratum I do not enter since the body having the responsibility of instruction must, after surveying the field, come to a conclusion as to what it considers best in the interests of the public which is really the test of the best interests of the neophytes.

Thus the responsibilities resting upon any Faculty of Law are onerous. In the past they have been met fully and with accomplishment at the University of New Brunswick and it is the firm conviction of all that in the future its Faculty will follow a noble tradition.

But if the teacher be important, as he is, the student body must be prepared to take full advantage of the opportunities afforded it. George Sharswood, in his Memoir of William Blackstone, justly points out that "the profession (of the law), like all others, demands of those who would succeed in it an earnest and entire devotion". In what other manner may a pupil justify the years he spends at such an institution as this? In some cases there have been sacrifices by parents and relatives. In every instance the student owes it to himself to utilize to the utmost the possibilities before him so that in time he may come to the Delectable Mountains; and there is an obligation to his future clients that no lack of preparation on his part may embroil them in needless litigation. This is not to say that all may bear the palm, but if each carries in his mind the words of another gifted son of this province his work will not have been in vain. In truth, anyone connected with the law must continue to pursue a studious course and therefore it is not only to the graduates of the Law School of the University of New Brunswick past, present and future, including today's recipients of your favour, but to each and all that these lines by Sir Charles G. D. Roberts are applicable: —

> Consider not my little worth, —
> The mean achievement, scamped in act,
> The high resolve and low result,
> The dream that durst not face the fact.
> But count the reach of my desire
> Let this be something in Thy sight —
> I have not, in the slothful dark,
> Forgot the Vision and the Height.

ADDRESS AT DINNER GIVEN BY
THE LAW SOCIETY OF UPPER CANADA
OSGOODE HALL
TO HONOUR OUR CHIEF JUSTICE
NOVEMBER 20, 1954

Mr. Treasurer,
Your Lordships,
Your Honours,
Ladies and Gentlemen: —

I would indeed be hypocritical if I did not admit at once the pleasure and satisfaction that tonight's gathering affords me. The remarks of the Treasurer have been flattering in the highest degree and, so far as they are personal, I trust that I shall cherish them with humility. I realize, of course, that they must also be taken as addressed to the office and, if my incumbency thereof merits but one-half the encomiums, then will I be satisfied and, I trust, not only the profession but the public at large. Nor can I proceed without publicly acknowledging my appreciation of the presence of so many members of the Bench and Bar. I have had the opportunity of meeting most of them during the evening and I hope to see the others before they leave, but now, to each individually, and particularly to those who have come from a distance, I extend my sincere thanks.

It was a gracious gesture on the part of the Treasurer and Benchers, not only to hold this event, but also to arrange that it take place in this building. Perhaps, in some future constitutional controversy learned counsel may argue that this is an example of the double aspect rule. In any event, if Bacon's statement be fact, as I believe it to be, — "The place of justice is a hallowed place", — then Osgoode Hall deserves that description not merely for the profession in general but certainly on this occasion for this speaker. Here I spent in Weekly Court, in Chambers, and in writing judgments what was left of three years after commercial travelling trips to almost every county and district centre in the province. But that was a mere interlude to the luncheons in the Judges' dining-room where the talk was high but the food content low. I understand that while the conversation is still good the physical inner man is better satisfied now than formerly. However, it is of this building I was speaking and since I also agree with Samuel Butler that "appropriate passages are intended to be appropriated", I quote from Mr. Charles Armstrong's sketch of the Honourable Society of Osgoode Hall:

> Convocation was first held in 1832 in the south part of the brick east wing of the present structure without the monumental stone facade on the south front.

Thus for one hundred and twenty-two years judges, barristers, solicitors and students-at-law have passed through the portals of this building intent on serving a jealous mistress. In Canada it is no mean achievement. But the governing body is older. You may remember, Mr. Treasurer, that when addressing the budding lawyers at a convocation a few years ago, I took the opportunity of referring to the Law Society of Upper Canada and pointed out that the title itself is a noble one and the Society's history one of which any body might well be proud. May I add that Mr. Armstrong's statement that its members have included one-half of the Chief Justices of Canada is still true. It has not been overlooked that there are institutions performing comparable functions in the other provinces, and I hasten to mention an organization (although of a different character), the Canadian Bar Association, so that it may not be suggested that the present holder of the position, particularly in the presence of the Solicitor General of Canada and the Attorney General of Ontario, expressed any inclination towards either federal jurisdiction or provincial autonomy.

I referred to the Law Society because I have known it actively as a student, as a practitioner, and (I understand to the discomfort of some) as an examiner at the Law School. I am not able to reach back into the distant past, as did Sir William Mulock on the occasion of the dinner in honour of his ninetieth birthday, but a remark a few months ago by one of my friends gave me pause. He suggested that before a few more suns should set over the dark hills of time I should put down on paper an account of the people I have known and such events in which I have participated. Only for a moment did it disturb my equanimity, because I have no immediate intention of departing this earth, and no thought of writing at any time an autobiography. You will, therefore, be relieved to know that to-night there will be no recollections, — save one, and it is mentioned because an open confession is good for the soul. It must now be related that once upon a time a rule of the Law Society was, perhaps, broken (this is merely judicial caution in not going beyond what is necessary). The script for a modest card to be inserted in a newspaper was confused by the type-setter with an advertisement of a laundry establishment so that all who ran might read: "Guthrie & Kerwin, Barristers, Solicitors, etc. Goods called for and delivered". I daresay more was promised in that notice than any lawyer could ever hope to sign, seal or deliver. In any event, any possible action by the Benchers is now outlawed, even if, under the circumstances, the notice would have been considered obnoxious.

I am afraid that I am now treading the well-known path paved with good intentions, but when I saw the smiling countenance of the Judge of the County Court of the County of Wellington, I felt that one of his stories should have a larger circulation. Many years ago John Galt, a famous Scotsman, with The Canada Company, founded Guelph and when, in 1927, the 100th anniversary of that event was celebrated, even the Irish and English together with all other sections of the community joined with Galt's countrymen in celebrating the occasion. You must understand that most of the lawyers' offices were on Douglas Street — banners were unfurled and flags erected and it was the suggestion of the then young practitioner that over the entrance to Douglas Street should be erected a banner bearing the inscription: "Abandon hope all ye who enter here".

And now enough of the first personal singular, or even, shall I say, of the "we", as it might appear in reasons for judgment. Most of you will agree that at a gathering of this nature an enjoyable evening might be spent by recalling the past, present and future of the legal profession in the most glowing terms. However, not all sections of the public regard us with complacency. In fact, at times we may look yellow to their jaundiced eye, as witness a statement heard some years ago to the effect that lawyers and judges do not understand mankind and social problems. That statement is, of course, without foundation, but, while you know it to be false, it expresses a view which is held by too many beyond the pale. It stems from a perversion of thought, — that law is purely legalistic and its votaries druids of naughty mien employing a jargon of their own. I do not propose to reiterate the reasons why every civilized community requires a system of law and hierarchy of courts. They are well known to all of you and, in fact, to each reasonably well informed person in every walk of life. True, from time to time, it is advisable to resurrect them and to explain them in the light of changing circumstances, but tonight they need not be elaborated.

The present quarrel is with the statement quoted. At first as to what appears to be the more easily answered of the underlying fallacies. There is no general complaint when physicians, surgeons, architects, scientists, operating in their particular spheres, use terms which have proved suitable to express their thoughts and carry on their investigations. Similarly it is necessary for the legal profession to employ a terminology which has developed through the ages, because, by trial and error, the right word or phrase has evolved to describe a situation or a problem. Surely it is not a matter for reproach that lawyers use those means to explain their client's cause in or out of court and thus enable his business to be brought to a conclusion in a shorter period of time. Legal terminology is a necessity, not merely for the practitioners but also in the best interests of the members of the public, whose servants they are.

The other fallacy is more firmly embedded. It is thought by some that law (including equity) has certain fixed rules permitting of no exceptions and suffering no easing of their rigours. What is overlooked is that law is made for mankind and not mankind for law. The exceptional cases where some lawyers fall by the wayside only prove that the great majority realize its truth and act accordingly, and the practical steps taken by that majority to assist those who may have been damnified by the unworthy actions of their fallen brethren emphasize that the profession realizes its obligations. The only justification for the law's existence is that the individual may pursue his avocation and, so far as it is possible in this world, in contentment. The rights of the individual are paramount until interfered with by some positive requirement; and that is the basis of the rule of law. Most of the transactions between human beings or their instruments, the corporations, are completed without any recourse to litigation, because the rules governing them have gradually come to fruition, whether by common law, by civil law or by statutory enactment, as a result of the democratic process. As occasion arises these rules must be amended or altered to meet new social conditions. The disputes that arise are, in most cases, as to the facts, and that is the reason so much depends upon the decision of the trial tribunal.

Let me say at once that no one need entertain a fear that I am moving a vote of want of confidence in appellate tribunals. Appeals are provided so that, if after one attempt to find the true circumstances a party is not satisfied, nothing reasonable may be left undone to justify the litigant thinking he has been unfairly dealt with. There are bound to be disputations in some instances as to the applicable law, because no one pretends that law is an exact science. I am speaking now of the great mass of disputes in which a knowledge of human nature is requisite; and it is at this precise point that I venture to affirm that in a purely worldly sense the legal profession by its training, by its experience, and by the mingling of its members in other groups is the most appropriate that has been devised to permit the work of the world to proceed in peace. While this may appear self-evident to us, it is my suggestion that, if the practicing members be prepared on all occasions to take part in the activities of their fellow citizens, the groundwork of the complaints on behalf of some of these disappears. This counsel of perfection applies to the Bar, because the holder of judicial office is restricted, and properly so, as to the fields of endeavour which he may pursue. But in our system, whereby the judiciary is drawn from the practitioners, the members of the former are able to bring to the discharge of their duties that training and experience which may have received as members of the latter. And, therefore, let all such come to the aid of their profession and by their interests outside their practice, — in their community's affairs — show to the laity that they are concerned with the lot of their fellow men. Not merely will that object be accomplished but the experience thereby gained will be of the greatest assistance in keeping our own house in order. Change for its own sake is not a desideratum, but continued surveys of our position from detached vantage points cannot fail to be illuminating and point the way more quickly to what should be done to make the machinery of justice work.

Perhaps the erroneous views which I have criticized are held because practically every individual at one time or another finds himself concerned with the law and its administration. Whatever may be the reason, I believe that if the suggestions made are carried out neither the timid newcomer nor the hardened litigant will fail to be impressed and benefited by their execution.

I shall not weary you by dilating upon the position of the judiciary in the opinion either of the profession militant or of outsiders. The experience of the labourer who sought employment from a farmer may serve to exemplify the responsibilities resting upon the holder of judicial office. He was hired for one day to cut wood. The job was done satisfactorily and he was engaged to build a fence the next day. That task having been completed in good order, the man was told on the third day to separate potatoes into three piles — (1) First class; (2) Second class but still edible; (3) Fit only for the soil heap. About noon the farmer went to see how the work was progressing and discovered that his man had fainted. Upon being revived and asked what had happened he at first declined to say. The farmer pointed out that his work on the first two days had been well done and that there was nothing difficult about the current job. Finally, after much persuasion, the man replied that he could not face the responsibility of deciding which potatoes went where. It is, of course, of capital importance that justice be swift, but if, on occasion, the time appears to lengthen between argument and judgment, you might bear in mind the struggle involved in reaching a conclusion, — and particularly if the coram consists of more than one.

The relative position of the Bench and Bar is akin to that of partners and, therefore, since an appreciation of the task of the occupants of the former has been suggested by the members of the latter, they in turn may reasonably expect a quid pro quo. It is generally true that in the past the members of the judiciary have understood the problems of the solicitor and advocate and have treated their efforts with consideration. In the future, so much, at least, should be accorded them. However, the Bench is required to decide between conflicting views, — whether as between man and man, or as between the public represented by the Crown, on the one hand, and an accused, on the other. The interests of the parties must be paramount and I am sure that none would wish it otherwise. This ultimate object may be attained if each on both sides of the border, in the spirit of Dr. Johnson, in his "Prayer before the study of the law", requests (and performs his good works accordingly): —

> Almighty God, the Giver of wisdom, without whose help resolutions are vain, without whose blessing study is ineffectual; enable me, if it by Thy will, to attain such knowledge as may qualify me to direct the doubtful, and instruct the ignorant; to prevent wrongs and terminate contentions.

ADDRESS TO THE CANADIAN CLUB, OTTAWA, MAY 11, 1955

When I was asked to address a meeting of the Men's Canadian Club of Ottawa, I found it difficult to decide upon a topic and I was reminded of Lord Morton's address to the Canadian Bar Association meeting in Banff in 1949. He had been confronted with a similar situation and stated that he had thought of something in the nature of a dissertation on some branch of the law, since such address might read well in the printed record which no doubt his audience and their families would read night after night during the long winter evenings; and he could well imagine the children clustering round and saying: "Now, daddy, do read us again that wonderful passage from Lord Morton's speech about the rights of a mortgagee in possession".

However, like Lord Morton, I decided against that idea and it was also impossible to adopt a suggestion that the office of the Chief Justice of Canada should be dealt with somewhat in the manner that Lord Simonds, in his address to this Club, had treated the position of Lord Chancellor. That office is not only one of great antiquity, having attached to it many powers and features that were gradually accumulated in the course of centuries, but, as Lord Simonds pointed out, his duties of presiding over the House of Lords in its judicial capacity and over the Judicial Committee of the Privy Council were combined with political obligations of a very high order, such as membership in the Cabinet and as Speaker of the House of Lords. Such is not the case with the Chief Justice of Canada and although duties not strictly judicial are from time to time involved, they are really not of a political nature. In addition to being the Chief Justice of the Supreme Court, the incumbent also acts upon request of His Excellency the Governor General as the latter's Deputy, but it is provided in the appointment that the Deputy may not dissolve Parliament. If His Excellency is temporarily absent from Canada for more than one month, or dies, or is incapacitated while he holds the position, the Chief Justice, by virtue of the Letters Patent constituting the office of Governor General, becomes what is termed Administrator of the Government of Canada upon taking the oaths of allegiance and for the due execution of the office of Governor General prescribed by the Letters Patent. The Governor General may appoint others to be his Deputy and in the case of the death, incapacity, or absence from Canada of the Chief Justice, the Senior Judge for the time being of the Supreme Court of Canada becomes Administrator.

There is but one more reference to the Chief Justice and that is because many have asked the correct mode of addressing, or referring to, him. Some may inquire, as did Mr. Ivor Brown, in an article published a few months ago, *What's in a Name?*; and he prefaced his remarks by stating that in a bus the conductor had called him Guv'nor when he asked for the fare and Mate when he received it. Well, it is not either of these, but neither is it Mr. Chief Justice. A tendency to use all these words presumably comes from the south where it is correct in the case of the Chief Justice of the United States. I presume that the fact that he is so-called and that each Associate Justice of the Supreme Court of the United States and each Puisne Judge of the Supreme Court of Canada is Mr. Justice, does not infer that the dignity inherent in "Mr." is lost merely because one happens to be the Chief Justice of Canada.

And now as to the Court itself. From remarks heard over the years its members gather that there are many things which are not self-evident. One query which has always surprised us is: — "May anyone attend a sitting of the Court?" May I immediately emphasize that all Canadian Courts of justice are open to the public, with some few exceptions, such as cases dealing with indecency and hearings against juveniles where the presiding Judge, or Magistrate, may, for obvious reasons, clear the Court. Ordinarily, however, the sessions of all Courts in this country are open and the Supreme Court of Canada is no exception. All Courts welcome the attendance of anyone so that not only will justice be done, it will have the appearance of being accomplished. Years ago a distinguished Lord Chancellor of Great Britain remarked that judicial proceedings in England are public and later one stated "Every Court of Justice is open to every subject of The King". Those remarks apply to every part of Canada.

If you attend a session you will find the Court consisting of its full complement of nine members, or perhaps seven, or, in the majority of cases, five, which is the quorum. Unless unavoidably absent all justices take part in the determination of constitutional questions and of murder cases. You will usually find that we sit in conventional black robes and white tabs. However, we appear in scarlet robes trimmed with ermine, black sash, and three cornered hats on the opening day of each Term; and also when hearing capital cases, and on the last day of a Term to which an adjournment has been made for the purpose only of giving judgments. The only other occasion on which you may see us in our full regalia is the Opening of Parliament. There is some question as to what model was followed when the robes and sash were adopted, but the prevailing opinion seems to be that they were copied from what the Judges of the Queen's Bench in England had used.

The ensuing reference to a few dates and episodes, will not result, I trust, in boring you, as so many young pupils have, I am sure, been bored with the date, for instance, of the Battle of Hastings, and with the regnal years. At that, I find that the learning by rote many years ago of all the counties and districts of Ontario, together with the county or district towns, can even now on occasion be of assistance. Furthermore, the genesis of the Court, its establishment and the position it now occupies are all part of the evolution of Canada from a colony to a member of the British Commonwealth of Nations. You may recollect that when Confederation came into force on July 1, 1867, the four provinces of Ontario, Quebec, Nova Scotia and New Brunswick had a total population of about three and one-half millions. Rupert's Land and the Northwest Territories were admitted in 1870, Manitoba in the same year, British Columbia in 1871, Prince Edward Island in 1873 and Alberta and Saskatchewan were established in 1905. Newfoundland was admitted in 1949 and the Court heard the first appeal from that province a short time ago. By the terms of *The British North America Act of 1867* the Governor General is to appoint the judges of the Superior, District and County Courts in each province, excepting the judges of the Courts of Probate in Nova Scotia and New Brunswick. The Members of the Courts of Quebec are to be selected from the Bar of that Province, and then comes section 101:

> The Parliament of Canada may, notwithstanding anything in this *Act*, from time to time, provide for the Constitution, Maintenance, and Organization of a General Court of Appeal for Canada, and for the Establishment of any additional Courts for the better Administration of the Laws of Canada.

That is the authority for Parliament to constitute the Supreme Court of Canada. Several attempts were made to exercise this authority, but it was not until 1875 that Parliament provided for the Supreme Court and Exchequer Court, the Members of the two Courts being the same. Two years later different persons were appointed to the Exchequer Court. Before the enactment of the 1875 statute copies of the proposed Bill had been sent to the

Members of the various provincial Courts and to others for their comment. In the Macdonald Papers in the Archives will be found a collection of answers from these individuals which indicated various points of view as to the constitutionality of the Bill's provisions and incorporated suggestions for alteration. Oliver Mowat (he had not then been knighted) wrote from Toronto a long exposé of his views. This is of particular interest, since we are told in Donald Creighton's "John A. Macdonald, The Young Politician" that while Mowat had been the latter's first articled student in his law office in Kingston, when both were in the Legislature under the *Act of Union* of 1845, Macdonald, angered by a speech by his former pupil, had confronted the latter after the Speaker had left the chair and roared "You damned pup, I'll slap your chops". However, in writing to Ottawa, Mowat discussed the proposed Bill in a serious and comprehensive manner.

There is also a letter from Alpheus Todd, Librarian of Parliament. The main comment by him and Mowat was directed to the power to be given the new Court to hear References by the Governor in Council as to the constitutionality of legislation, actual or proposed. Throughout the years there have been many References of this nature, but it was not until 1912 that the power of Parliament to provide for such proceedings was attacked in the Judicial Committee of the Privy Council in England. In decisions handed down in that and in the following year the Committee decided that Parliament had such power. It was natural that the Members of the Charlottetown and Quebec conferences and of the London meetings should have present to their minds the constitution of the United States. While in that country all powers not conferred upon the central government were reserved to the States, the opposite approach was made in drafting and having enacted the constitution of Canada. The Supreme Court of the United States was established in 1789, but, while suggestions were made from time to time there that it should have power to consider References of the nature mentioned, these did not meet with approval. On the other hand, it was considered advisable to do so in this country and the fear expressed by many that because the Court was created by Parliament its Members might be more likely to be influenced by Parliament than Judges of the provincial Courts is without foundation.

The appointments of all Superior, County and District Court Judges are made in the same way as appointments of the Members of the Supreme Court of Canada. At present three are from Ontario, three from Quebec, one from the Maritimes, one from the Middle

West and one from British Columbia. The *Act* constituting the Court in 1875 had in it a provision that the judgment of the Court should in all cases be final and conclusive "saving any right which Her Majesty may be graciously pleased to exercise by virtue of Her Royal Prerogative". However, in the course of constitutional development, the Statute of Westminster was passed in England in 1931 to carry out the declarations and resolutions set forth in the Reports of the Imperial Conferences held at Westminster in 1926 and 1930, and in 1935 the Judicial Committee of the Privy Council decided that Parliament had the power to make the Supreme Court of Canada the final Court in criminal cases. Later a Bill was introduced into Parliament to provide that it should also be the final Court in civil matters and that appeals to the Judicial Committee from any Court in Canada should be abolished, and upon a Reference to the Supreme Court of Canada that Court held that it was within the Legislative competence of Parliament to enact such a provision. By arrangement an appeal from that decision was not argued during the war, but in 1947 the Judicial Committee affirmed the decision of the Supreme Court and the Bill was passed in December, 1949. Except, therefore, as to civil matters commenced before that date, it is the final Court of Appeal in Canada.

The result is that the work of the Court has increased considerably. Not merely are appeals taken to it that would otherwise have gone direct from the provincial Courts to London, but many are now taken that otherwise would not have materialized since a loser in a provincial Court might previously have feared that even if he succeeded this Court his opponent might then obtain leave to go to the Judicial Committee.

A few years ago, in order to cope with the increased business, the Members of the Court recommended, and Parliament enacted, that the First Term of the Court should commence earlier than theretofore and now it commences on the fourth Tuesday in January, the Second on the fourth Tuesday in April and the Third on the first Tuesday in October. Sittings are now almost continuous, save for short adjournments for Christmas and Easter and a longer one for the summer. It is impossible for the Court to decide each appeal immediately upon the conclusion of the argument, or even in the few hours which are available before and after the actual time spent on the bench. A period is required to consider the arguments adduced and in many instances to make further research, particularly when constitutional questions are involved. The greater part of this necessary time can only be found during these recesses.

The Court has an original jurisdiction in connection with certain applications for *habeas corpus*, the details of which are at the moment unimportant, because the main business of the Court, in addition to References, is appellate, that is, no witnesses are heard and the appeals are disposed of on a record of what has occurred in the Courts below. The parties file factums, or written arguments, and then the oral arguments are heard when the case is reached on the list. This list is made up in view of the tremendous distances in this country and in order, so far as possible, to meet the conveniences of the litigants. The first part consists of election cases, the second of Western Provinces cases, including appeals from the Northwest Territories and the Yukon, the third, appeals from the Maritimes, the fourth from the Province of Quebec and the fifth from Ontario. Constitutional references, capital cases and, in fact, all criminal appeals where the accused is in custody are given priority. The factums and oral arguments may be in either English or French and the record in many cases from Quebec is entirely in French with the assistance of the record, the factums, the arguments and the books in the library, the Members of the Court proceed to decide the appeals. In order that in a proper case no one may be deprived of having his rights determined by the highest authority merely because of financial considerations, provision is made that if such a person swears that he is not worth $500 in the world except his wearing apparel and his interest in the subject matter of the intended appeal and that he is unable to provide the usual security for costs, a Member of the Court may make an order permitting him to appeal in *forma pauperis*. The application must be accompanied by a certificate of counsel that the appellant has reasonable grounds of appeal. A respondent may also secure leave to oppose an appeal under similar conditions. If the order is granted, an appellant need not give the security for costs ordinarily required, nor need he pay any fees by way of Government law stamps. If either appellant or respondent ultimately succeeds in this Court, he is not entitled to any counsel fees, but only to out-of-pocket expenses and three-eighths of the usual charges under the other items in the tariff. These remarks as to appeals in *forma pauperis* apply to civil cases. No security is required in criminal appeals. As to these either the accused or the Attorney General may appeal upon any question of law upon which there has been a dissent in the provincial Court of Appeal and in other criminal cases a Member of the Court, or the full Court, has power to grant leave to appeal on a question of law.

I shall not attempt to describe the building in which the Court operates — in the hope that those who have not already visited shall shortly remedy that situation. On May 20th, 1939, Her Majesty the Queen, upon the occasion of laying the foundation stone of this edifice devoted to "the administration of Justice in Canada", remarked: —

> It is fitting that on these heights above the Ottawa —
> surely one of the noblest situations in the world — you
> should add to the imposing group of buildings which house
> your parliament and the executive branch of government, a
> worthy home for your Supreme Court.

In that addition to space for the Exchequer Court, there is, of course, the Courtroom, and accommodation is supplied for the Members of the Court and the necessary staff and also a library of about 135,000 volumes, which should be a source of pride to every Canadian and as to which I give a few details. There are to be found copies of all the statutes of Canada and of every province and of Great Britain and of Ireland and from the various countries of the Commonwealth, the reports of decisions of the Supreme Court of Canada and the Exchequer Court and of all the Provincial Courts. There is a comprehensive collection of reports of the Courts of Great Britain, Ireland, Scotland and of the Commonwealth countries. There is a separate division comprising nearly 40,000 volumes and containing reports of every State in the United States of America. There are practically all the legal textbooks published in Great Britain and Canada and a great number from every part of the Commonwealth and from the United States, as well as about 15,000 law treatises and reports from France and Belgium. In addition there is a precious collection of rare law books and folios of the sixteenth, seventeenth and eighteenth centuries pertaining to the common law and the law of France, the latter of which, particularly, are of great importance in considering the civil code of the Province of Quebec. The Library contains a number of biographies and autobiographies of men known to the law, as well as volumes of a more general nature.

I trust that what I have said has not appeared to be either too legalistic or historical. However, agriculturists, merchants, manu-facturers, businessmen and housewives, in fact all in Canada, have an interest in the administration of justice. All Courts constitute a strong arm of the constitution and in many cases their decisions govern many more than those who are intimately concerned in particular pieces of litigation, or in a prosecution. Anyone may find that his method of earning a livelihood or even his mode of living has been affected by a decision to which he is not a party.

What is justice in particular circumstances may not be easy to discover and, therefore, it is that in all civilized countries the matter is not always left to the sole arbitrament of one individual, but appeals are provided in many cases to an Appeal Court and thence to a final Court which, in Canada, is the Supreme Court of Canada. That Court was established to ensure that there should be one ultimate tribunal to determine the law between subject and subject and between the various governments and the subject so that the results might be uniform. The civil law of the Province of Quebec applies in civil cases arising in that province and the common law in the other provinces; in each case, as varied by provincial enactments, — where the subject matter does not fall within the jurisdiction of the Parliament of Canada. Some questions arise which are common to all, but others depend upon the construction of valid provincial or municipal enactments. In each system, the common law and the civil law, the object is to do justice between man and man and between government and governed.

Gilbert and Sullivan may not have been quite accurate in saying that in every respect the law is the embodiment of everything that is excellent, but it is the endeavour of the Supreme Court of Canada and of all Canadian Courts to keep pace with changing conditions because, as Sir Edward Coke pointed out many years ago, "Reason is the life of the law". In the sixteenth century Richard Hooker put it thus: "Of Law there can be no less acknowledged, than that her seat is the bosom of God, her voice the harmony of the world: all things in heaven and earth do her homage, the very least as feeling her care, and the greatest as not exempted from her power". With these goals before us, and with the spirit of God hovering over us, the Members of the Supreme Court of Canada echo the words of Daniel Webster: "The Law: It has honoured us, may we honour it".

ADDRESS AT HARVARD UNIVERSITY IN CELEBRATION OF THE TWO HUNDREDTH ANNIVERSARY OF THE BIRTH OF JOHN MARSHALL SEPTEMBER 25, 1955

This session of the Conference was held in the Ames Court-room in Austin Hall. Professor Arthur Sutherland of the Harvard Law School was chairman. Again the proceeding consisted of two parts — an address by the Chief Justice of Canada*, a discussion of the papers written by Judge Charles Wyzanski, Jr. and Mr. John Lord O'Brian on the fourth theme of the conference, *The Value of Constitutionalism Today.*

The members of the Conference first heard Chief Justice Patrick Kerwin, of Canada, present his address,

Constitutionalism in Canada.[262]

*Hon. Patrick Kerwin, Chief Justice of Canada. Chief Justice Kerwin was born in 1889. He studied law at Osgoode Hall in Toronto, was called to the bar of Ontario in 1911, became King's Counsel in 1928, and became a Justice of the Supreme Court of Ontario in 1932. In 1935, he became a Justice of the Supreme Court of Canada, and in 1954 he became Chief Justice.

A facsimile of the full text of this Address is presented on the following pages.

---

262 Arthur E. Sutherland, "Government Under Law – A Conference Held at Harvard Law School on the Occasion of the Bicentennial of JOHN MARSHALL, Chief Justice of the United States, 1801-1835" (Harvard University Press, 1956).`

-73-

ADDRESS AT HARVARD UNIVERSITY, SEPTEMBER,
1955, IN CELEBRATION OF THE TWO HUNDREDTH
ANNIVERSARY OF THE BIRTH OF JOHN MARSHALL

May I first say how gratified I was to receive
the invitation to attend and take part in the celebration
of the two hundredth anniversary of the birth of John Marshall.   It is a privilege and a pleasure to do honour to
the memory of the great Chief Justice whose judgments are
so often quoted not only in the United States, but in many
other countries and not least in Canada. Throughout the
length and breadth of Canada his opinions are from time to
time referred to and particularly those dealing with the
construction of the Constitution of the United States. He
had a robust mind which, coupled with a felicity of expression, enabled him to put in trenchant terms the philosophy
of the Constitution and to infuse its majestic outlines with
a living spirit. The free peoples of the world are indebted
to him and are happy to take part in a discussion of the
general subject of this conference.

It is apparent from a perusal of the papers published for the purpose of this gathering under the heading
"Government Under Law" that more than one meaning may be
attached to the term "Constitutionalism" in the United
States and that when one goes beyond the confines of the
Republic even greater variations may be found. As it was
intimated that a discussion of The British North America

Act, 1867, as amended, might be of some interest that suggestion will be followed although it must be immediately emphasized that it is only the written Constitution of Canada, and, as will subsequently appear, there are other matters to be considered in applying the term to that country.

The British North America Act was enacted by the Parliament of Great Britain and Ireland in 1867 following conferences at Charlottetown, in Prince Edward Island, Quebec City and London, England, but it is impossible to understand what was accomplished thereby without a brief historical summary. Following the wars between France and England, the latter became the sovereign power over a great part of what is now Canada, although certain areas had been settled and not conquered. The Treaty of Paris of 1763 was followed by the Quebec Act of 1774 and then by the Constitutional Act of 1791, under which Upper Canada and Lower Canada were established. These were united by the Act of Union of 1840 and became the Province of Canada, so that the title of The British North America Act, 1867, is "An Act for the Union of Canada, Nova Scotia, and New Brunswick, and the Government thereof; and for Purposes connected therewith". Provision was made and steps subsequently taken for the admission and creation of other provinces so that at the present time there are ten in all. Nova Scotia and New Brunswick, as well as

-75-

the others now forming part of Canada, had a long and eventful history as colonies or as parts of the old Northwest
Territories. The old Province of Canada was re-subdivided
to form two separate provinces under the names of Ontario
and Quebec.

After the establishment of the United States of
America its history and development and that of the colonies
to the north proceeded along different paths. Many of the
battles for representative and responsible government had
been fought and won before 1867. While the war of 1812 had
passed into history, the Union would, in the words of one of
the recitals of The British North America Act, "conduce to
the Welfare of the Provinces and promote the Interests of
the British Empire". Conditions varied in the four provinces, particularly in Quebec where the overwhelming majority
of the population were French and Roman Catholic, while in
the other provinces the great majority were English-speaking
and Protestants. In the former, the basis of the civil law
was French, while in the latter, save as altered by statute,
the English Common Law held full sway. In all the Criminal
Law was English as varied by local enactments.

At the conferences preceding the enactment of The
British North America Act considerable attention was directed
to the Constitution of the United States but it was considered advisable to endow the legislatures of the provinces

exclusively with power to make laws in relation to matters
coming within certain enumerated classes of subjects, being,
in general, local matters which solely affect a province (s.
92) and to confer the residue of legislative authority upon
the Parliament of the new entity, Canada (s.91), although
in that section there is also an enumeration. Nowhere does
the Act empower any Court to declare an Act of Parliament,
or of a legislature, ultra vires. However, the authority
of the Privy Council in England had for years been exercised
in deciding appeals from colonial courts, -- in conjunction
with a legislative and executive authority exerted by the
disallowance of colonial legislation. The Privy Council
treated as invalid and void ordinances and statutes of
colonial legislatures when they exceeded the powers committed to them, or when they had neglected to observe a prohi-
bition contained in the charter of government. In fact, the
colonial courts themselves declined to give effect to legislation which had been enacted in contravention of some such
restriction. Although considerably amplified, that would
appear to be one of the bases of the argument of James Otis
in the case of General Warrants, and it is considered by some
that this practice of the Privy Council and of the colonial
courts prepared the way for the ultimate adoption by the
people of the United States of the principle and practice
of the judicial review of legislation. In colonial days

the superior authority was the Sovereign, either in Council or in Parliament, but after the Revolution that became in the new Republic the sovereignty of the people.

Whatever the origin, the power was exercised during Chief Justice Marshall's incumbency with respect to State and Federal legislation. In Canada the Courts have exercised a similar jurisdiction in connection with legislation of the Parliament of Canada and of the Legislatures of the Provinces. There is allotted to the latter by Head 14 of s. 92 authority to make laws in relation to "The Administration of Justice in the Province, including the Constitution, Maintenance, and Organization of Provincial Courts, both of Civil and Criminal Jurisdiction, and including Procedure in Civil Matters in those Courts". By Head 27 of s. 91 Parliament is empowered to make laws in relation to "The Criminal Law, except the Constitution of Courts of Criminal Jurisdiction, but including the Procedure in Criminal Matters". By another section (96), the Governor General, which means the representative of the Monarch acting on the advice of the Canadian Cabinet, is to appoint the Judges of the Superior, District, and County Courts in each province, except those of the Courts of Probate in Nova Scotia and New Brunswick. Magistrates, Justices of the Peace, and some others may be appointed by a province. S. 101 enacts:-

"The Parliament of Canada may, notwithstanding

-78-

"anything in this Act, from Time to Time, provide for
the Constitution, Maintenance, and Organization of a
general Court of Appeal for Canada, and for the Establishment of any additional Courts for the better ·
Administration of the Laws of Canada".

Pursuant thereto the Supreme Court of Canada was established
in 1875.

Subject to what is later stated as to the Exchequer
Court, the provincial Courts, whether the members are appointed by Canada or the provinces, deal with federal and provincial matters alike and the Supreme Court Act provides for and
regulates appeals from their decisions, so that the Supreme
Court of Canada is a general Court of Appeal. At first appeals could be taken to the Judicial Committee of the Privy
Council from the provincial Courts of Appeal and, by leave
of the Committee, from the Supreme Court of Canada. Pursuant to the Imperial Statute of Westminster of 1931, enacted
as a result of conferences among representatives of Great
Bratain and the Dominions, an amendment to The Supreme Court
Act was passed by Parliament in 1933 abolishing appeals to
the Privy Council in criminal cases and in 1935 this amendment was held valid by the Judicial Committee. (1)   In Decem-

---

(1) British Coal Corporation v. The King (1935) A.C., 500.

295

-79-

ber, 1949, another amendment was enacted abolishing appeals
in civil cases from any Court in Canada, which the Courts,
including the Judicial Committee, also upheld, (2) and, therefore, at the present time, The Supreme Court of Canada is the
final Court of Appeal for the country, except as to civil matters commenced before that time. It has a qualified original
jurisdiction by which every Member of the Court "except in
matters arising out of any claim for extradition under any
treaty, has concurrent jurisdiction with the courts or judges
of the several provinces, to issue the writ of habeas corpus
ad subjiciendum, for the purpose of any inquiry into the
cause of commitment in any criminal case under any Act of
the Parliament of Canada". (3)

The only other additional Court for the better
administration of the laws of Canada established by Parliament is the Exchequer Court, dealing with such matters as
patents, trademarks, copyrights, revenue, and expropriations
by, and claims against, Canada. It also has jurisdiction in
admiralty cases. Appeals lie in most cases from the decisions
of that Court to the Supreme Court of Canada.

---

(2) Reference Re An Act to Amend the Supreme Court Act (1940)
S.C.R., 49; (1947) A.C., 127.

(3) Supreme Court Act, R.S.C. 1952 c. 259, s. 57.

In all Courts the question may be raised as to the
validity of Canadian or Provincial statutes and, in addition
thereto, the Supreme Court Act from its very inception pro-
viided for the giving of advice by the Court upon certain
questions that might be submitted to it by the Governor
General-in-Council. This provision is now to be found in
s. 55 of the Supreme Court Act, s-s.(1) of which reads:-

"(1) Important questions of law or fact touching

    (a) the interpretation of the British North
        America Acts;

    (b) the constitutionality or interpretation of
        any Dominion or provincial legislation;

    (c) the appellate jurisdiction as to educational
        matters, by the British North America Act,
        1867, or by any other Act or law vested in
        the Governor in Council;

    (d) the powers of the Parliament of Canada, or
        of the legislatures of the provinces, or of
        the respective governments thereof, whether
        or not the particular power in question has
        been or is proposed to be exercised; or

    (e) any other matter, whether or not in the opin-
        ion of the Court ejusdem generis with the
        foregoing enumerations, with reference to
        which the Governor in Council sees fit to
        submit any such question;

-81-

> "may be referred by the Governor in Council to
> the Supreme Court for hearing and considera-
> tion; and any question touching any of the
> matters aforesaid, so referred by the Gover-
> nor in Council, shall be conclusively deemed
> to be an important question".

Considerable discussion occurred before this was written in
the Act, but it was acted upon in a number of cases and when
the question was squarely raised it was held that the provision was _intra vires_ Parliament. (4)

#The system was adopted notwithstanding the fact
that in the United States it had been decided to confer no
such power upon any Court in your country. Difficulties
sometime arise, caused by the generality of the questions
put but, on the whole, the jurisdiction has not been used
extensively and it has served the useful purpose of obtaining an authoritative pronouncement upon the legality of
actual, or proposed legislation, without putting a litigant
to the trouble and expense of raising the issue and carry-

↑ *Above paragraph [between square brackets] omitted by Patrick Kerwin.*

---

(4)   A.G. of Ontario v. A.G. of Canada, (1912) A.C., 571.
(4a) Reference re Industrial Relations and Disputes Act,
       not yet reported.

I had written here, before I arrived at Harvard
that that system was adopted notwithstanding the fact that in
the United States it had been decided to confer no such power
upon any court in your country. Since my arrival here, I take
it that that statement must be qualified, certainly so far as
Massachusetts, as I am informed, is concerned, because of
certain powers that exist in this state. Difficulties sometime
arise, caused by the generality of the questions put, but, on
the whole, the jurisdiction has not been used extensively and
it has served the useful purpose of obtaining an authoritative
pronouncement upon the legality of actual, or proposed,
legislation, without putting a litigant to the trouble and
expense of raising the issue and carrying it through several
courts. For the same reason that I indicated a moment ago, I
give you a recent example, in fact, so recent that the judgment
has not yet been reported. [5.]

↑ *Above note inserted by Patrick Kerwin.*

5

Reference Re Industrial Relations and Disputes Act, (1955)
Sup. Ct. Can. 529.

be found in a dispute that had occurred as to the labour
union which should represent the employees of a stevedoring
company at Toronto whose operations consisted exclusively of
services rendered in connection with the loading and unload-
ing of ships, all of which were operated on regular schedules
between ports, in Canada and ports outside of Canada.   Collec-
tive agreements had been entered into by the company and one
union but another applied to the Ontario Labour Relations
Board for certification as the bargaining agent of the same
employees and that Board decided that it had jurisdiction to
hear the application and to deal with it on its merits.   The
first union applied to the Supreme Court of Ontario for an
order quashing that decision, or in the alternative, for an
order prohibiting the Board from taking proceedings with respect to the application.   The Attorney General of Ontario
interviewed and notified the Attorney General of Canada that
in those proceedings the constitutional validity would be
brought into question of an Act of the Parliament of Canada
to provide for the investigation, conciliation and settlement
of industrial disputes.   An order of reference by the Governor
General-in-Council was made in order to settle the dispute
and obtain the opinion of the Supreme Court of Canada as to
the jurisdiction of Parliament to enact the statute.

   All of the provinces have enacted similar clauses
authorizing references by the Lieutenant Governor-in-Council

to the Provincial Court of Appeal. Coupled with these clauses is a provision that the opinion is to be considered a judgment, and, therefore, by virtue of a section of the Supreme Court Act of Canada an appeal may be taken to the Supreme Court from the Provincial Court of Appeal. (5)

Thus the British North America Act provides a division of legislative authority between Parliament and Legislature and the all-pervading jurisdiction of the Court warrants that neither may encroach upon the territory of the other with impunity. That is one example of constitutionalism, or government under law. That branch is important in a federation even if, as has been asserted, The British North America Act is a highly specialized kind of federalism. (6) It is indeed necessary in a country covering such a large area and following different traditions and possession diversified economies. And while every decision of the Courts has not met with unqualified approval from the Bar and the commentators, that is merely an indication that any form of federalism and judicial supervision is subject to strain and stress

---

(5)   Supreme Court Act, R.S.C. 1952, c. 259, s. 37.

(6)   Professor Scott, The Special Nature of Canadian Federalism, (1943) 13 Can. Journal of Economics and Political Science-13, referred to by Hon. Mr. Justice Vincent C. Macdonald in "The Privy Council and the Canadian Constitution", (1951) 29 Can. Bar Review, 1021 at 1031.

-84-

Few amendments to the Act have been made altering
the allocation of legislative jurisdiction. One, 1940,
was the insertion of Head 2(a) in s. 91 conferring power
upon Parliament to make laws in relation to unemployment
insurance. (7) Another was in 1949 by the enactment of
Head 1 reading as follows:-

"The amendment from time to time of the Constitution of Canada, except as regards matters coming
within the classes of subjects by this Act assigned
exclusively to the Legislatures of the provinces,
or as regards rights or privileges by this or any
other Constitutional Act granted or secured to the
Legislature or the Government of a province, or to
any class of persons with respect to schools or as
regards the use of the English or the French language or as regards the requirements that there
shall be a session of the Parliament of Canada at
least once each year, and that no House of Commons
shall continue for more than five years from the
day of the return of the Writs for choosing the
House:

Provided, however, that a House of Commons may
in time real or apprehended war, invasion

---

(7) U.K. Statutes of 1940, c. 36.

or insurrection be continued by the Parliament
of Canada if such continuation is not opposed
by the votes of more than one-third of the
members of such House". (8)

The object of this last amendment is to permit
Canada to amend the Constitution, subject to the qualifi-
cations stated, so far as relates to the powers of the
Nation as distinguished from those of the Provinces.
Exactly what will be done under it is a matter awaiting
development. You will have noticed in it a reference to
schools and languages. The position of each of these subjects in the various provinces cannot be adequately covered
on this occasion and it must suffice to state that The British North America Act, 1867, and later Acts dealing with the
admission or creation of other provinces, contain provisions
relating to education; and that as to language, s. 133 provides:-

> "Either the English or the French language may be
> used by any Person in the Debates of the Houses of the
> Parliament of Canada and of the Houses of the Legislat-
> ure of Quebec; and both those Languages shall be used
> in the respective Records and Journals of those Houses;
> and either of those languages may be used by any Person

---

(8) U.K. Statutes 1949, c. 81.

or in any Pleading or Process in or issuing from any
Court of Canada established under this Act, and in or
from all or any of the Courts of Quebec.

The Acts of the Parliament of Canada and of the
Legislature of Quebec shall be printed and published
in both those Languages".

Two other points might be mentioned: (1) Under s.
95 of the Act concurrent powers of legislation respecting
agriculture and immigration are vested in the provincial
Legislatures and in Parliament, but, in case of repugnancy,
enactments of the latter prevail; (2) By s. 125, "No lands
or property belonging to Canada or any Province shall be
liable to Taxation".

Legislative jurisdiction being thus divided and
the power of the Courts to ensure its continuation being
present, what is the position of the individual or corporation desirous of questioning any proceeding purportedly taken
under intra vires enactments of Parliament or a Legislature ?
In these days of delegated authority it is particularly important that the delegate should be restricted to the authority
conferred upon him and jurisdiction exists by way of the well-
known writs of habeas corpus, certiorari, mandamus and quo
warranto in a hierarchy of Courts to determine the rights
under such enactments.   These methods are recognized and
authorized by other statutory provisions of the proper

legislative authorities. Thus, no man is made to suffer in body, or mind, or goods, except for a distinct breach of law established in a legal manner before the ordinary tribunals.

The legislative power in Canada is conferred upon the Houses of Parliament consisting of an elected House of Commons and a Senate whose members are appointed for life by the Government from the different sections of the country in a fixed proportion. In the provinces there is only a Legislative Assembly, save in Quebec, where there is a Legislative Council consisting of members appointed by the Lieutenant Governor-in-Council. Within the ambit of their respective powers the Parliament of Canada and the provincial Legislatures are supreme.

The agitation as to the incorporation of a Bill of Rights in the Canadian Constitution led to an Order of Reference by the Senate in 1950 to a Special Committee of that body on Human Rights and Fundamental Freedoms. Witnesses were heard and briefs submitted to the Committee which reported to the Senate in favour of the inclusion of certain recommendations into the written Constitution. The difficulty was ralized of meeting the wishes of the provinces in providing for such matters and that it would, therefore, be necessary for conferences to be held between representatives of Canada and of the provinces. The Committee's Report was adopted by the Senate and there the matter rests.

-88-

The contention against these endeavours is based
upon the effect in practice of the first recital in The British North America Act:

> "WHEREAS the Provinces of Canada, Nova Scotia, and
> New Brunswick have expressed their Desire to be feder-
> ally united into One Dominion under the Crown of the
> United Kingdom of Great Britain and Ireland, with a
> Constitution similar in Principle to that of the Uni-
> ted Kingdom:".

Except for the radical differences between a federation and a
unitary state like Great Britain, the Constitution of the United Kingdom applies not only to Canada but also to each of
its ten provinces.   Sir Ivor W. Jennings has appointed out that
with the exception of the Instrument of Government which made
Cromwell Lord Protector and established a new legislature,
Britain has never had a written Constitution, and that "if
a Constitution consists of institutions and not of the paper
that describes them, the British Constitution had not been
made but has grown -- and there is no paper". (9)   In his
lectures delivered at the University of Toronto, in 1921,
under the Marfleet Foundation Sir Robert Borden pointed out
that the great constitutional change in various provinces
before Confederation by which responsibility of the execu-

---

(9) The Law and the Constitution, 3rd Ed., pp. 7-8.

tive to the legislative body came to be established was not
based upon any statutory provision but was consumated by
the adoption of a recognized convention. (10)   Since 1921
other constitutional changes have occurred but it must be
noted that The British North America Act itself provides
that Bills for appropriating any part of the public revenue
or for imposing any tax or impost shall originate in the
House of Commons (11) and that that House may not adopt or
pass any vote, resolution, address, or Bill for the appro-
priation of any part of the public revenue or of any tax or
impost to any purpose that has not been first recommended to
it by message of the Governor General in the session in which
such vote, resolution, address or Bill is proposed. (12)   This
ensures that no Bill which might be termed "a money Bill" may
be introduced except by the Government.

In connection with the gradual evolution of the
Canadian Constitution, it is interesting to notice that for
various reasons some of Chief Justice Marshall's opinions
on the written Constitution of the United States have been
distinguished even in the Republic.   His famous dictum that

---

(10)   Canadian Constitutional Studies, 1922, pp. 45-46.

(11)   s. 53;

(12)   s. 54.

-90-

The power to tax involves the power to destroy". (13) was
capped by Mr. Justice Holmes' epogram (14) "The power to
tax is not the power to destroy so long as this Court sits",
and several decisions of the Supreme Court of the United
States based upon the dictum were finally reversed by that
Court in Graves v. New York. (15). In the meantime in Abbott
v. St. John, (16) the Supreme Court of Canada had held that
s-s. 2 of s. 92 of The British North America Act giving provincial legislatures exclusive powers of legislation in respect to "direct taxation within the province", was not in
conflict with s-s. 8 of s. 91 which provides that the Parliament of Canada shall have exclusive legislative authority
over "the fixing of and providing for the salaries and allowances of civil and other officers of the Government of Canada",
and, therefore, the legislature of a province had the right
to impose income tax upon Canadian officials' salaries paid
to them in that province. In Caron v. The King (17) it was

---

(13)   McCulloch v. Maryland (1819) 4 Wheaton, 316 at 431;

(14)   Pan Handle Oil Company v. Mississippi (1927) 277 U.S.,
       218 at 223.

(15)   (1939) 306 u.s., 466;

(16)   (1908) 40 S.C.R., 597;

(17)   (1922) 64 S.C.R., 255.

decided that Parliament had the right to impose income taxes
upon the salaries of provincial officials.   This was affirmed
by the Judicial Committee of the Privy Council (18) and followed in Worthington v. A.G. of Manitoba (19) and also in
Judges v. A.G. of Saskatchewan (20) the last of which decided
that judicial emoluments are not protected by any paramount
principle making inapplicable to such income a tax imposed
by a statute in terms wide enough to include it.   Neither
the independence, nor any other attribute of the judiciary
could be affected by a general income tax which charged
their official incomes on the same footing as the incomes
of other citizens.

To turn to another field, it was pointed out in
one of the opinions in In re Storgoff (21) a decision of the
Supreme Court of Canada in 1945 that a statement by Chief
Justice Marshall in Ex parte Bollman and Swartwout (22) could
not be justified in view of a more thorough investigation
than had been possible in 1807.   That statement reads:-

---

(18)   Caron v. The King (1924) A.C., 999;

(19)   (1936) S.C.R., 40; (1937) A.C., 260;

(20) (1937) 53 T.L.R., 464;

(21) (1945) S.C.R., 526;

(22) (1807) 4 Cranch, 75.

-92-

"It has been demonstrated at the bar, that the
question brought forward on a habeas corpus, is always distinct from that which is involved in the
cause itself. The question whether the individual
shall be imprisoned is always distinct from the
question whether he shall be convicted or acquitted
of the charge on which he is to be tried, and therefore these questions are separated, and may be decided in different courts".

The Supreme Court of Canada held that certain provisions in
The British Columbia Court of Appeal Act granting a right to
the Provincial Attorney General to appeal to the Provincial
Court of Appeal from an order of a single judge in habeas
corpus proceedings freeing an individual were inoperative,
if the applicant for that writ be detained in custody by
virtue of a conviction for a criminal offence under the
Criminal Code of Canada. Leaving aside the use of the
Writ of Habeas Corpus to determine questions of nurture
and education of infants, a more comprehensive research
had shown that while the writ is one to enforce a right
to personal liberty, that right may have been infringed
by process in criminal, or civil proceedings, and that in
the instant case it was merely a step in the proceedings
under which the applicant was imprisoned.

The growth of the British and Canadian Constitu-

311

tions from the days of the absolute sovereigns disputing
with the barons has continued to the present era of constitutional monarchy.   Under this system the Government of the
day executes the authority conferred upon it, but its very
life depends upon its retention of the confidence of the
legislative body.   When it is apparent that this condition
no longer exists, the question of who shall carry on the
Government is finally determined by the electors at the poll.
This close affinity between the wishes of the ultimate mas-
ters and the resulting enactments is what may be described
as a government of opinion.   The preservation of fundamental rights, except as they are covered by The British North
America Act, as amended, depends upon an enlightened public
opinion and a history which, while it has had its dark days,
has gradually evolved a system in which it is taken for
granted that an alert public will see that the legislators
keep an even balance between the rights and duties of the
individual.   The individual is the most important fact in
the world in all enlightened systems and it must be the aim
of the State to preserve his natural rights while at the
same time ensuring that the rights of one do not interfere
with those of another.

Some of the provisions of The British North Ameri-
ica Act must be read in view of the similarity in principle
of the Canadian Constitution to that of the United Kingdom.

For instance, s. 9: "The executive government and authority of and over Canada is hereby declared to continue and be vested in the Queen". But this means that, in a constitutional monarchy, while the Sovereign is the head of the state constitutional usage now demands that the executive power be exercised by and with the advice of Her advisers. These constitute the Government for the time being in Canada or the Provinces, as the case may be. The Governor General, for whose appointment provision is made, represents the Sovereign and a stranger to the Constitution might be pardoned for thinking that his power as to assenting to Bills is absolute, if attention were directed only to ss. 55, 56 and 57 of The British North America Act. S. 55 reads:-

> "Where a Bill passed by the Houses of the Parliament is presented to the Governor General for the Queen's Assent, he shall declare, according to his Discretion, but subject to the Provisions of this Act and Her Majesty's Instructions, either that he assents thereto in the Queen's Name, or that he withholds the Queen's Assent, or that he reserves the Bill for the Signification of the Queen's Pleasure".

S. 56 provides for disallowance of any Act assented to by the Governor General within two years after receipt thereof by the Secretary of State in Britain and s. 57 enacts that

any Bill reserved by the Governor General for the signification of the Queen's Pleasure is not to have any force
unless within two years from the day on which it was presented to him the Governor General signifies that it has
received the assent of the Queen-in-Council.

The Letters Patent appointing the Governor General
were formerly either accompanied, or succeeded, by instructions suitable to the constitutional practice that was then
in vogue as expressed by the sections mentioned. While it
was not suggested in 1867 that the Sovereign might appoint
a Governor General without the advice of the Imperial Cabinet, it is now settled that the appointment is made by the
Sovereign on the recommendation of the Canadian Government.
The form of the Letters Patent has been altered to meet the
new conditions and at the present time assent to the Bills
passed by Parliament is given as a matter of course. There
is no power of reservation by the Governor General or of
disallowance by the British Government.

By another section (90), the provisions of the
Act respecting the Parliament of Canada as to assent to
Bills, the disallowance of Acts an/ the signification of
pleasure on Bills reserved shall extend and apply to the
Legislatures of the Provinces. While in provincial affairs
the Lieutenant Governor of each province, who is appointed
by the Canadian Government, represents the Sovereign, the

Supreme Court of Canada has held(23) that the power of the
Diminion to disallow within two years Bills passed by the
legislative authority of a Province is still a subsisting
power and its exercise is not subject to any legal limitations or restrictions. The Court, of course, was not concerned with the constitutional exercise of that power.

You may be interested in s. 5 of The Canada Evidence Act.(24) The first sub-section speaks for itself:-

"No witness shall be excused from answering
any question upon the ground that the answer to
such question may tend to criminate him, or may
tend to establish the liability to a civil proceeding at the instance of the Crown or of any
person."

S-s.(2) is in these words:-

"Where with respect to any question a witness
objects to answer upon the ground that his answer
may tend to criminate him, or may tend to establish
his liability to a civil proceeding at the instance
of the Crown or of any person, and if but for this
Act, or the Act of any provincial legislature, the

(23)   Reference Re Power to Disallow Acts passed by Provincial Legislatures (1938) S.C.R., 71; An appeal
to the Judicial Committee was abandoned.

(24)   R.S.C. 1952, c. 307

-97-

"witness would therefore have been excused from answering such question, then although the witness is by reason of this Act, or by reason of such provincial Act, compelled to answer, the answer so given shall not be used or receivable in evidence against him in any criminal trial, or other criminal proceeding against him thereafter taking place, other than a prosecution for perjury in the giving of such evidence."

As long ago as 1873 it was held by the Judicial Committee of the Privy Council(25):-

"that the depositions on Oath of a Witness legally taken are evidence against him, should he be subsequently tried on a criminal charge, except so much of them as consist of answers to questions to which he has objected as tending to criminate him, but which he has been improperly compelled to answer. The exception depends upon the principle 'nemo tenetur seipsum accusare', but does not apply to answers given without objection, which are to be deemed voluntary."

In 1947 this decision was applied by the Supreme Court of

....

(25)   Regina v. Coote, (1873) L.R., 4 P.C., 599 at 607.

-98-

Canada in a case arising under the Criminal Code of Canada
(26) and it was held that, if a person testifying does not
claim the exemption, the evidence so given may be later
used against him and this notwithstanding the fact that
he may not have known of his rights.

In all of the Provinces the Legislatures have enacted provisions presumably with the same object in mind, but
in 1955 the Supreme Court of Canada decided, (27) with reference to the British Columbia statute:- (1) The Legislature
could legislate only with reference to proceedings over which
it had legislative authority. (2) Since it had coupled with
the obligation to answer a proviso that the answer could not
be used against him in proceedings under the Criminal Code
of Canada, the proviso could not be severed from the rest .
of the section and, therefore, the whole was <u>ultra vires</u>,
and the witness was entitled to rely upon his common law
right to refuse to answer on the ground that to the best
of his belief his answers to particular questions would
tend to criminate him. It should be observed that this
case was decided upon the provisions of the British Columbia statute and without considering the terms of any other
provincial enactment.

(26)   <u>Tass v. The King</u>, (1947) S.C.R. 103;
(27)   <u>Klein v. Bell</u>, (1955) 2 D.L.R., 513.

A word might be added as to the operation of the
Constitution in time of crisis. On the outbreak of war in
1914, Parliament passed the War Measures Act, (28) by s. 6
of which

> "The Governor-in-Council shall have power
> to do and authorize such acts and things and to
> make from time to time such orders and regula-
> tions, as he may by reason of the existence of
> real or apprehended war, invasion or insurrec-
> tion, deem necessary or advisable for the secu-
> rity, defence, peace, order and welfare of Can-
> ada;"

and for greater certainty there follows an enumeration of
powers. It was held by the Supreme Council of Canada (29)
that certain Orders-in-Council passed under the authority
of this Act were intra vires. By The War Measures Act
Parliament absorbed practically the whole legislative
field of the provinces for the purposes of the conduct of
the war, and, in 1923, the Judicial Committee of the Privy
Council held (30) that, under ss. 91 and 92 of The British

(28) Statutes of Canada, 1914, c.2;

(29) Re George Edwin Gray, (1918) 57 S.C.R., 150;

(30) Fort Frances Pulp & Power Company Limited v. Mani-
      toba Free Press Company, Limited, (1923) A.C., 695.

- 100 -

North America Act, Parliament had an implied power for the
safety of the Dominion as a whole to deal with a sufficiently great emergency such as that arising from war,
although in so doing it trenches upon property and civil
rights in the Provinces from which subjects it is excluded
in normal circumstances. It was accordingly held that The
War Measures Act and Orders-in-Council made thereunder during the war for controlling throughout Canada the supply of
newsprint paper by manufacturers and its price, and also an
Act of Parliament passed after the cessation of hostilities
for continuing the control until the proclamation of peace
with power to conclude matters then pending were intra vires.
Finally, in the case of the Japanese Canadians, (31) Orders-
in-Council passed under the authority of The War Measures
Act and continued in force by an Order-in-Council passed
pursuant to a section of The National Emergency Transi-
tional Powers Act of 1935, were intra vires. The judgement
of the Privy Council states:-

"The Parliament of the Dominion in a sufficiently great emergency, such as that arising out
of war, has power to deal adequately with that emergency for the safety of the Dominion as a whole".

---

(31)   Cooperative Committee on Japanese Canadians v. A.G.
       for Canada, (1947) A.C., 87.

- 102 -

"Prayer for cloudless vision,
And the valiant hand,
That the right may triumph
To the last demand." (33)

---

(33)   In the Day of Battle, Collected Poems, P. 383.

ADDRESS AT DINNER MEETING OF THE LAWYERS' CLUB, OSGOODE HALL, TORONTO, JANUARY 12, 1956

On behalf of the Members of the Supreme Court of Canada may I first thank the Officers and Members of the Lawyers' Club of Toronto for their invitation to this gathering. We welcome the opportunity of foregathering with the profession, including the Judiciary. Owing to the vast distances in Canada, Judges and lawyers are not able to congregate to the same extent as is done in Britain and, therefore, such occasions are indeed highly prized. For some of us it is a chance to revisit old haunts and for others a means of appreciating what Chief Justice Armour used to call the metropolis, — and in order to avoid any misconception I hasten to add "of Ontario"; and also of viewing at closer quarters than from the dais a number of active practitioners.

After the glowing words of Chief Justice Pickup and Chief Justice McRuer there is really very little for me to say. In fact I expected that the Members of the Club came to enjoy themselves and not to listen to me. However, as has been pointed out, while all the Members of our Court were unable to attend for various reasons which have been made known to your President, there is a quorum present and we are prepared to affirm without argument any decision that the Court of Appeal might make tonight. Of course, it sometimes happens that we disagree with the judgments in the Courts of Appeal or with those at the trial, but that is to be expected since law is not an exact science and all one can do is use his training and knowledge in coming to a conclusion in any particular dispute.

That, however, does not interfere with the personal friendships between the Members of the various Courts and I am sure that in most instances the same spirit prevails amongst the practitioners. While lawyers on opposite sides do the best for their clients it is in the majority accomplished with a sense of the fitness of things.

You may have read the *Canons of Ethics* prepared by the Canadian Bar Association and may have noticed that one of them reads that the lawyer should always bear in mind that the profession is a branch of the administration of justice and not a mere money getting trade.

As long as that idea is kept before the profession and followed the public need have no fear of being enmeshed in what some unthinking laymen describe as "the lawyer's wiles". We do belong to a profession the members of which, particularly because of their close association with the joys and sorrows and aspirations of man in general, must ever bear them in mind. Of such stuff is the everyday life of the citizens of Canada, and if we weave the warp and weave the woof we shall not have laboured in vain, whether advising in the office, or arguing or deciding in court.

These propositions are self-evident and they point to the Arcanum in the Canon to which I have referred. If the Members of the Bar keep this in mind it may be taken for granted that the judiciary will do likewise. And if, notwithstanding all this, complaints are by disappointed litigants, all of us will be able to bear them with equanimity and proceed to do our duty according to the ambit of our activities.

It should not be too much to expect that in those circumstances we will have the satisfaction of something tried, something accomplished, and we may even hope that the discontented will in time admit the justification of our existence.

Many years ago Cicero, although in rather oratorical style, put the matter thus: —

> For the law is the bond which secures our privileges in the commonwealth, the foundation of justice. Within the law are reposed the mind, the heart, the judgment and the conviction of the state. The state without law would be like the human body without mind — unable to employ the parts which are to it as sinews, blood, and limbs. The magistrates who administer the law, the judges who interpret it — all of us in short — obey the law to the end that we may be free.

And I add, — free to live our lives under God in our own way and without interfering with the like rights of others. It is in these higher realms and, I might say, not only in what Sir Edward Beatty once described facetiously as the rarefied atmosphere of Ottawa that the true functions of the profession persist.

We all know from the story of this Club that these have always been the ideals of its Members. Your President has done well in reminding us of its long and honourable history. We feel sure that under his guidance and that of his successors the same traditions will be carried on; that the members of the public will be well served and that the profession will be held in that esteem which their efforts deserve.

The law is part of the
warp and woof of our civilization.

—Chief Justice Patrick Kerwin, Address to
Boston University Law School,
June 1, 1957

www.ingramcontent.com/pod-product-compliance
Lightning Source LLC
Chambersburg PA
CBHW071707120626
46550CB00001B/139